LENTEN REFLECTIONS

From the Desert to the Resurrection

MILTON E. LOPES

WESTBOW°
PRESS
A DIVISION OF THOMAS NELSON
& ZONDERVAN

WestBow Press books may be ordered through booksellers or by contacting:

WestBow Press
A Division of Thomas Nelson & Zondervan
1663 Liberty Drive
Bloomington, IN 47403
www.westbowpress.com
1 (866) 928-1240

ISBN: 978-1-4908-5151-8 (sc)
ISBN: 978-1-4908-5153-2 (hc)
ISBN: 9781-4908-5152-5 (e)

Library of Congress Control Number: 2014916301

Printed in the United States of America.

WestBow Press rev. date: 10/02/2014

The deep secrecy of my own being is often hidden from me by my own estimate of what I am. My idea of what I am is falsified by admiration for what I do. And my illusions about myself are bred by the contagion from the illusions of other men. We all seek to imitate one another's imagined greatness.

If I do not know who I am, it is because I think I am the sort of person everyone around me wants me to be. Perhaps I have never asked myself whether I really wanted to become what everybody else seems to want to become. Perhaps if I only realized that I do not admire what everyone seems to admire, I would really begin to live after all. I would be liberated from the painful duty of saying what I really do not think and acting in a way that betrays God's truth and the integrity of my own soul.

—Thomas Merton, *No Man Is an Island*

To Mary, the mother of God, who in joy nursed the child Jesus at her breast and who in grief cradled the lifeless body of the man Jesus in her arms. To Mary, the wife of Joseph, with whom she shared the everyday moments of nurturing, feeding, clothing, and loving this extraordinary man, our Redeemer. "Holy Mary, Mother of God, pray for us sinners now and at the hour of our death. Amen."

and

To my brother and sister Lay-Cistercians of the Monastery of the Holy Spirit in Conyers, GA., particularly Jeanne Krebs, my veritable "Soul Sister." May she rest in eternal peace! Also our intrepid and blessed Fr. Anthony Delisi OCSO, who labors so mightily among us. Let us pray for one another!

CONTENTS

ACKNOWLEDGMENTS

There are several people to whom I owe much in writing this book. First and foremost is my wife and life mate, Gail Gray Lopes, who encouraged me from the onset, and my daughters, Teresa and Dominique, both of whom kept me *honest* when I moved too far into *la-la land*.

I am also indebted to those who read portions of the book and offered their sage and always constructive criticism. Thank you.

PREFACE
FOR WHOM IS THIS BOOK WRITTEN?

This book is written for those of us who want to be more spiritual but realize that we must first become more human, for it is through our humanity that we become divine.

Lent is about coming to grips with the reality that we are creatures fashioned from a scoop of dirt into which God breathed life. Man and woman he created us in his very image and likeness. He blessed us with his grace and saw that we were good. We are humans by virtue of the fact that we came originally from dirt (*humus* in Latin). But we are divine by virtue of his breathing into us and placing a divine spark that marks us as his sons and daughters.

During this holy season we catch a glimpse of who God would have us to be and what we have become. Lent is about remembering that we came from dirt and we will return to dirt, but the breath and spark that God breathed into us continues into eternity either in paradise or in a far different place or state of being.

This book is written for those of us who have weathered life's storms and are troubled by a sense of a nagging emptiness in our spiritual well-being. This will not be our first Lent. We know that there is more to it than simply giving up chocolate. We go to church on Sundays and sometimes during the course of the week. We have religion and believe we are religious. Yet we are not convinced that having religion is enough. We suspect we have lost our focus; we harbor a deep uneasiness. We know we are sinners.

Something tells us that what we are doing is treading water. On Sunday we listen to the sermons and homilies of our priests and ministers, and for a brief moment we are moved by them. Yet on Monday we act as if we heard nothing.

Notwithstanding, many of us continue to seek the Lord in prayer, song, worship, petition, and acts of kindness and mercy. We give alms. We try to be good people. But deep within us we know that all too often we miss the mark of Christian life. When it is all said and done, we have to admit that we are a mystery unto ourselves. We do not know who or what or why we are. If we are truly honest, many of us have ceased to have a true desire to have the Spirit of God and his goodness within us. This is a message to those of us of the body of Christ, those of us who know that this is the unvarnished truth.

This is a message for those of us who are hurting and weak and often confused. For some it will prove hard to bear, and for others it will be a challenge, perhaps an affront; however, it is a message for sinners—you and me.

Lent is an opportunity to go deep inside ourselves to find the aforementioned spark of God within, to find out who we are. It is a time for each of us to discover the "I am who I am." This is not easy. Fortunately, there are maps or guides that have been provided us. It is my prayer that in some small way this book might serve in a similar capacity.

In Shakespeare's *Hamlet* we hear Polonius's advice to Laertes, "To thine own self be true, and it must follow as the night the day, thou canst not be false to any man." This presumes that I know who I am and that at a minimum I know who I am becoming. How do I know this? To whom can I turn to help me? I offer two ways, which is really one way.

First each one of us is unique. There is no one else in history or on the planet quite like you or me. Yes, there are similarities, but deep down we are all different. It is up to each of us to discover our own uniqueness and to build on it. By the same token we are told that each one of us was created "in the image and likeness of God." Is this contradictory to the first assertion? I think not. We are not able to plume the length, breadth, or depth of our God. Yet it is possible that each of us in a unique way reflects some aspect of God. Hence, our second task is to get in touch with that aspect and to allow God to nurture our deepest reality. It is in the desert where he purges us of our evil and sinful inclinations and cleanses or illuminates us so that we emerge as a new creation at the resurrection of his Son from the filth of the world, the flesh and evil personified by Satan. In a word, through the desert experience we become Christocentric. We experience a new and higher dimension of consciousness.

I do not pretend that this is the only way to this new consciousness. Nor do I suggest that this should be the only treatment of Lent that you should read. My intention is to encourage you to embark on, renew, and enrich your journey into your reality. I hope to suggest a path or to provoke in you a new dialogue with God. I want to help you get in touch with and allow the Holy Spirit to make this Lent not only meaningful but also productive. It is my prayer that the same Spirit that drove Jesus into the desert will drive you there as well. Just as the Holy Spirit manifested himself in all of Jesus' words and deeds during his earthly ministry, so it is that I pray that he animate you these forty days.

So let us go forward and with the help of our Savior, Jesus Christ, stand up to and excise from our beings all traces of sin and any tendencies that are displeasing to our God. As fellow travelers, wounded and weakened by life's vicissitudes, let us both go forward and reclaim our humanness so that we can ready ourselves to realize our divinity. But first let me give you a brief outline of what to expect in this book.

It is divided into four parts. Part 1 sets the framework for our treatment of the study of our salvation. It is devoted to the historical roots of Lent, its purpose, and its theology. To that end this section also provides the reader with an overview of the creation story, prompts a discussion of evil and sin, and ends with a summary of the Trinity and the Incarnation. Part 2 sets the stage for our initial reflections on Lent, while part 3 introduces us to the disciplines we will require to successfully pass through the desert to spiritual wholeness. Here we will begin by asking ourselves four seminal questions: Where are we? What are we? Who are we? Why are we? Having addressed these questions, we will next enter into what many spiritual masters call the purgative way, where we will begin to employ the twelve-step program of Alcoholic Anonymous as a framework to our first steps into spiritual wholeness. We will move into what these same spiritual masters call the illuminative and unitive ways. In the illuminative way we begin to sense the presence of and a deep union with Jesus. Our faith begins to be strengthened. We begin to grow in understanding and wisdom. In time we start to have a taste of the unitive stage and begin to experience a spiritual transformation which continues into the next life.

Part 4 is titled the agony and exultation. Here we will reach the zenith of our Lenten journey as we join Jesus on the road to Calvary, as he is nailed to the cross, and after he rises from the tomb. We end our reflections with him leaving the disciples and the coming of the Paraclete to be with us until end-times.

The season of Lent is upon us. Let us set out to find our Lord and our true selves. To do this we must first lose ourselves.

PART 1

FIRST THINGS

CHAPTER 1

THE ORIGIN, PURPOSE, AND THEOLOGY OF LENT

The time is fulfilled and the kingdom of God has come near;
repent, and believe the good news.

—Mark 1:15

The Origin of Lent

The word *Lent* comes from a Teutonic (Germanic) word meaning *spring*. The Latin name for this period is *Quadragesima*, which means the "forty days" or "the fortieth day" prior to the feast of the resurrection. It is specifically used to denote a forty-hour or forty-days fast. Another term associated with this period is the *ante-Paschal fast*. The earliest reference to this period is found in a letter attributed to St. Irenaeus (circa 115–142 CE) by the early church historian Eusebius (260-340 CE). As a very young man Irenaeus had seen and been a devotee of St. Polycarp (91–155 CE), a disciple of the apostle St. John. He is a key figure between the apostolic and patristic age. In his church history[1] Eusebius cites a letter written by Irenaeus to Victor, bishop of Rome (circa 189–199 CE), who was embroiled in a controversy with several Eastern bishops concerning the date of the feast of Pascha (Easter). The Eastern bishops promoted the practice of celebrating the Pascha on the fourteenth of the Jewish month of Nisan (March through April). Irenaeus[2] is reputed to have written that the "mystery of the resurrection of the Lord should be observed only on the Lord's day and ... the controversy is not only concerning the day (i.e., Easter) but also concerning the very manner of the fast (i.e., the fast before Easter). For some think that they should fast one day, others two, yet others more; some moreover count their day as consisting of forty hours, day and night. And his variety in its observance has not originated in our time, but long before in that of our ancestors." This quotation implies that some form of the ancient fast must have been observed by the beginning of the patristic period, conceivably during the time of the apostle. However, Thurston[3] gives short shrift to this last assertion and suggests that there is little evidence of anything more than a two-day fast during either the apostolic or patristic periods. He further asserts that there was substantial evidence of a diversity of practices throughout the first three centuries of the Common Era despite the inferences drawn from Eusebius' *Histories*. He traces these assertions to Rufinus (circa 340–410 CE), the monk and historian who translated Eusebius into Latin toward the end of the fourth century.

Another reference to the origin of the ancient fast can be found in the writings of Tertullian[4] (160–220 CE), an African church father and contemporary of Eusebius. He writes of a two-day period prior to celebrating the Pascha. This period was in remembrance of the forty hours in which the Lord is believed to have laid in the sepulcher. By the beginning of the fourth century the observance of Lent was widespread in both the Eastern and Western churches, albeit with a variety of durations. During the first general or ecumenical council of the church, Nicea (325 CE), which was convened by Emperor Constantine, the assembled bishops alluded to the keeping of a period of fasting and prayer in their discussions concerning the proper dating of the Paschal/Easter celebration.[5] The fifth canon of this council refers to this period chiefly as "a preparation for baptism, of absolution of penitents or of retreat and recollection." Constantine[6], at the conclusion of the council, wrote a letter to the bishops urging not only uniformity in celebrating this great and solemn feast but also the observance of an ante-Paschal fast. He wrote, "Let your pious sagacity, (i.e., bishop) reflect how evil and improper it is, that days devoted by some to fasting should be spent by others in convivial feasting; and that after the paschal feast, some are rejoicing in festivals and relaxations, while others give themselves up to the appointed fasts."

At about the same time St. Athanasius of Alexandria[7] (circa 296–373 CE) bade his followers to keep a forty-day fast prior to the fast of Holy Week. He urged this practice throughout the empire and Egypt. Over time the length of the Lenten fast increased throughout the church. The Eastern historian Socrates of Constantinople[8] (circa 380 CE–unknown) writes, "One may observe how the ante-paschal fast is differently observed by men of different churches. The Romans fast three weeks before Easter, only the Sabbaths and Lord's Days excepted; the Illyrians and all Greece and the Alexandrians fast six weeks; others (i.e., the Church of Constantinople) begin their fast seven weeks before Easter, but only fast fifteen days by intervals."

John Cassian[9] (360–435 CE), an ascetic monk, theologian, and historian, adds, "Though some churches kept their Lent six weeks, and some seven, yet none of them made their fast above thirty-six days in the whole." He posited that the reason the fast was for thirty-six days was because that is equivalent to one-tenth of the year, a tithe of time that should be devoted to God just as one-tenth of a Christian's income should be tithed as alms to God.

By the close of the sixth century and the beginning of the seventh, thirty-six days had become the established custom of the Western church. Sometime in the late seventh or early eighth century, Ash Wednesday and three extra days were added to make forty days. Since then, it has become common belief that the number forty is the traditional biblical period of fasting and prayer. Upon his ascent of Mount Sinai (or Horeb) Moses fasted forty days and forty nights. Upon witnessing the apostasy of the Hebrews, he prostrated himself on the ground for forty days and forty nights without bread or water. The Israelites languished in the desert for forty years. The Ninevites repented for forty days. Similarly Elijah fasted forty days. Before either Moses or Elijah forty days were the number of days attributed to the flood. However, our primary example is Jesus being led into the desert by the Spirit to be tempted and to fast for forty days and forty nights in preparation for his ministry. Hence, the name of the season itself—Quadragesima.

In sum, the origin of Lent as a season of fasting, penitence, almsgiving, and prayer is conceivably of apostolic origins. It is more probable that it is a custom promulgated during the patristic era by the early church in its faithfulness to Scripture, particularly the Gospels and the example of the likes of Moses, Elijah, and our Hebrew forefathers. It also owes much to the councils and customs of the church fathers and their followers in Northern Africa and medieval Eurasia.

The Purpose of Lent

As we have seen, Lent has been observed by Christians perhaps from the time of the apostles for more than two millennia. Aside from being a special time of fasting, penitence, almsgiving, and prayer, it is also a time of self-denial, spiritual growth, and good works. It is a time of preparation and renewal, a time when we undertake a spiritual inventory and address our individual and corporate relationship with God. It is season of transformation of body, soul, and spirit. It is also a season of joy. It is a season whose disciplines help us become more like Jesus. Eastern Christians call this process *theosis*, of which St. Athanasius[10] writes, "He [Christ], indeed, assumed humanity that we might become God. He manifested Himself by means of a body in order that we might perceive the mind of the unseen father. He endured shame from men that we might inherit immortality." Our role during this season is to cooperate with God's grace and initiatives that we might become gods by virtue of God's grace. Our role during this season is to cooperate with God's grace and initiatives.

These dimensions of Lent are underscored in the Second Vatican Council's Constitution on the Sacred Liturgy[11].

> 109. The season of Lent has a twofold character: primarily by recalling or preparing for baptism and by penance, it disposes the faithful, who more diligently hear the word of God and devote themselves to prayer, to celebrate the paschal mystery
>
> (b)… it is important to impress on the minds of the faithful not only the social consequences of sin but also that essence of the virtue of penance which leads to the detestation of sin as an offence against God; the role of the Church in penitential practices is not to be passed over, and the people must be exhorted to pray for sinners.
>
> 110. During Lent penance should not be only internal and individual, but also external and social. The practice of penance should be fostered in ways that are possible in our own times and in different regions, and according to the circumstances of the faithful.

In addition to being a season of preparation, Lent is also one of joy. This last point may be a bit strange to us of a certain age, particularly those of us who attended parochial school. Preparation, yes … but joy? We scarcely remember the first preface for the Mass in Lent that makes the point, "Each year you give us this joyful season when we prepare to celebrate the paschal mystery with mind and heart renewed. You give us a spirit of loving reverence for you, our Father, and of willing service to our neighbor. As we recall the great events that gave us a new life in Christ, you bring to perfection within us the image of your Son."[12]

Yes, Lent is a time for joy, but let us not forget that it is also a time of penance. Jesus tells us of the necessity to do penance, "Repent, for the kingdom of heaven is close at hand." (Mat. 4:17) He adds that he had come to call sinners to repentance by saying, "I came not to call the just, but sinners to repent. Except you do penance, you shall all … perish."

The Wages of Sin

The above notwithstanding, there is another purpose behind this season. Lent is as much about death as it is about repentance. This is a subject that we shun. We fear death. Our whole culture defies or denies it, yet it is a major part of modern man's psychological makeup. We build around it all sorts of subterfuges or barriers. Hollywood and the entertainment industry has created an entire genre of goblins, ghosts, zombies or walking dead, and other ghoulish, deathlike, or death-defying characters. In the American gun-loving culture murder is an everyday occurrence, often involving scores of innocent individuals. Throughout history people have been maimed or killed over political, economic, or religious reasons in senseless and at times sizeable conflicts in different parts of the world. Still it is always something that is going to happen to another, not me. From time to time we shudder at its thought as deep down within us we know that there will come a time when we will cease to exist on this earth. Deep down, as our end draws near, we experience considerable existential fear of what lies on the other side.

And so Lent is also a time to contemplate the fact that each of us is going to die. We are told by Scripture that the wage of sin is death. Each of us will be called before the judgment seat of God for an accounting of all we have done and left undone in this life. We know not when this will happen, but we know that it will. We know that the saints trembled in anticipation of this moment, not knowing the severity of his or her sentence or the extent of God's mercy. In this modern age little thought is given to this moment. Few of us have uttered the words of Job, "What shall I do if God arise to judge me? What am I that I should answer Him? I cannot answer Him one for a thousand." We know that the judgment of God is very different from the judgment of man.

Hence, when it comes time for our souls to leave our bodies and pass beyond the unknown into eternity, when we come face-to-face with our maker and we see our sins clearly with new eyes, we hope that we are able to give a good account of our thoughts, words, deeds, and omissions. We hope we are not counted among those hapless sinners who will stand convicted of pride, anger, avarice, greed, sloth, envy, lust, or other willful transgressions of God's laws. We fear his justice even as we see how laden we are with a multitude of impurities. We realize that our only defense is to throw ourselves at the feet of this judge and beg that his mercy will extend to each of us and that we will not be consigned to hell for all eternity even as Satan and his minions stand ready to accuse us by bringing to light all of our sins.

Welcome to the holy season of Lent. Repent now of your sins. Don't wait until you are no longer in good health and are on your deathbed. Turn away for your sinful ways while there is still time. Prepare yourself for that eventful moment when you will stand before the heavenly court for an accounting of all you have done and left undone in this life.

The Theology behind Lent

Metanoia

In the word *metanoia* or *repent*, we have the essence of the theology behind Lent. *Metanoia* literally means "change of mind." To the Semite this same word connotes "turning away" from one's wrongdoing and striking out in a new direction. In the context of Lent it calls for the reorientation of one's life and behavior, changing one's way of thinking and turning from sin. Metanoia leads to a radical change of heart and/or change of consciousness. It results in a new way of envisioning one's self in relation to God and the world. It suggests conversion, repentance, sorrow for one's sins, the avoidance of self-righteousness, presumption, pride, and much more.

To Merton[13] metanoia means more than repentance or sorrow for one's sins. It is a radical mind shift with respect to our relationship to sin as an obstacle to our experience of God. It speaks to our failure to see sin as an evil in our own being. It speaks to being "deeply and deliberately false to my inmost reality, my likeness to God" and his laws, which dwell within me. Lent calls me to become attuned to the sense of sin within me, to realize that this sin is a "radical evil and sickness of [my] spirit and conceivably renders me morally and spiritually dead. This spiritual death separates me from all that I am, from truth, and from the love of God. Metanoia leads me to a sense of this sin within me, to the realization that I am a liar, and a false being, that I am on the path to spiritual self-destruction, and yes, Hell." This is the focus of Lent—to bring about this realization and give us the wherewithal to remove the abovementioned obstacles to our experience of God.

Accordingly Lent is traditionally viewed as the penitential season. It is that time of the year reminiscent of the Hebrew Day of Atonement, Yom Kippur, a period wherein the Jew is expected to make reparations for his or her sins. It recalls the call to atonement in Leviticus 16:29–30, "In the seventh month, on the tenth day of the month, you shall afflict your souls, and you shall not do any work … For on that day he shall provide atonement for you to cleanse you from all your sins before the Lord." Probably the most important holyday of the Jewish year, Yom Kippur is observed by refraining from work, fasting, and/or attending synagogue services. It is a day set aside to *afflict the soul*, to atone for the sins of the past year between man and God, to appeal to God's mercy, to demonstrate repentance, and to make amends. Before the onset of Yom Kippur the devout Jew is expected to seek reconciliation with anyone against whom he or she has committed a wrong or an injury.

For the Christian church Lent is not unlike the Jewish period of atonement, where the Hebrews sought cleansing, forgiveness, and purification from their transgressions, iniquities, and sins as a people. However, for Christians it is also a time of preparation, individual and collective, for the paschal mystery where Christ *atones* for our sins by sacrificing himself on the cross. Just as with the Jews, both ancient and modern, it is a time set aside to bring to mind our sins against God, our brothers and sisters, and ourselves. But metanoia is more than a negative concept. It is also a call to bring about a positive change in our lives and in our communities. It is an urging to "love God with our whole hearts, our whole soul, our whole minds and our whole strength; and to love our brothers and sisters as we love ourselves."

Kerestzy[14] likens metanoia to a complete change of heart and way of life that begins with our acceptance of Jesus' invitation to a festive banquet to which all are invited—the repentant sinner and the law-abiding Pharisee. When we accept his invitation, we also implicitly accept his forgiveness of our sins and acknowledge his forgiveness of the sins of those who have sinned against us. We also realize that like Jesus we must go further and forgive those who have sinned against us. If we do not imitate God's forgiveness toward those who have offended us, God will revoke the forgiveness of our own sins (Matthew 18:21–35). I must love my enemies. This is what metanoia demands. Only in this way can I give credence to Matthew's observation that I have understood and accepted the love of God who "makes his sun rise on the evil and the good and causes rain to fall on the just and the unjust" (Matthew 6:45).

Another aspect of metanoia is Jesus' desire that we become "like little children," unconditionally trusting, loving, and joyfully surrendering to God as our Father. In a later chapter we will return to this theme when we discuss the Sermon on the Mount. Hence, Lent is a time in which to live out the letter and spirit of this urging, which was made manifest to the Hebrews at Sinai and in the gospel when Jesus spoke with Nicodemus and told him he was not far from paradise. Here we sense that Jesus is telling us to seek the kingdom of God by not only being cognizant of our sinfulness but also by fostering and becoming the change we want to bring within ourselves and in our world. This change must begin within ourselves so that we might become who God created us to be. Once we acknowledge the *log* in our eyes, only then are we able to extract the speck in the eye of our brother or sister. Only then can we love our brothers and sisters regardless of their race, economic status, or what have you. Only then can we promote metanoia throughout our society and world.

Kenosis

The second theological concept undergirding the season of Lent is the idea of emptying one's self of ego, persona, or whatever is inconsistent with who or what we are in the sight of God. It is about acknowledging that we have lost our innocence. In Jungian terms metanoia connotes radical transformation particularly when connected with kenosis. This speaks to coming to terms with what is false in my ego and persona. It means dealing with my shadow, sorting through the long bag I carry behind me,[15] and acknowledging those parts of myself that have become tarnished through the agency of society (the world), my inner and prurient desires (the flesh), and those evil or malevolent forces aligned against me (the Devil). We have additionally lost a sense of the reality and mystery of sin. Merton[16] describes modern man as "so full of sin that he no longer experiences contrition and is consumed with guilt only for what is relatively inoffensive."

Merton draws a distinction between sin and guilt. He defines the latter as a fear that we will be called to account for our misdeeds. I am guilty when someone thinks I am wrong. Sin, on the other hand, is deeper and more existential. It is the loss of our bearings and our liberty to be who we really are. Merton couches this observation in a distinction between our real and false selves. Our real selves are a mystery to us, known only in their entirety to God. Our false selves, on the other hand, are what Jung calls our persona, that part of ourselves which we present to the world. It is the mask or superficial social role and facade behind which we define who we are, how we relate to others, the kind of clothes we wear, and how we express ourselves. It also enables us to protect our ego and psyche from the social forces and attitudes such as cultural prejudices and social rejection that are constantly bombarding us through the media, our families and associates, the various institutions with which we identify, and society in general. The persona is important as we develop our ego. But unfortunately there often comes a time when we so identify our ego with our persona that we lose sight of who we really are. Merton[17] ruefully observes that herein lays a great irony of human existence. We have cauterized our sense of sin. When we violate the inmost laws of our being (i.e., the infused laws of the God within), we are being "deeply and deliberately false" to our inmost reality, our likeness to this God. Sin leads ultimately not only to moral degradation and death but worse and more likely to spiritual death. The more we pursue a life of pleasure and desire to be powerful and knowledgeable as well as rich and famous, the more likely is it that our life choices enhance a trajectory to sin and self-love and a destiny of destruction and ultimately nothingness.

In a word, Lent is a time to come to grips with and to accept with humility our human status and to set aside our own will, becoming totally receptive to God's divine will. We are reminded of Paul's description of Christ becoming man. "Being in the form of God [he] did not count equality with God something to be grasped. But he emptied himself, taking the form of a slave, becoming as human beings are; and being in every way like a human being, he was humbler yet, even accepting death, death on a cross" (Philippians 2:6–8).

Although Paul applies the term kenosis to Jesus as he became man, it has deep relevance to our spiritual life during this season. The presumption is that if we are empty of self, then we are open and receptive to the Spirit's *movements* within us. We cease to be preoccupied or absorbed by our petty fixations. We are amenable to becoming persons conformed—or better yet re-conformed—into the image of the God within us. We look to being who God originally intended us to be.

This idea of the "emptying of the self" calls to mind the story of the young monk who sought from an older monk the secret to wisdom and enlightenment. The older monk invited the younger man to tea. He commenced to pour tea into the cup of the younger man. He poured and poured until the tea flowed not only over the cup but also over the saucer to the ground. The young man was perplexed but eventually felt compelled to tell the old monk that his cup was overflowing, that it was more than full. The elder simply responded, "And so it is!"

All too frequently both you and I are like that young monk. We are so full of ourselves that there is no room for what God wants to plant in us. We must make room for him and his Spirit. We must empty ourselves of all that is not pleasing to him. We must let go of those attachments that are obstacles to loving God with all our heart and soul and mind and strength and loving our neighbors as we love ourselves. We must find a way to empty ourselves of our illusions and attachments to whatever is either delimiting or debilitating. Kenosis is a call to nothingness, to the point where we are totally at God's mercy and his intention to shape his will within us. It is not a one-time process but ongoing as long as we walk this plane.

Although Karl Rahner,[18] a major influence on twentieth-century Roman Catholic thought, does not explicitly describe *kenosis* as a process of self-emptying, he does imply in his concept of "self-surrender" that we realize the inner life of the spirit when we lead our lives in such a way as to forget ourselves in and for God. This means waiting for eternity in faith, hope, and love, bearing the darkness of human existence. It also means not identifying ourselves solely with this world but rather the world to come.

Ingvild Røsok[19] writes that the key to grasping Rahner's perception of kenosis is to be found in his comments on the *Spiritual Exercises of Ignatius Loyola*,[20] (a set of meditations, prayers, and mental exercises composed from 1522 to 1524). In the *First Principle and Foundation*, Loyola concentrates on the term *indifference*, with the statement, "We need to make ourselves indifferent to all created things." According to him, we must do this in order to move toward the end for which we are created (i.e., to praise, revere, and serve God, our Lord). Rahner considers indifference to be a process that should be integrated into all parts of our lives. It is a process that aims at freeing ourselves of preconceptions and allows for an opening up of ourselves to God's good pleasure.

The second key to his perception of kenosis is Loyola's *Call of the King*, wherein we accept or are ready to follow Jesus no matter the insults, injuries, or poverty that might ensue. We are convinced that Jesus' call is the will of his Father. We are ready and prepared to follow Jesus wherever his Father commands—unto death if need be. We are committed to a radical surrender and abandonment to his will.

The third and final aspect of Rahner's concept of kenosis is found in the exercise *Contemplation to Attain Love*. Love is the goal and focal point of the entire Ignatian retreat. We know that this world in which we live and die comes from God. Here is where we meet him, and here is where we connect the descent of God into the world through the incarnation and the cross, at which point we not only accept the truth of Christ but also empty ourselves so that we are able to share in his mission.

There is another side to self-emptying. It is realized when we lose someone we love to death, when we retire and no longer enjoy the companionship of colleagues, when our children grow up and leave home, when we experience a diminishing of our youthful vigor and energy, or when we reach old age and impending death. Merton[21] describes this time in our lives by reminding us that the resurrection was only possible after the crucifixion. "A man cannot enter into the deepest center of himself and pass through that center into God, unless he is able to pass entirely out of himself and empty himself and give himself to other people in the purity of a selfless love." Unless we empty ourselves, we are unable to receive and accept what God has in store for us, the possibilities that are ours for the asking.

The Shema, Another Gloss On Metanoia

> Hear, O Israel! The lord is our God, the Lord Alone. You shall love the Lord your God with all your heart, and with all your soul and with all your might.
> —Deuteronomy 6:4–5

> Listen, Israel, the Lord our God is the one, only Lord, and you must love the Lord your God with all your heart, with all your soul, with all your mind, and with all your strength … You must love your neighbor as yourself.
> —Mark 12:29–31

> You must love the Lord your God with all your heart, with all your soul, and with all your mind … You must love your neighbor as yourself.
> —Matthew 22:37–39

The Shema, the central or fundamental prayer of the ancient Hebrew and contemporary Jew, is a summation of metanoia as a process of radical and the fundamental transformation of one's relationship with God or YHWH. Each word in the Shema has a particular relevance and meaning with respect to Judeo-Christianity. In its first rendition the specific reference to *mind* was absent. The word *heart* indicated that one should love the Lord from the very core of one's existence or life. The word *soul* commands that one's spirit should love God with every power at its disposal—physical, mental, and spiritual. The word *might* or *strength* calls on us to love God with every resource, capacity, authority, or stature we possess internally as well as externally. At first the ancient Hebrews drew no distinction between heart and emotion, soul and strength, or mind and intellect. Each was related or connected. Life, breath, and energy affected one another. This is seen very clearly in Psalm 24:3–4, which says, "Who may ascend the mountain of the LORD? Who may stand in his holy place? He who has clean hands, and a pure heart, who has not taken a false oath or sworn deceitfully."

The hands represent action or might/strength. The heart relates to thought or mind/emotion, while the soul or breath/spirit/life makes the other two possible. The Hebrews clearly understood that they had power and control, (i.e., bodily strength over the workings of the heart as mind and emotion), but God controlled their souls.

By the time of Christ, for those who lived in a Greco-Roman world and its Hellenistic culture, the Shema took on a slightly different gloss. Whereas the ancient Hebrews used the words *heart, soul,* and *strength,* now the word *mind* is added. This word *mind* was decidedly Platonic (from Plato who lived circa 428–348 BCE). According to Plato, mind was related to the idea that humans could understand things through pure reason and gain knowledge through the senses and the intellect or intelligence. Thus, at some point in biblical times the construct *mind* is explicitly added to the Shema, even though it was always implied. The bottom line is that the heart, soul, mind, and strength are a complex, interconnected, and concentric totality. The Hebrew usage of the word *heart* is consistently used wherever thought or intent is implied. The word for soul generally connotes the whole being, both body and thought. The word for strength or might relates to one's power in living the Shema.

By medieval times and Thomas Aquinas, *heart* came to refer to the center of one's personality, wherein human free will and decision-making power resides and where one communes with the Christ within us. *Soul* means the essence of who we are as human beings, the source of our passions, appetites, and powers that move us to some action, whether good or evil. It is in and through the soul that we are aware of our very being, of who and what we could really become, and through which we see the essence of God. Finally it is in the soul where we are the created and vital image and likeness of God. *Mind* subsists as one's intellect (i.e., to know and to understand). It is the center and totality of one's mental and psychic powers and is clearly allied to the heart in terms of a knowledge of God. *Strength* speaks to the somatic or physical connect between the preceding elements and the body. It refers to the power and commitment to carry through with the difficult task of living the gospel.

Hence, love means directing all our desires toward God by involving our whole being, heart, soul, mind, strength or will, desires, intellect, and bodily might. Those who freely and joyously obey this commandment in addition to loving one's neighbor in the same way that one loves one's self are drawn into God's love. "Anyone who loves me will keep my word, and my Father will love him, and we will come to him and make a home with him" (John 14:23).

Asceticism, Spiritual Direction, and the Lenten Journey

There is another dimension to Lent that is rarely discussed, and that is the concept of asceticism, the science of saints, spiritual science, spiritual theology, or the art of perfection. It is to the spiritual life what physical exercises are to the athletic life. It subscribes to Jesus' mandate that we be perfect as our heavenly father is perfect. Although related to and dependent upon moral and dogmatic theology, asceticism is a distinct branch of theology. Tanquerey[22] defines it as "that part of spiritual doctrine whose proper object is both the theory and practice of Christian perfection, from its very beginnings up to the threshold of infused contemplation [or mysticism]." Aumann[23] defines it as "that part of theology that, proceeding from the truths of divine revelation and the religious experience of individual persons, defines the nature of the supernatural life, formulates directives for its growth and development, and explains the process by which souls advance from the beginning of the spiritual life to its full perfection."

It is this science that is practiced by spiritual directors or companions who accompany others in their journey to holiness. Suffice it to say that spiritual directors are dedicated to helping individuals who sense that there is a deeper meaning to their lives. These individuals want to wake up to God's reality, to establish focus, and to discover possibilities in their lives, while at the same time they want to respond in a deep and sustained way to God's call to holiness. This ministry is based on the belief that deep within the ground of one's very being God is to be found as a *divine spark*. The job of the spiritual director is to help men and women discover this spark, to help you discern or recognize the movement of the Holy Spirit within your heart. It is all about you and God. If truth be known, the real spiritual director is the Holy Spirit. Hence, the spiritual director's real job is to facilitate the interaction between you and the Holy Spirit and know when to get out of the way and be silent. What better time than Lent to seek out a spiritual director.

Conclusion

To conclude this chapter, I am reminded of a story about the successful businessman who feels that his life is not going in the right direction. He decides to return to the faith. After some thought he determines that his sins are great and only the pope can absolve him. He decides to go to Rome, where the Holy Father agrees to hear his confession.

After his confession the pope says to him, "You have broken every one of God's commandments, and I must give you an appropriate penance. For your penance I want you to go to Mass every morning for six months."

But the businessman replies, "Holy Father, I am a very busy man. I simply don't have time to go to Mass every morning. Could you give me some other penance?"

After some thought he responds, "All right, for your penance I want you to fast every day for three months."

Once again the businessman has a problem. This time he pleads that as a businessman he needs to muster considerable energy just to survive. "This penance is just too hard."

The Holy Father smiles and says, "For your penance you may read one chapter from the Holy Bible each day for one year."

Once again the confessor has another excuse. He has poor eyesight and is unable to read in the evening because of artificial light. With amazing patience the pope takes off his ring and gives it to the man with the statement, "For your penance I want you to wear this ring, and every day I want you to read the inscription on it, *Memento Mori*, which means *remember death*."

This time the very busy, low-energy businessman with poor eyesight takes the ring, and we are told that he read the inscription every day. Within a few months we hear that his neighbors and associates have noticed that he attends

Mass every day during the week and fasts three days each week. He also reads a chapter of the Holy Bible every day.[24]

There is a lesson for each of us in this story. "In all thy works, O Man, remember thy last end, and thou shall never sin" (Ecclesiasticus 7:40). Let us pray for one another. May God rekindle in each of us the spark he has planted deep within us. May we find therein our selves and our purpose. May we find peace and joy when we cry out on resurrection day, "The Lord, He Has Risen! Alleluia!" And at Pentecost, may tongues of fire rest on our heads to enervate the new beings that we have become.

Endnotes

[1] Eusebius, *Ecclesiastical History,* Kindle Electronic Edition: Chapter 24, Paragraph 11-18; 114-115 Location 2636 -2663.

[2] Lonsdale, Herman Lilienthal, *Lent Past and Present: A Study of the Primitive Origin of Lent, Its Purpose and Usages,* (Princeton, NJ: Princeton University Internet Archives, 1895; reissued Memphis, TN: General Books, LLC, 2009), 17.

[3] Thurston, H., "Lent," The Catholic Encyclopedia (New York: Robert Appleton Company, 1910), retrieved April 6, 2014 from New Advent at http://www.newadvent.org/cathen/09152a.htm.

[4] Tertullian, "On Fasting," Translated by S. Thelwall. In The Catholic Encyclopedia: From Ante-Nicene Fathers, Vol. 4. Edited by Alexander Roberts, James Donaldson, and A. Cleveland Coxe. (Buffalo, NY: Christian Literature Publishing Co., 1885.) Revised and edited for New Advent by Kevin Knight. <http://www.newadvent.org/fathers/0408.htm>.

[5] At the Council all the Churches agreed that Easter, the Christian Passover, should be celebrated on the Sunday following the first full moon (14 Nisan) after the vernal equinox. See the Catechism of the Catholic Church, (Libreria Editrice Vaticana, Vatican City, 1994), Paragraph 1170, 303.

[6] Ibid, Lonsdale, 21.

[7] St. Athanasius, "Celebrating Easter – The Paschal Feast", An Excerpt from an Easter Letter by Saint Athanasius written circa 340 CE to prepare the people of Alexandria for the celebration of the Paschal Feast of Easter. http://www.crossroadsinitiative.com/pics/Celebrating_Easter.pdf (Accessed August 1, 1014).

[8] Thurston. "Lent" The Catholic Encyclopedia.

[9] Russo, Nicholas V. "The Early History of Lent," in *Christian Reflection* (Waco, TX: The Center for Christian Ethics at Baylor University, 2013) 18-26.

10   Athanasius, "On the Incarnation" Kindle Electronic Edition: Chapter VIII, Paragraph 54, Location 1039

11   Second Vatican Council's Constitution of the Sacred Liturgy, *Sacrosanctum Concilium*, (Washington, DC: National Catholic Welfare Conference, 1963) Para 109–111.

12   Preface (P8) for First Week in Lent, in *Daily Roman Missal*, ed. James Socias (Princeton, NJ: Scepter Publishers; Chicago, Ill: Midwest Theological Forum, 1993), 594.

13   Merton, Thomas, *The Inner Experience, Notes on Contemplation,* (San Francisco: HarperSanFrancisco, Harper Collins Publishers, 2003), 119.

14   Kerestzy, Roch A., *Jesus Christ, Fundamentals of Christology* (Staten Island, NY: the Society of St. Paul, Abba House, 2002), 109.

15   Bly, Robert, *A Little Book on the Human Shadow* (New York: HarperCollins Publishers, 1988), 17.

16   Merton, *The Inner Experience*, 118.

17   Ibid, 119.

18   Rahner, Karl, *Spiritual Exercises* (New York: Herder and Herder, 1956), 318.

19   Røsok, Ingvild, "Unconditional Surrender and Love, How Spirituality Illuminates the Theology of Karl Rahner," The Way, vol. 50/4 (October 2011): 121–132.

20   Ignatius Loyola, The Spiritual Exercises of St. Ignatius, translated by Motola, Anthony (New York: Doubleday Image, 1964).

21   Merton, Thomas, Seeds of Contemplation (New York: Dell Publishing Company, 1960), 41.

22   Tanquerey, Adolphe, The Spiritual Life: A Treatise on Ascetical and Mystical Theology. (CreateSpace Independent Publishing Platform, April 9, 2013) 5.

23   Aumann, Jordan, Spiritual Theology, (London: Continuum, 1980) 22.

24   Scannell, John W., "The Real Purpose of Lent," http://www.fatherscannell.org/index.php. accessed March 2014.

CHAPTER 2

IN THE BEGINNING—

And God created man in His image,
in the image of God he created him:
male and female He created them.
—Genesis 1:27

Anthropologists tell us that every grouping of people have stories of their beginnings. These stories are generally in the form of myths. Myths in contemporary times have the connotation of fabrications, fictional, untrue accounts of supposed realities. However, in archaic or primitive societies myths were thought of as true stories. Indeed, they were considered significant accounts of sacred and primordial revelations of *beginnings* and proper behavior. Eliade[1] defines a myth as the narration of a sacred history, of a true event that took place in primordial time, the fabled time of *beginnings*. He goes on to say,

> In other words, myth tells how, through the deeds of Supernatural Beings, a reality came into existence, be it the whole of reality, the Cosmos, or only a fragment of reality— an island, a species of plant, a particular kind of human behavior, an institution. Myth, then, is always an account of a "creation;" it relates how something was produced, began to *be*. Myth tells only of that which *really* happened, which manifested itself completely. The actors in myths are Supernatural Beings. They are known primarily by what they did in the transcendent times of the "beginnings."

Eliade[2] adds that myths speak to not only the origin of the world but also the creative and sacred, sometimes dramatic breakthroughs of the sacred into this world. Through the intervention of a supernatural being man becomes a "mortal, sexed, and cultural being ... organized in a society, obliged to work in order to live, and working in accordance with certain rules." In a word, myth teaches man "the primordial 'stories' that have constituted him existentially."

Joseph Campbell[3] further adds that myths serve four functions—the mystical (the transcendent or God), the cosmos (science), the society (the social order), and the pedagogical (how to live a human life under any circumstance). Marius[4] writes,

> In the pre-modern world people talked and wrote of events, not in order to describe what actually happened. They were concerned with what an event meant. The myth is a meaningful event that happened but is happening all the time as well. Due to modern man's restriction of a chronological view of history, no word exists for such an occurrence.

Myths in the biblical context are concerned more with the truth about God than with precisely recorded events.

All the great Mediterranean, Middle Eastern, and Indian religions have mythologies that were at first transmitted orally. However, in time they were reduced to written texts that have been the subject of reinterpretation and elaboration by the creative genius of exceptionally gifted theologians, anthropologists, ethnographers, and historians.

Judeo-Christianity boasts its own mythology in the story of the creation and its immediate aftermath (i.e., the sin of Cain, the flood, and the building of the tower of Babel) as told in chapters 1 through 11 in the book of Genesis. The biblical authors used these familiar patterns as teaching devices to convey profound religious rather than historical or scientific truths. These religious truths speak to the human attempt to play God and its consequences.

At this point we would do well to explore how this Judeo-Christian myth came to be written. We begin in Babylon and the beginnings of Judaism. We then move to a discussion of their relevance to Christianity.

The Mythical Beginnings of Judaism

For more than seventy years the Jews (Judeans) were held captive by the Babylonians, who in 609 BCE first imprisoned Daniel and other members of Judah's elite (Daniel 1:1; 2 Kings 24:1, 2). In 597, they took captive Johoiakim and other members of his royal family (2 Chronicles 36:9, 10; 2 Kings 24:15–17). In 586, after a three-year siege the Babylonians conquered Jerusalem, destroyed its temple, and took most of the remaining people into captivity along with articles from the temple, leaving behind only the poorest of the poor. In 538, Cyrus II of Persia conquered Babylon, and six years later by royal decree he allowed the Jews to return to Jerusalem, thus ending more than seventy years of exile.

While in Babylon they maintained their identity and culture by relying on their sacred writings and initiated the practice of the Sabbath by gathering periodically to read from these writings and pray to their God. This practice evolved into a tradition where they would meet at a specific place—a synagogue—to conduct their worship services. They also began to produce a body of writings that would recount the story of the Hebrew people. Beginning with the patriarchs, Abraham, Isaac, and Jacob, they traced back some four thousand years when they were but wandering nomads. Circa 1700 BCE, these nomads found themselves in Egypt, where they stayed for more than four hundred years, a good portion of which they spent as slaves. They followed a certain Moses out of Egypt to Mt. Sinai, where God gave them the Decalogue or Ten Commandments. For forty years they wandered in the wilderness. Over time they occupied the land (called Canaan) in which they lived under judges and kings until they were conquered by the Babylonians.

Upon their return to Jerusalem in 532 BCE, their first order of business was to rebuild their temple and to construct a narrative or myth that would explain the genesis or beginnings of the Hebrew people. Though their attempt to rebuild their temple proved ineffectual, this period saw the formation of Judaism, which flourished with the construction and study of the *Torah* (the "law") which refers to the first five books of the Bible: Genesis, Exodus, Leviticus, Numbers, and Deuteronomy. Their exposure to several Mesopotamian myths, particularly Babylonian stories, provided these returning Jews with an outline.

Of particular relevance to them were those myths that separated reality into two competing realms—one good and the other evil. Throughout Mesopotamia and the Mediterranean these myths espoused a dualism of good and evil through competing divine forces. Creation was an admixture of light versus darkness, heaven versus earth, good powers versus evil powers, spirit versus flesh. The Babylonian epic *Enuma Elish* epitomizes these myths.

According to this myth, in the beginning the universe was in a formless state. Nothing is named as yet because nothing is created. With the appearance of two gods, Apsu (male) and Tiamat (female), the Lahmu and Lahamu (meaning *slime* or *mud*) emerge, and from them come Anshar (the sky) and Kishar (the earth). Apsu is slain by Tiamat. Soon many other gods and goddesses, palace intrigues, usurpations of power by upstart gods, and the appearance of Marduk set in motion the creation of the universe. Marduk is acclaimed as king of the gods and goes forth to slay Tiamat and her consort and second husband, Kingu, and their retinue of monsters. The struggle between them is basically a fight over the power to shape the universe. Marduk is successful and becomes the chief Babylonian deity.

Having defeated Tiamat and Kingu, Marduk creates the heavens and the world and sets the stars in the heavens as lights. From two ribs of Tiamat he creates east and west, and with her liver he creates the pole star. He also creates the sun and moon and organizes their daily and monthly cycles. From Tiamat's spittle he forms clouds, rain, and fog. Placing a mountain over Tiamat's head, he pierces her eyes, from which spring the sources for the Tigris and Euphrates rivers. He also places several other mountains over her breasts, piercing them "to make the rivers from the eastern mountains which flow into the Tigris. Her tail he bends up to the sky to make the Milky Way, and uses her crotch to support the sky. He then rests and is recognized as king of the gods of heaven and earth. He decides to build his dwelling in a place he called Babylon, which means 'gate of god.' All the other gods bow down before him, repeating their praises and promising to obey his commands. With this he has one of Kingu's arteries cut and creates from his blood mankind. Mankind is forced to build Babylon and Marduk is firmly entrenched as its chief deity."[5]

Several other Mesopotamian myths are connected to the creation story. One myth is the story of *Atrahasis*, in which the gods send a flood to wipe out the human race because of their evil ways, with the exception of one good man from whom the human race will begin anew. Another is the epic poem *Gilgamesh*, where the hero loses his opportunity to become immortal and must come to terms with his humanity. In his search for immortality the hero Gilgamesh is told by the gods that he would first have to successfully pass a series of ordeals. According to the story, beyond the Waters of Death there is a magic, life-giving plant that renews a person's youth. Gilgamesh gathers it, but an evil snake snatches it away, ending our hero's hope of eternal life. He fails. Instead the snake receives the benefit of possessing the plant and lives on as evidenced by shedding its old skin and receiving a new lease on life. The epic of Gilgamesh is also seen as an illustration of the human condition. Death becomes a reality and is inevitable.[6]

One other persona in this drama is the image of the serpent, an image of tremendous significance in the ancient world. Two highly significant roles are attributed to the serpent. One role is its connection to the heavens. The serpent represents deity, creative powers, and healing. The other role connects the serpent to the underworld, where it is associated with evil, harm, and destruction. The Sumerian god of spring vegetation, Tammuz, who is represented by a snake, is said to spring from the god Anu. The companion of Tammuz, Ningizzida (a horned serpent), was also in Sumerian mythology the guardian at the door of heaven and had the power to bestow fertility, protect the living, ward off death, and heal disease. The Mesopotamian corn goddess, Nidaba, was represented with serpents springing from her shoulders. Throughout Mesopotamia the serpent symbolized regenerative and healing properties of certain elements and produce of the earth. In certain circumstances the serpent could also reflect primeval struggles such as we found in the *Enuma Elish* and *Gilgamesh*.

In *Enuma Elish*, Tiamat's retinue of monsters is made up of serpents that represent the forces of chaos in the primeval world of the gods. They are described as "sharp-toothed, with fang unsparing," possessing bodies filled "with poison for blood." Tiamat is herself a female dragon. Thus, each one of these myths plays a similar role in Genesis, preventing Adam and Eve from immortality, particularly the myth about the Serpent as adversary or tempter. Later in Scripture we learn of a beneficial role for the serpent (i.e., the "brass serpent" that Moses erected on a pole in the wilderness for the protection and healing of the Israelites as indicated in Numbers 21:4–9).

Of particular interest to the returning Jews was not only to put forth a Judaic version of creation that would be in contrast to the Babylonian version but also to institute the peculiar Jewish Sabbath (or Shabbot) day custom as a day of rest in commemoration of the seventh day of creation, on which God rested and the Israelites gained redemption from slavery in ancient Egypt. In time the Sabbath became not only their first but also their most sacred institution. It also became a defining mark of all Jewish people distinguishing them from all other people.

It was also thought that the emphasis on the Sabbath as a fundamental characteristic of their belief system and their refusal to work on that day would keep them from losing their identity by intermingling and ultimately intermarrying with members of other ethnic groups. Only in a strictly observed separation could the continuity of the Jewish people be guaranteed, and only in this separation could they fulfill what was, they believed, their

God-given vocation, namely to be the people through whom all the nations of the world would be blessed. That was their calling, their messianic role, and their divine, historical destiny. The creation story was designed to affirm the oneness of God and the goodness of creation and to justify the stance of separation in which their hope of survival as a people rested.

The Judaic Creation Story

The authors of the Judaic *creation story* constructed the first eleven chapters of the book of Genesis around four accounts of what Scripture scholars now call "the primal story," which begins with two distinct accounts of the creation and ends with the building of the Tower of Babel (Genesis 1–11). The pattern of each of these stories or myths are arranged so as to teach a fundamental lesson, namely that God made man and woman in his own likeness and image. But they and their progeny wanted to play God and rejected him. They sinned by defying God's purpose. Punishment follows. But God will ultimately have the last word. His will, will be done. He will prevail. This story begins with the creation of man.

The first of the creation stories to appear in Genesis is the story written in Babylon by that group of writers identified by Scripture scholars as "P" (priestly). It is an account that is actually preceded by the second account in Genesis written some four hundred years earlier by that group of writers identified by the same scholars as "J" (those who wrote the name of God as YHWH).

The primary concern of the priests in the first creation story was order and clear boundaries. Modern readers—particularly Christians—construe this account to read that God created the world out of nothing. To the ancients, God created the world out of malevolent forces or chaos represented by an undifferentiated mass of primeval waters and deep darkness. To say that a deity had subdued chaos was to accord him or her high praise. This creation story also speaks to the creation of man in God's image. In Genesis 1:26, we read that God said, "Let us make man in our own image, after our likeness."

In Genesis 1:27–28, we read, "And God created man in His image, in the image of God He created him; male and female He created them. God blessed them and God said to them, 'Be fertile and increase, fill the earth and master it; and rule the fish of the sea, the birds of the sky and all the living things that creep on earth."

Not only was man created in the image and likeness of his maker, but he was given a commission to rule over the animal kingdom not as the owner of nature but as its steward. Later at Genesis 1:31, we read, "God saw all He had made, and found it very good."

Still later in Genesis 2:7—this account was written by J—we find another account of the creation of man, this time one that does not seem to be as lofty. Man has a lower origin than what man created in the first creation story. Here he is made of dust and not in the image and likeness of God. However, there is a more intimate and close relationship with God. "The Lord God formed man from the dust of the earth. He blew into his nostrils the breath of life, and man became a living being."

In Genesis 2:15–17, we read, "The Lord God took the man and placed him in the garden of Eden to till it and tend it. And the Lord God commanded the man, saying, 'Of every tree in the garden you are free to eat; but as for the tree of the knowledge of good and bad, you must not eat of it; for as soon as you eat of it, you shall die.'"

Noting that it was not good for him to be alone, God created woman from Adam's rib, whom Adam named Eve. The two of them, "the man and his wife," were naked and "felt no shame." Nudity attests to their innocence and ignorance.

With the second account of man's creation we see a greater emphasis on the human attributes of Adam and Eve as well as an indication of a close intimate relationship between them and God, with whom they walked each day at the "breezy time of the day." They were "friends" of God (Genesis 3:8). They were created in a state of holiness. By the same token, they were indeed fully human and fully divine, yet they were limited by their creatureness, which was dependent on and subject to God's laws of creation.

Lest we get ahead of ourselves, let's recount what happened in the garden. Genesis 3:1–7 says,

> Now the serpent was the shrewdest of all the wild beasts that Lord God had made. He said to the woman, "Did God really say you shall not to eat of the fruit of the other trees of the garden?" The woman replied to the serpent, "We may eat of the fruit of the other trees of the garden. It is only about fruit of the tree in the middle of the garden that God said, 'You shall not eat of it, or touch it, lest you die.'"

> And the serpent said to the woman, "You are not going
> to die, but God knows that as soon as you eat of it your eyes
> will be opened and you will be like divine things who know
> good and evil." When the woman saw that the tree was good
> to eat and a delight to the eyes, and that the tree was desirable
> as a source of wisdom, she took of its fruit and ate. She also
> gave some to her husband and he ate. Then the eyes of both
> were opened and they perceived that they were naked. So they
> sewed together fig-leaves and made themselves loincloths.

This gives the Serpent his opportunity to convince her to touch the tree and shake it until its fruit drops to the ground. At this point we all know what happened. She touches and finds the fruit to be a delight to her eyes. She realizes that it is a source of wisdom and of the knowledge of good and evil. She eats and gives some to Adam, who in turn eats. Their eyes are opened, and they realize that they are naked and experience shame, guilt, and a strange sense of estrangement from God.

God comes into the garden at his customary time and calls out for them. When they appear, he asks Adam where he was. Adam responds, "I heard the sound of You in the garden, and I was afraid because I was naked, so I hid" (Genesis 3:10).

Of course God knew all along that Adam had disobeyed him. "Who told you that you were naked? Did you eat of the tree from which I had forbidden you to eat?" (Genesis 3:15).

And Adam passed the blame on to his wife and indirectly to God himself. Eve blamed the Serpent. The Serpent did not respond. In the end all three were punished—the Serpent to crawl on its belly and "the woman to bear her children in pain and to cling to her husband" and the man to earn his bread by the sweat of his face.

> And the Lord God said, "Now that the man has become like
> one of us, knowing good and bad what if he should stretch
> out his hand and take also from the tree of life and eat, and
> live forever!" So the Lord God banished him from the garden
> of Eden, to till the soil from which he was taken. He drove
> the man out, and stationed east of the garden of Eden the
> cherubim and the fiery ever-turning sword, to guard the way
> to the tree of life. (Genesis 3:21–23)

By preferring their will to that of God, Adam and Eve underwent a transformation that resulted in the loss of both supernatural and preternatural gifts, keeping only those natural gifts proper to their humanness, (i.e., memory, intellect, free will, and physical well-being). They became susceptible to character flaws, confusion, and psychosomatic disorders. They were also removed from the garden and consigned to a life of toil, pain, disease, and death. God's final verdict was thus: "For dust you are, and to dust you shall return" (Genesis 3:19). And their descendants are subject to the same consequences.

But the story does not end here. Before evicting the couple from the garden and upon hearing the woman's plea, "The serpent duped me, and I ate," God turned to the serpent and said, "Because you did this, more cursed shall you be than all cattle and all the wild beasts; On your belly you crawl and dirt shall you eat all the days of your life. I will put enmity between you and the woman, and between your offspring and hers; they shall strike at your head and you shall strike at their heel" (Genesis 3:14–15).

Adam and Eve were deprived of their glory, which was not to be regained until the coming of the offspring of the woman, when God's Word ("I will put enmity between you and the woman") becomes flesh. Note that initially the Serpent was simply described as the "tempter." Only much later did Jews and still later Christians identify him as Satan.

In this chapter we have given rise to several questions, probably the most vexing of which is this: Why is all this important? I submit it is fundamental to an understanding of salvation history wherein Christians believe that Mary is that woman and her offspring is he who became her birth child, Jesus. Any understanding of this history calls for a coming to grips with the reality of evil and its offspring, sin. Let us first turn to a discussion of evil.

Endnotes

[1]   Eliade, Mercea, *Myth and Reality* (New York: Harper Row, 1963), 6.

[2]   Ibid, 11–12.

[3]   Campbell, Joseph, *The Power of Myth* (New York: Anchor Books, 1991), 38-39.

[4]   Marius, Nel. Daniel 7, "Mythology and the Creation Combat Myths," OTE 1 (2006): 156-170.

[5]   Eliade, Mercea, A History of Religious Ideas, vol. 1, translated by Willard R. Trask (Chicago: The University of Chicago Press, 1978), 70–73.

[6]   Ibid, 77–80.

CHAPTER 3

FROM WHERE DOES EVIL COME?

They burn villages, murder, rape women and children,
they nail their prisoners to the fences by the ears,
leave them so till morning, and in the morning they hang them
—all sorts of things you can't imagine. People talked
sometimes of
bestial cruelty, but that's a great injustice and insult to the beast;
a beast can never be so cruel as a man, so artistically cruel.
The tiger only tears and gnaws, that's all he can do.
He would never think of nailing people by the ears, even
if he were able to do it. These (men) took
pleasure in torturing children, too; cutting the
unborn child from the mother's womb, and
tossing babies up in the air and catching them
on the points of their bayonets before their mothers' eyes.

—Ivan in *The Brothers Karamazov*
by Fyodor Dostoevsky

Introduction

Some time ago I was sitting in the cafeteria of a local university with a Greek Orthodox Catholic priest and several young people who were members of his parish. The conversation was about the fasting regulations of their church. Somehow the discussion turned to sin and evil. There seemed to be a general consensus that sin was an offense either against an individual or God. But one of the students was particularly interested in evil. She wanted to know where it came from. The priest looked at me, expecting a response. I hesitated. Seeing my hesitancy, he responded, "It began with man. Man brought evil into the world." I voiced my doubt whether or not this was true. We did not have time to continue our conversation, but an uneasiness with his reply has remained with me. Is man the source of evil? Given our earlier discussion of the incarnation, it is appropriate to return to this conversation.

This is not an idle concern. Evil is real. We have tangible evidence that it exists in this world, (e.g., slavery and its aftermath, racism in the United States, Hitler's Nazi Germany and the Holocaust, Stalin's cruel dictatorship and communism, Pol Pot and the Cambodian genocide, ethnic cleansing in Rwanda and the Balkans, the atrocities committed by the Taliban in Afghanistan, wanton acts of murder of its own citizenry by Syria, and rampant crime in large urban areas throughout the world, etc.). Conversely we also have tangible evidence that good is found in countless individuals, some unknown but others like Mother Teresa, Martin Luther King, and Dag Hammarskjöld. We read of God and his goodness in the Hebrew Scriptures, the Christian apostolic writings, and other holy writings of other faith traditions. In these writings we also find many answers to the question of evil, generally personified by the name Satan or the Devil. Let us first discuss the Jewish concept of evil. After all, the ancestors of the Jews were the authors of the Hebrew Bible or TANAKH and, if truth be told, most of what Christians call the New Testament.

The Jewish Concept of Evil

The preceding chapter inferred that our Christian idea of evil was built on a myth that was constructed by a group of Hebrew or Jewish priests who, while exiled in Babylon from 609 to 538 BCE, were exposed to a variety of other myths that separated reality into two competing realms, one good and the other evil. Throughout Mesopotamia and the Mediterranean these myths espoused a dualism of good and evil through competing divine forces. Creation was an admixture of light versus darkness, heaven versus earth, good powers versus evil powers, and spirit versus flesh. We have seen how the Babylonian epic *Enuma Elish* symbolizes this dualism.

Jewish theology has approached the problem of evil with two perspectives in mind. First God is the source of all existence, and secondly in that God is all good, he cannot be the source of evil. It follows that evil could not possibly coexist in a creation that God looked upon as good to very good. Thus, "evil must be a lack or deficiency in what is rather than a part of it." Hence, borrowing from Hellenistic philosophy, Jewish theologians, particularly those of the Middle Ages, taught that the evil we find in creation are really privations—darkness as opposed to light, emptiness rather than fullness, disease instead of health, ignorance and not knowledge, blindness in place of sight, etc.[1]

Contemporary Judaism considers good and evil through the eyes of God. Ecclesiastes 7:14 tells us, "So in time of good fortune enjoy the good fortune; and in a time of misfortune, reflect: The one no less than the other was God's doing; consequently, man may find no fault with Him." In Isaiah 45:7, the prophet claims, "I form light and create darkness, I make weal and create woe—I the Lord do all these things."

The Jewish theologian Abraham Herschel[2] writes,

> "Seen from God, the good is identical with life and organic to the world; wickedness is a disease, and evil identical with death. For evil is divergence, confusion, that which alienates man from man, man from God, while good is convergence, togetherness, union. Good and evil are not qualities of the mind but relations within reality. Evil is division, contest, lack of unity and as the unity of all being is prior to the plurality of things, so is the good prior to evil.
>
> Good and evil persist regardless of whether or not we pay attention to them. We are not born into a vacuum, but stand *nolens volens (whether willing or not)*, in relation to all men and to one God. Just as we do not create the dimensions of space in order to construct geometrical figures, so we do not create the moral and the spiritual relations; they are given with existence. All we do is try to find our way in them. The good does not begin in the consciousness of man. It is being realized in the natural co-operation of all beings, in what they are for each other."

Judaism also teaches that there is an evil impulse in the human race that it calls *yetzer ha'ra*. In Genesis, this impulse is called *evil*, in Psalms *unclean*, in Proverbs *a fiend*, in Isaiah *a stumbling block*, and in Joel *a hidden object in the heart of man*. Conversely there is also in each of us a good impulse or inclination called *yetzer ha'tov*. Both of these tendencies come from God, yet there is constant tension between them in that man is endowed with free will or moral freedom. Hence, the importance of these two options. Only by doing good deeds can the Jew counteract the *yetzer ha'ra*. The rabbis clearly preferred and advocated the choice of *yetzer ha'tov*, the good inclination, but at the same time saw a value in the evil inclination, *yetzer ha'ra*. Not only did it support the idea of free will, but it also played a significant role in kindling the passions that drive a man to get married and build a house for his bride, to beget children, to ply a trade, or to pursue a profession.[3] For the ancient Jew at Sinai, it was the covenant that was at stake in every man. The supreme issue was not good and evil but God and his commandment to love good and to hate evil. Evil was not the ultimate problem. The ultimate problem was man's relation to God. The biblical answer to evil is not the good but the holy. The essence of right living was summarized by Psalm 34:15, "Shun evil and do good." Recall Deuteronomy 30:15–20.

> See, I set before you this day life and prosperity, death and adversity. For I command you this day to love the Lord your God, to walk in His ways, and to keep His commandments, His laws, and His rules, that you may thrive and increase, and that the Lord your God may bless you … But if your heart turns away and you give no heed, and are lured into the worship and service of other gods, I declare to you this day that you shall certainly perish … I have put before you life and death, blessing and curse. Choose life … by loving the Lord your God, heeding His commands, and holding fast to Him."

The Jew was also commanded to be humble, serve God, do good by helping his brother Jew, be pure, and love life in this world—in a word, do the will of God and obey him. This was and continues in modern times to be the law.

Evil and the Onset of Western Theology

The early Christians saw evil in a somewhat different light. St. Paul saw it as an external force that somehow held him in its grip. He explained its presence by saying, "It was sin, working death in me through what is good" (Romans 7:13). Later but in a similar vein he explained that when he knows what is evil and still chooses to do it, "It is no longer I that do it, but sin

31

which dwells within me" (Romans 7:17). Since the early patristic period of Christianity evil has been a major concern of theology. Its particular study is known as theodicy. Two of its most prominent students are Irenaeus and Augustine.

Irenaeus (c. 115–202 CE)

Born in Smyrna in Asia Minor (what is most of modern-day Turkey), St. Irenaeus studied under Polycarp, who in turn had been a disciple of the apostle John. He became bishop of Lyons in Southern Gaul (France) about 178 CE. He is best known for his refutation of Gnosticism, an esoteric or quasi-intuitive doctrine of salvation by knowledge, that held that one is saved from damnation by virtue of superior knowledge of the universe and its mysteries rather than obedience to and love of God. He also set out to explain, using the Scriptures, the creation of man and his fall.[4] He hypothesized that Adam and Eve were created as children.

> "So having made the man lord of the earth and everything in it, he made him in secret lord also of the servants in it. They, however, were in their full development, while the lord, that is, the man, was a little one; for he was a child and had need to grow so as to come to his full perfection. … the man was a little one, and his discretion still undeveloped, wherefore also he was easily misled by the deceiver."[5]

Adam and Eve possessed what Irenaeus described as a primal innocence. They were *naked and not ashamed*.

> "Their thoughts were innocent and childlike, and they had no conception or imagination of the sort that is engendered in the soul by evil, through concupiscence, and by lust. For they were then in their integrity, preserving their natural state, for what had been breathed into their frame was the spirit of life, now so long as the spirit still remains in proper order and vigor, it is without imagination or conception of what is shameful. For this reason they *were not ashamed* as they kissed each other and embraced with the innocence of childhood."[6]

Irenaeus describes Adam and Eve as infants[7] who were not created as either wise or holy. Contrary to later theologians who postulated that they were fully developed individuals upon their creation, Irenaeus and many of his contemporaries contended that they were like children possessing only limited intellectual or moral capabilities. What is more, they were inexperienced. They were innocent and childlike, though created in God's "image" or form. They were not perfect. Their intellectual abilities had not yet developed to the level of adults. One author argues that "the notion that Adam was not created perfect, but rather... intended to come to be in the likeness of God at the end of a process of development, is Irenaeus' most characteristic understanding of Genesis 1:26, and the one that most coheres with the rest of his theological scheme."[8] In a word, Adam and Eve needed time to grow into maturity.

God intended that they would grow in grace, submit to his commands, and in time reach the point where they would be confirmed in the Holy Spirit, becoming like God, and thereby his adopted sons and daughters. Irenaeus added that Adam and Eve in their innocence had been "injured" and "corrupted" by the cunning of the serpent, causing them to sin "under color of immortality" and thus incurring the consequences of death.[9] Notwithstanding, Irenaeus considered their sin as a necessary step in learning to cope with these consequence. Note that even after Adam's sin God did not pronounce a curse against him personally, but against the ground. As his punishment, man was consigned to toil and sweat, tilling the earth for his food, and returning to the earth from which he had been taken. Similarly Eve, his wife, was to experience the pains of labor and subjection to her husband. But God does not abandon them. All was not lost. His image and likeness will be restored.

It is to the Serpent that God turned his full wrath. God clearly laid the blame for Adam and Eve's sin upon it. He realized that they had been deceived. And he also saw that their sin of disobedience would become the source of the general sinfulness and immorality of their descendants. He knew the Serpent had beguiled Eve and Adam. He was the prime mover in the dastard deed. Hence God cursed him, but mitigated his rebuke of Adam and Eve, showing them compassion by providing something more comfortable than fig leaves to cover their nakedness prior to dismissing them from the Garden of Eden.[10]

Irenaeus also contended that good and evil are not limited to the thoughts, words, or deeds of individuals, nor do they originate solely in the human will. It is in their rationality and inherent freedom that Adam and Eve have within themselves a weakened capacity to participate in God's will and thus become like him and to be instruments through which goodness is performed upon the earth. This weakness he traced to their disobedience and the resultant curse of God upon their work and vocation in the world.

God is the fount of all goodness, which is focused on counseling and instructing his human creature to embrace life, growth, maturity, righteousness, and perfection. It is the Serpent (or Devil) who is the origin of sin and evil. The Devil directs his counsel and instruction toward evil (i.e., hatred, selfishness, and pride). While Satan is the cause and source of evil and sin, Adam and Eve are victims of his deception and malicious manipulation into participating in Satan's rebellion against God

In Adam and Eve sin entered into the world. Within his offspring there is a profound, dynamic, and continuous struggle toward life or toward sinful corruption and death that is cosmological and eschatological. Adam and Eve's sin led to cosmological consequences as they bear the burden of a cursed earth. But nonetheless, they and their posterity continue to enjoy God's compassion and love in the promise to send a Savior who will overpower the Serpent and his retinue, bind them up and crush all their power while restoring goodness and grace to humankind.[11] This Savior will engage Satan in an eschatological conflict wherein the power of God to create and the power of Satan to destroy intersect with the human will. For God seeks to bring creation to perfection and glorification and to diminish the power of Satan to destroy, leading to his eventual demise. At end time God will demonstrate his power by using sin and evil in the service of his own eschatological purposes.

What is more, Irenaeus taught that the ultimate purpose of this conflict is soul-making, the moral and spiritual growth of man and woman into perfected beings "capable of personal relationships with their creator."[12] Only by joining God in this conflict does evil and suffering begin to make sense. It is in this struggle that man and woman become truly free and begin to grow in maturity, perfection, the knowledge of God and reconciliation with him.

Finally, Irenaeus recognized and understood that man's imperfections, weaknesses, and vulnerabilities provide an "opportunity for a sinful and evil will to pervert the world." This evil consists in a will or power whose purpose is to reverse the will of God. Whereas God's will is to create, protect, and bring us to the fullness of a good destiny and a newness of life, evil—a noncreative power—strives to bring God's creation to death, corruption, and nothingness. In the final analysis, the creation story is ongoing and did not end in the Garden of Eden.[13]

Augustine (354–430 CE)

Fast-forward to the fourth century of the Common Era and the most significant theologian of his day, Augustine, the bishop of a North African city known as Hippo (in modern-day Libya). In fact, with due respect to Irenaeus, he was the most significant theologian of the first twelve hundred years of the Christian era until the appearance of Thomas Aquinas in the early thirteenth century. A convert to Christianity, decidedly a Platonist and at one time a follower of a Middle Eastern dualist named Mani (his followers being called Manicheans), Augustine looked to the Hebrew Scriptures to find the key to understanding evil and its source. Noting the two stories of creation, he blended them to develop his theory.

In reading the first story, he found that the creation of living things came in an orderly manner from plants to animals to human life. From the first account of the creation (Genesis 1:1–2:4a) he took the idea of the perfection and completion of creation. He zeroed in on the end of the story where God pronounced that everything he had made was good, thus establishing that there was no dualism between good and evil. All was good, all of creation. All was complete and perfect. It is here that present-day creationists rest their case against evolution. God was satisfied with his work, and so he rested from his labors on the seventh day. In the first story the perfection of creation is asserted. God finds that all is good.

In the second story he noted that its primary focus was on the creation of man out of the dust of the earth after he had created a beautiful garden in which the man could live. Made in God's image from the mud of the earth, God breathed on man and gave him a soul endowed with such reason and intelligence as to place him above all the other creatures that would live within this garden.[14] The man became known as Adam. Seeking to find companions for him, God created the animals, each of which received a name from Adam. When it was obvious that the animals were unable to meet his needs for companionship, God created from the ribs of Adam a woman. She was to be his helpmate. Adam named her Eve. Adam was decidedly the one to whom was given the power to name and control. But to both, according to Augustine, God gave another gift, free will. Augustine opined that

> "… He [God] created man with a nature midway between angels and bests, so that man, provided he should remain subject to his true Lord and Creator and dutifully obey His

commandments might pass into the company of the angels, without the intervention of death, thus to attain a blessed and eternal immortality. But should he offend his Lord and God by a proud and disobedient use of his free will, then subject to death and a slave to his appetites, he would then have to live like a beast and be destined to eternal punishment after death." [15]

Augustine hypothesized that not only did God endow man from the start with wisdom and knowledge, natural qualities and perfections, forces and energies, dignities and rights proper to their nature but that he also endowed them with *supernatural gifts* over and above their nature. These gifts were those infused qualities of holiness, graces, perfections, energies, and dignities that supersede the natural qualities proper to man per se. In addition to being fully human, they were also fully divine (i.e., holy as God himself is holy and perfect as God himself is perfect). Beyond the reach of all men and women, these gifts elevated Adam and Eve to the status of adopted sons, daughters, and heirs of God himself. Man was also given what theologians call preternatural gifts, which exempted him from death, sickness, ignorance, and sensuous appetites like lust and other natural weaknesses of the flesh.

Placing Adam in the garden, he charged him not to eat of the fruit of a particular tree lest he die. The inference here is that Adam was presented with a choice to live or not to live. All was well in the garden until Eve encountered the Serpent, who suggested to her that she should eat some of the fruit from the Tree of Knowledge of Good and Evil so that she could become like God himself "knowing good from evil." Eve looked at the fruit and found it "good to eat and a delight to the eyes, and that the tree was desirable as a source of wisdom." She took some and gave some to her husband to eat. The eyes of both were opened. The upshot of their choice was to choose to die and become like God, knowing good and evil? In a word, they were disobedient and to God's explicit directive. As a result they were immediately deprived of divine grace and became ashamed of their nakedness. They covered themselves with fig leaves to hide their nakedness. They had lost mastery over their own bodies. Augustine posited that from their fateful decision the flesh began to experience lust, and death loomed as their destiny. But they were not the only ones to suffer the consequences of Eve's curiosity. Augustine adds that,

"… when the first couple were punished by the judgment of God, the whole human race, which was to become Adam's posterity through the first woman, was present in the first man. And what was born was not human nature as it was originally created but as it became after the first parents' sin and punishment – as far, at least, as concerns the origin of sin and death.[16]

In addition It is through this singular act of disobedience that evil emerges. But what is evil per se?

Augustine defined evil as the privation of an inherent good. "… evil has no positive nature; what we call evil is merely the lack of something that is good."[17] In that human beings have free will, it arises when humans freely choose to follow their own desires or those of a lesser being rather than God. It is a turning away by a finite human being who possesses and exercises his or her free will from the immutable and infinite good, namely God. Hence, evil enters the world through free will. Adam and Eve in exercising their free will turned away from God.

It is here where Augustine put forth a novel theory. He suggested that this concept of free will embraces two elements, free choice (*liberum arbitrium*) and the wherewithal whereby human beings are innately enabled to make good choices (*libertas*). His argument appealed to a first person perspective which ties the vocabulary of free will and free choice to a concept of freedom. He argued that human beings are sufficiently free to do evil under their own power (*liberum arbitrium*). However, after the fall, although humans still have free will, they are no longer able to exercise this free will to innately make good choices. They are increasingly in need of the assistance of grace that restores the ability to make good choices.[18] Hence, Augustine divided freedom of choice into two categories: (1) the freedom of post-fall human beings who fail to cooperate with grace, and (2) the freedom of post-fall human beings who do cooperate with grace."[19] Human beings are increasingly in need of some sort of "guidance control" to do the right thing, to do other than evil. We are in need of grace to achieve some good choices and acts. As for the first category it is by rejecting grace that we limit ourselves to nothing more than the freedom to sin.

As for the freedom (*libertas*) with which human beings were initially created, it will be restored in the after-life and will be comparable to the freedom of the angels and the blessed in heaven. Libertas is true freedom to exercise one's ability to do good and an inability to sin.[20]

Finally, Augustine noted that though man was made from dust, he is not unfit for heaven. God was quite aware that Adam and Eve would succumb to the machinations of the Serpent and disregard his law. He knew that the punishment he would mete out to Adam and his descendants would result in a change in his human nature making it subject to concupiscence and the curse of death. But he also knew that it was also possible to turn man from evil to good and that is why he promised to redeem Adam's progeny.

Thomas Aquinas (AD 1225–1274)

Thomas Aquinas, on the other hand, approached the question of evil by equating or defining *good* as God, in that all things – including man - have their source in him. What God has created is necessarily good. But in essence, only he is perfect goodness. Aquinas contended that though the goodness in man is an adherence to God's good purpose, it is deficient in terms of a limited perfection. This deficiency Aquinas terms "a privation." Evil is then "a privation of perfect goodness." It is a departure from God's good purpose and a rejection of his will. It is a corruption of free will. Like darkness is a lack of light, so is evil a lack of goodness.

Yet nothing is totally or pure evil. For it to exist there must be some share of goodness in it. Absolute evil would be the total lack of good. It necessarily follows that if this were the case, it would also lack existence. (It would be nothing.) Ordinary evil is real. It is a privation in the sense that it is an absence or deficiency of goodness in human nature, a consequence of man's freedom and free choice.[21]

Another way of looking at Aquinas's concept of evil is to consider it as the opposite of good. Whatever lacks perfection is evil—that is to say that it lacks something that it should have had. For example, a man who is blind, deprived of sight, lacks the ability to see, which is proper to normal men. This is not to say that the blind man is intrinsically evil, but he is deprived of what he should by his very nature possess. Hence, Aquinas suggests that one can study evil in a number of ways—evil in nature (*malum naturale*), evil in human work (*malum artificale*), and moral evil in human actions (*malum morale*). In these instances evil is always a privation of a good in a subject.[22]

Evil in nature is simply a privation that takes the form of decay, malformations, or the death of organisms like animals or plants so as to make way for the sustenance, birth, and generation of new animals or plants.

Natural disasters like hurricanes, flooding, or earthquakes might well be a deprivation for a particular group of people or geographic area but might well be necessary in the long run because they provide rivers and fertile lands and regulate energy exchanges and temperature within the oceans. Another natural evil is pain and suffering in body and in mind. When caused by man, it might well be a moral evil. But one can readily see that the pain and suffering that result from a removal of a life-threatening tumor is not the same thing as that caused by a criminal act such as an assault or act of thievery. Of course, there are considerable gradations of pain and suffering among animals and human beings. Hence, the willful causing of pain and suffering up to the privation of life in a human being is not of the same magnitude as the willful causing of pain and suffering or privation of life of an animal. The former is patently evil.

Aquinas further teaches that an action is morally evil whenever man knowingly and freely deviates from what he is obliged to do as a human being. Whenever one fails to do what he or she knows to be good and chooses evil, we are in the realm of moral evil or sin. Deagan[23] writes, "Moral evil is the most total form of evil because it deprives man of his perfection as man and is a conscious free choice of evil (under the form of a limited good which stands in separation from man's duties)."

Most Christians accept the Augustinian and Thomist view that evil is nothing more than the privation of good. Evil is not a positive thing but merely the absence of good. There is no trace of evil in God, who is perfect. Hence, he cannot be blamed for bringing evil into existence. Even though the world contains evil, this fact cannot be reconciled with the idea that it was created by a God who simply cannot create evil, only good.

The Story of Two Trees

There is more to our discussion than our treatment of good and evil per se. Perhaps we might benefit from an account of the *two* trees in the garden, the Tree of Life and the Tree of the Knowledge of Good and Evil. The words with which God expelled Adam and Eve from the garden say it all. "And the Lord God said, 'Now that the man has become like one of us, knowing good and bad, what if he stretch out his hand and take also from the tree of life and eat, and live forever!' So the Lord drove the man out" (Genesis 3:22–23).

What is the significance of this Tree of Life? It is safe to say that the Tree of the Knowledge of Good and Evil represents a mixture of good and evil. It symbolizes man's decision to discover for himself what is good and what is evil and to assume the consequences of his decision. By choosing this tree Adam sought to become as God. On the other hand, the Tree of Life symbolizes many other things, including wisdom, strength, and obedience to God and hence, the way to eternal life. It leads to truth, the good, and love. In other words, had Adam and Eve chosen the fruit of the Tree of Life, they would have lived forever in addition to knowing good and evil.

In the mystical tradition underlying modern day Judaism, Kabbalah, there are two different trees of life. One is depicted as upside down with its roots flowing from the heavens the source of divinity and infinite goodness. Its trunk and branches reach out toward us, penetrating our spirits, psyches, and physical existence. Kabbalists call this the Tree of Emanation. The other tree symbol is similar to what we normally visualize as a tree whose roots are deep in the earth, its trunk and branches flowing upward back to the sky. Kabbalists call this the Tree of Evolution or Initiation. As the initiated man climbs this tree to the source, he evolves and awakens to who he really is, penetrating the worlds of psyche, spirit, and divine unity and ultimately reconnecting with the divine source of his existence, God. Hence, the Tree of Life situated in the middle of the garden and from whose roots stream milk, honey, wine, and oil, according to the Hebrew creation myth and Jewish commentators, is the ultimate symbol of the life-giving source of that which sustains and nourishes us. In psychology this tree is a symbol of one's true self and model of how both psyche and spirit unfold. We have seen that through the Tree of Knowledge of Good and Evil, sin came into the world. But it was also through a tree that we have been redeemed. The cross upon which Jesus was crucified has become the new Tree of Life. But we digress. Let us return to our discussion.

In the final analysis Adam's decision leads to expulsion from the garden.

> And to the woman He said, "I will make most severe your pangs in childbearing. In pain shall you bear children. Yet your urge shall be for your husband, and he shall rule over you."
>
> To Adam He said, "Because you did as your wife said and ate of the tree about which I commanded you, 'You shall not eat of it,' cursed be the ground because of you; by toil shall you eat of it all the days of your life; thorns and

thistles shall it sprout for you. But your food shall be the grasses of the field; by the sweat of your brow shall you get the bread to eat, until you return to the ground—for from it you were taken, for dust your are, and to dust you shall return. (Genesis 3:14–19)

Yet even after being expelled from the garden, God's initial gift of free will remains. Man now must live according to his own decisions as to whether or not to abide by what is right and/or what is evil. Does this act of disobedience constitute the introduction of evil into the world? Perhaps we should look elsewhere or at least ask a few more questions, particularly as it relates to the principal protagonist in the creation story, the serpent.

The Serpent

We have seen that it was through a singular act of disobedience that evil emerges. Hence, the source of evil is the desire to be like divine beings who know good and bad. Is the priest right that man brought evil into the world? Many believe this to be the case. But wait. It took another entity to stoke that desire, the Serpent.

Just as God created man, he also created the Serpent. So the real question is this: Who is the Serpent? Who is this who encouraged Adam and Eve to disobey their Creator? Tradition would have him be Lucifer, the fallen archangel whom we now know as Satan or the Devil. But actually how do we really know?

In any discussion of Satan one should bear in mind the fact that early Judaism, as has been mentioned earlier, was heavily influenced by the dualism of Babylonian and later Persian religion, which held that the powers of good and evil were in perpetual struggle with each other over the control of the universe and created human beings. However, the initial meaning of Satan among each group was "the Adversary." God created Satan so that he might seduce man "for the sake of heaven." The best description of Satan at work is found in the book of Job, where as a member of a divine counsel, his job was to observe human activity, to search out sinners, and to accuse them before God. In this, the oldest book of the Hebrew Bible, God permits Satan to tempt Job to curse God by heaping misfortune after misfortune upon him. In the end Satan does his job, yet Job remains faithful to the Almighty.

According to contemporary Jewish thinkers, this continues to be Satan's job. He is simply doing a dirty job, trying to destroy us spiritually.[24] According to Rabbi Heschel[25], "There is a holy spark of God even in the dark recesses of evil. If not for the spark, evil would lose its power and reality, and would turn to nothingness."

When God's judgment that the Serpent would be consigned to crawling on his belly is combined with his proclamation that there would be an enmity between the Serpent and his seed and the seed of the woman, this passage lends credence to the creation story writers' belief that the Serpent was the personification of evil.

The Problem of Satan

Contemporary Judaism has a different take from Western Christianity in recognizing Satan as an angel with a particular job. According to Singer, in the same article cited previously[26], Satan's specific purpose is to hinder us or prevent us from doing something, to make things difficult for us, to tempt us, or to test us. This purpose has been determined by God. Satan, whose name in Hebrew means *hinderer*, presents us with the ability to look at evil and refuse to succumb to it or to choose between good and evil. To help us meet this challenge, God gives us free will. We exercise that free will when we remove ourselves from evil and choose to do good. Satan offers us death and curse. God offers us life and blessing. We have the power to overcome Satan and choose God.

Rabbi Singer recalls reading of a man who was very troubled coming to a rabbi to ask for his prayers. He wanted God to stop his evil inclinations and temptations. He knew he was a sinner, but he wanted to stop sinning. The rabbi answered (and I paraphrase), "If you had no evil inclinations, what would your purpose in life be? You were created to overcome your temptations, to choose to do good, to improve yourself by being godly. Your reward will come when you hear the words upon your death, 'Well done, good and faithful servant.'"

The rabbi goes on to say that whenever we are tempted by another or tempt our brother or sister to sin, we have chosen to join Satan, failed to resist him, and done evil by sinning. We have lost a battle. We must pick ourselves up, dust ourselves off, seek God's forgiveness, and ask for his help and the means with which to overcome our evil inclinations. At the end of time Satan's work will be done. There will no longer be a need for a tempting angel, an angel of death, or a prosecuting angel.

Christians, on the other hand, see Satan as "the prince of darkness, ruler of all evil spirits, enemy of both God and humankind, and source of treachery and wickedness."[27] It is he who in the guise of the Serpent tempted Adam and Eve. With the writing of the New Testament, Satan's role as the Devil was well established among Christians.

The previous notwithstanding, this does not let man off the hook. To what extent is man the source of evil? After all, it could be argued that Adam and Eve had the propensity to harbor the desire to be like God in the eating of the forbidden fruit. They were apparently willing and able to commit the act thereof. Augustine begins this discussion by suggesting that it was God who created the world and promised man's redemption after the fall. The existence of evil in creation cannot be ascribed to God. He created the world as good. It was free of evil. Therefore, evil is a direct consequence of the misuse of human freedom. Now God created humanity with the freedom to choose good or evil. Unfortunately humanity chose the latter. As a result, the world is sullied by evil.

How could humans choose evil if there was no evil to choose? Evil had to be an option within the world if it were to be accessible to human choice. Augustine concludes that the origin of evil lies in the temptation by the Serpent—who tradition recognizes as Satan—by which he lured Adam and Eve into disobedience. God, therefore, cannot be responsible for evil. Alas, Augustine failed to realize that the existence of the Tree of Knowledge of Good and Evil was known to be in the middle of the garden by both Adam and Eve, therefore putting into question his point about the option being accessible to human choice.

Another question is this: Did he not create Satan? Granted he created the world good. But did he not originally create Satan or Lucifer good? How is it that this archangel and others like him succumb to the temptation to become like God and assume supreme authority by rebelling against God and spreading that rebellion to the world? How is this possible? In creating Lucifer as one of his archangels, did God create evil? How could he have not known that through an act of disobedience evil would corrupt the goodness of his creation?

From the first to the last book of the Bible, the Devil appears as the purveyor of evil, the one who sows discord, wreaking havoc and adversely affecting the history of mankind even until this day. This would seem to imply that I consider Satan to be the source of evil, one who influences the commission of sin and evil acts by human beings. Is it possible, given

Rabbi Singer's assertions, that Satan was really the first of God's creations to embody all that is inimical to God's character? Truth was not in him. He is a murderer and the father of lies (John 8:44). He was the epitome of evil, "forever prowling like a roaring lion looking for someone to devour." (1 Peter 5:8). Or was he totally depraved and corrupt?

An interesting starting point in this discussion is the name of Satan found in Hebrew Scripture, Lucifer, which in Hebrew means *brightness*. The following passage is taken from Isaiah:

> How are you fallen from heaven,
> O Shining One, son of Dawn!
> How are you felled to earth,
> O vanquisher of nations!
> Once you thought in your heart,
> "I will climb to the sky;
> Higher than the stars of God
> I will set on my throne.
> O will sit in the mount of the assembly,
> On the summit of Zaphon;
> I will mount the back of a cloud—
> I will match the most High."
> Instead, you are brought down to Sheol,
> To the bottom of the Pit. (Isaiah 14:12–15)

On the surface its context refers to the fall of the king of Babylon, who is purported to have been strident in his pride and splendor and evil. Isaiah seems to be addressing the power behind this evil Babylonian king, who claimed that his throne was above that of God or that he was equal to God. This power was none other than Lucifer.

The fathers of the church applied this passage to Lucifer. Isaiah was aware of many Canaanite myths, particularly one about a lesser god's attempt to become head of the pantheon of gods. This served him well to illustrate the pride of an earthly king. No less familiar were the fathers of the church who, along with Isaiah, were also aware of the book of Enoch[28], a Jewish pseudepigrapha (apocryphal) of the Hebrew Bible. In this book Enoch writes of one of the angels created by God who went by the name of Satan. "And one of the angels, having turned away with the order that was under him, conceived an impossible thought" to place his throne higher than the clouds above the earth that he might become equal in rank to my power. And I threw him out from the height" (2 Enoch, 5).

In a later passage Enoch writes,

> The Devil is the evil spirit of the lower places, a fugitive … his name was Satan. Thus he became different from the angels, but his nature did not change his intelligence in regard to understanding right and wrong. And he understood his condemnation and the sin which he had sinned. Therefore he nurtured thoughts against Adam. He entered his world and seduced Eva but did not touch Adam. (2 Enoch, 6)

From Enoch we learn that Satan was of high rank in the angelic order. But he wanted more. He wanted to be God or at least his equal. This having been said, the real concern of the church fathers and other commentators of these passages in not about Lucifer (Satan) per se but how he works to seduce not only earthly kings and other high officials of government and those of other walks of life—even men and women of the church and synagogue—to abrogate to themselves divine honors and in this way to be like God. This calls to mind St. Paul's warning, "For it is not against human enemies that we have to struggle, but against the principalities and the ruling forces who are masters of the darkness in this world, the spirits of evil in the heavens" (Ephesians 6:12).

St. John adds much to this discussion. Turning to the book of Revelation, Satan is called by name at least seven times and is equated to evil (Revelation 2:9, 13, 24; 3:9; 12:7–9; 20:1–3, 7–10). He is also referred to as the Dragon, the primal Serpent (who had beguiled Eve), and the false prophet. His minions are called the beast, the great prostitute, and the angels of the abyss. Illustrative of Revelation's treatment of Satan are the following passages:

> And now war broke out in heaven, when Michael with his angels attacked the dragon. The dragon fought back with his angels, but they were defeated and driven out of heaven. The great dragon, the primeval serpent, known as the devil or Satan, who had led all the world astray, was hurled down to the earth and his angels were hurled down with him. (Revelation 12:7–9)

> Then I saw an angel come down from heaven with the key of the Abyss in his hand and an enormous chain. He overpowered the dragon, that primeval serpent which is the devil and Satan, and chained him up for a thousand years. He hurled him into the Abyss and shut the entrance and sealed it over him, to make sure he would not lead the nations astray again until the thousand years had passed. At the end of that time he must be released, but only for a short while. (Revelation 20:1–3)

> When the thousand years are over, Satan will be released from his prison and will come out to lead astray all the nations in the four quarters of the earth, God and Magog, and mobilize them for war, his armies being as many as the sands of the sea. They came swarming over the entire country and besieged the camp of the saints, which is the beloved City. But fire rained down on them from heaven and consumed them. Then the devil, who led the astray, was hurled into the lake of fire and sulphur, where the beast and the false prophet are, and their torture will not come to an end, day or night, for ever and ever. (Revelation 20:7–10)

What I have attempted to do up to this point is to posit—rather tentatively—that the instigator of evil is the Devil. Fortunately God has not left man defenseless in his encounters with Satan. He has given us free will to choose good or evil. Through natural law, his prophets, experience, and other means, he has given us the wherewithal to choose between the two alternatives. Alas, unless we are vigilant and seek God's protection and grace, all too frequently do we opt for an act that rejects him.

But there is still another point that needs to be made in this discussion. The jury is still out with respect to the question whether Lucifer or man brought evil into the world? Is God the source, the origin of evil? Just as God gave man a free will, did he also give it to his angels? If so, did Lucifer and several of his fellow angels choose to be like God? If not, could there be some truth to Rabbi Singer's assertion? Do the angels simply have *standing*? Are they simply the way they are because that is the way God created them? Why is this important? Did Adam know what he was doing? Did he and Eve really know what they were choosing? If you believe that they had reached a state of perfection as complete human beings fully cognizant of the consequences of their action, then perhaps so. But if you believe that man evolved over long periods of time, I think they did not fully comprehend those consequences just as we today also fail in this respect because we are still evolving. One thing is still certain. Evil is "alive and well." But what is it?

What Is Evil?

When it is all said and done, what is evil and from whence does it come? It is markedly easier to answer the first question. The second question has been an ongoing debate that will continue for millennia. Simply stated, *Webster's* associates evil with all that is "angry ... wrathful, [and] malignant." Jungian analyst Liliane Frey-Rohn[29] contends that "evil is a phenomenon that exists and has always existed in the human world." It is an existential reality. Freud described evil as a duel between an evil "death instinct" (thanatos) and a good "life instinct" (eros). Jung's "shadow" speaks to the certainty of personal and collective evil.

Evil is the conscious, deliberate, and indiscriminate wrongdoing or violence designed to harm others, diminish their psychological well-being and dignity, or cause pain or suffering to another for selfish or malicious reasons. According to Diamond[30], it is that tendency which – whether in oneself or others – "would inhibit personal growth and expansion, destroy or limit innate potentialities, curtail freedom, fragment or disintegrate the personality, and diminish the quality of interpersonal relationships." At a religious or theological level – based on values, ethics and morals—evil is associated with human moral turpitude or attitudes and behaviors that promote "excessive interpersonal aggression, cruelty, hostility, hatred, disregard for the integrity of others, self-destructiveness, psychopathology, and human misery in general ... It is manifested in homicide, suicide, sexual perversion, assaults, abuse, or addictions 1510—such as alcoholic, pornographic, or otherwise destructive behaviors directed at oneself or another.

History—past and present—has seen evil perpetrated by a single individual, group, country, or entire collective (culture).

Evil goes to the core of our being. It is like an abscess, a cancer that bores into our souls, weakening the very fibers of our being of our will. We are absorbed by and into a spirit that if not initially rebuffed, takes over us not unlike Mr. Hyde taking over the persona and soul of Dr. Jekyll. You will

47

recall the latter's fateful decision to experiment with the duality of good and evil within his psyche, expressing thereby its deep spiritual and moral aspects. When Mr. Hyde's morally reprehensible acts begin to overcome Dr. Jekyll's Victorian sensibilities and subsequently his image of himself as a moral and spiritual person, the inner conflict between good and evil, i.e. Dr. Jekyll and Mr. Hyde, results in the triumph of the latter, with its consequent effects and implications upon not only Dr. Jekyll, but also society writ large. Two examples include pornography and how it wraps one in its filthy arms as well as alcoholism, which eradicates our will to the point where we become monsters or demons to our loved ones. In these addictions we choose evil over good. We know better, but we are powerless.

All people seem to know intuitively at a deep level when they are in the presence of evil, even though they cannot quite explain it other than to make statements like, "The hair on my back stood up," "I broke into a cold sweat," or "I could not breathe." Most of us know when someone or something is not *holy* or *good* or *pure*. We feel dirty or filthy. From this all people know that evil is real and at times overpowering. But we also know that it thrives best when it is disguised as good or coexists with the holy.

Noting that the problem of evil has been central to religious thought for millennia, the contemporary psychologist and spiritual director M. Scott Peck[31] adds that we cannot separate it from the problem of goodness or the question of God and creation. He notes that evil spelled backward is *live*. He infers from this that evil is in opposition to life. It opposes the life force. It is tantamount to killing or murdering without destroying the body, the essential attribute of human life (i.e., the spirit). It weakens man's nobility, autonomy, and will. Referencing Eric Fromm, he goes on to say that it gives rise to the desire to control others, to discourage their capacity to think for themselves, to diminish their unpredictability and originality, and to keep them in slavery to sin, causing them to become obedient automata, robbing them of their humanity, making them simple chattel.

Quoting Jesus' statement "I have come that they might have life, and they might have it abundantly," Peck equates goodness with that which promotes life and liveliness. Quoting Jesus' description of Satan as "a murderer from the beginning," he underscores the aforementioned murder of the spirit if not the body. So Satan is the instigator of evil and sin. But man, given his free choice between doing good or evil, is the perpetrator of the dastard deed when he chooses the latter. For God being is intrinsically good. It speaks to life and hence "convergence, togetherness, union, and community." Evil is disease and death. It speaks to divergence, confusion, and the alienation of man from man and man from God. Additionally Adam's choice introduces disharmony and death.

Concluding Comments

Teilhard de Chardin[32] provides an interesting gloss on evil in a world that is still evolving. Speaking of the negative essence or shadow of the biological process of hominization or "becoming man," he suggests that evil is to be found in "every nook and cranny, through every joint and sinew of Christian existence." He speaks of

- the evil of disorder and failure where there is much misery, sinfulness, sentient suffering, wickedness, and torture of spirit;
- the evil of decomposition where there is sickness and corruption and death; and,
- the evil of solitude and anxiety where man's consciousness wakens to reflection in a dark universe in which light takes centuries and centuries to reach it and where we have not yet succeeded in either understanding either it or its demands on us;

In addition he also thought that because there is a general consensus that evolution is a reality, evil is simply an incompleteness of man, who is steadily progressing toward a higher state of unity. It is not an unforeseen accident in an Aristotelian sense but "the shadow that God raises by his very decision to create." It speaks to disunity and disharmony, even physical decomposition, manifested by sin, a deliberate movement of the will away from unity. Accordingly it is an evil at the level of moral consciousness that affects the well-being of the soul and makes a mockery of the commandment to love God with one's whole heart, soul, mind, and strength. In summation, it is a precursor of human suffering, a lack of freedom, and disorder.

On a more prosaic level evil is all around us. Read the local newspaper or listen to television news anchors and commentators as they *inform* us of euthanasia, lies, theft, greed, promiscuity, fornication, and abortion. Read of any number of crimes and other wrongs committed within families and by neighbor against neighbor, businessmen and women mistreating their employees by not paying a just wage or selling shoddy merchandise at obscene prices to low-income consumers, politicians, clergy, and other so-called upstanding citizens engaging in questionable and immoral practices, and the list goes on. Listen also to the graphic and disturbing language that poses as lyrics in contemporary music. See the tawdry behavior and actions of entertainers, starlets, and other theater or film types.

What is common to all is the belief that "no one will see me." All believe that darkness will hide their sin and complicity. All are children of the dark, or as Peck declares "people of the lie." Yes, the sons and daughters of man have chosen darkness over light. Many have chosen to become children of darkness, as Reinhold Niebuhr would say in his commentary on the following:

> The people that walked in darkness have seen a brilliant Light. (Isaiah 9:2)

> Though the light has come into the world, people have preferred darkness to the light because their deeds were evil. (John 3:19)

> I am the light of the world; anyone who follows me will not be walking in the dark, but will have the light of life. (John 8:12)

Evil thrives in the dark. It cannot tolerate the brightness of the light. It thrives on the absence of light to survive. Not unlike roaches, which scurry under a refrigerator when the light goes on in the kitchen, so too does evil seek the safety of secrets, collusions, and lies. We read in Job 24:13–17:

> They are rebels against the light;
> They are strangers to its ways,
> And do not stay in its path.
> The murderer arises in the evening
> To kill the poor and needy,
> And at night he acts the thief.
> The eyes of the adulterer watch for twilight,
> Thinking, "No one will glimpse me then."
> He masks his face.
> In the dark they break into houses;
> By day they shut themselves in;

They do not know the light.
For all of them morning is darkness;
It is then that they discern the terror of darkness.

To compound matters, the very environment in which we are born and nurtured produces in us an inability to see clearly through the darkness that permeates our consciousness, preventing us from seeing and appreciating reality. We are not unlike those individuals of whom Plato wrote in his Allegory of the Cave. You will recall that Plato, through a conversation between Socrates and one Glaucon, describes a cave in which prisoners are chained facing the cave's back wall. They are prevented somehow from turning around. Behind them is a bridge upon which a number of puppeteers are lying down. Behind the puppeteers is a fire. Beneath the bridge is an opening that leads to the entry to the cave. Using wooden and iron objects together with their puppets to approximate reality as close as possible, the puppeteers produce shadows that resemble objects and people. Of course the prisoners who are unable to turn their heads have no idea that what they are seeing as shadows is anything but reality. They think that what they see on the walls is real.

In time one of the prisoners is released and forced to look at the fire and the puppeteers and their objects by which they produced the shadows, dictating his perception of reality. He begins to realize that what he is now looking at is actual reality. Once the prisoner climbs out of the cave and stands in full daylight, he finds the sun's rays at first blinding. He becomes bewildered and fearful as he gazes about him to see what is really real. He begins to recognize shadows and reflections, items and people, even the sun, which he realizes is according to Plato the "form of the good." He now is aware not only of reality but also truth, and he ultimately begins to *understand*.

Although fearful, he reluctantly returns to his fellow prisoners to apprize them of his discovery. He realizes and feels keenly that his is returning to a world of darkness. Only a few believe him. Others simply do not understand something they have never experienced. Still others laugh at him, ridicule him, and abuse him. They question his veracity and attempt to dissuade him of the certainty of what he has seen. Of course, in time there is always the possibility that he might begin to doubt what he has seen and to adjust his view of reality.

We live in a time when it is fashionable to deny the existence of evil, of sin, of hell, of Satan. We love the darkness more than we love the light.

And this applies even to those of us who would not think of missing church on Sundays, for the very next day we are back to our sinful ways. We park our consciences and sense of morality at the doorstep of our workplaces and engage in questionable and oftentimes unethical behavior in our business dealings. We say we subscribe to the teaching of Jesus, but when was the last time we got beyond pious platitudes and visited the sick, gave drink to the thirsty, clothed the naked, visited our brother and sister in prison, gave shelter to the homeless, gave a meal to the hungry, or buried the dead. Jesus referred to those of us who failed to do any of these as goats to be cast into hell.

Toward the end of his long pontificate Pope Leo XIII was saying a mass in his private chapel. His secretary was his altar server. Suddenly, as his secretary reports, the Holy Father's face turned pale and ashen. He began to stare out into space, becoming almost catatonic, not saying a word. He was that way for a long time before he finally came out of it. He finished the Mass, and without any conversation the pope went to his study and his desk and started writing. Later he told his secretary and several of his advisors that he had experienced a very strong, almost overpowering premonition that the twentieth century was to be Satan's own handpicked century.

And it would seem that there was truth in that premonition when you consider the scale of violence and mayhem in the twentieth century (i.e., World War I, the Great War, followed in short order by World War II and Hitler with his concentration camps and the killing of six million Jews, the atomic bomb and Hiroshima, Mao Tse-Tung's China, the Korean War, Vietnam, Pol Pot's killing fields, the genocide in Bosnia, Serbia, and Uganda, and the list goes on). Truly the sons of man have chosen the darkness over the light.

By the way, remember my eastern orthodox priest friend and his contention that man is the source of evil. Given the discussion thus far, do you agree with him? Perhaps you might want to refrain from commenting until you have read the following chapter on sin.

Endnotes

[1]   Seeskin, Kenneth, *Searching for a Distant God* (New York: Oxford University Press, 2000), 177–188.

[2]   Heschel, Abraham Joshua, *Man Is Not Alone: A Philosophy of Religion* (New York: Farrar, Strauss and Giroux, 1951), 121–122.

[3] Apple, Raymond Rabbi, "Evil in Man: The Jewish Point of View," (*The Australian Journal of Forensic Sciences*, Volume 15, Issue 3, 1983), 125–132.

[4] Irenaeus, Proof of the Apostolic Preaching, Translated and Annotated by Joseph P. Smith, S.J., Ancient Christian Writers Volume 16 (Mahweh, NJ: Paulist Press, 1956), 54-57

[5] Ibid, 53

[6] Ibid, 56

[7] Ireneaus, Against Heresies, Book IV, Chapter XXXVIII, Kindle Electronic Edition: Paragraphs 1 - 2 Location 8661 - 8676

[8] Minns, Dennis Irenaeus, An Introduction (London, England: T & T Clark International, 2010), 61

[9] Irenaeus, Against Heresies, *Ante-Nicene Fathers* Volume 1, Book III, Chapter XXIII, Kindle Electronic Edition: Paragraphs 1, 2 Location 32382 - 32415

[10] Irenaeus, Against Heresies, Book III, Chapter XXIII, Kindle Electronic Edition: Paragraphs 3-5 Location 6353-6413

[11] Ibid, Book XXIII Paragraph 7.

[12] John Hick, Evil and the God of Love ((Houndmills, Basingstoke, Hampshire, England: Palgrave Macmillan, 2010), 212

[13] Clark, Mary T., "Irenaeus," Everett Ferguson, ed., *Encyclopedia of Early Christianity* (New York: Garland Press, 1990), 471–472.

[14] St. Augustine, City of God, translators: Gerald Walsh, S.J. Demetrius B. Zema, S.J. Grace Monahan, OO.S.U, Daniel J. Honnan (Garden City, NY: Image Book, 1958), 263

[15] Ibid, 262

[16] Ibid, 263

[17] Ibid, 217

[18] Augustine, *Confessions Book XIII, Chapter* 21, Kindle Electronic Edition, Location 12710.

[19] Gilbert, Christopher, Grades of Freedom: Augustine and Descartes, in *Pacific Philosophical Quarterly* 86 (2005): 201-224

[20] ibid

[21] Aquinas, Thomas, Summa Contra Gentiles Book III, Chapter VII in Basic Writings of Saint Thomas Aquinas Volume 2, ed. Anton Pegis, New York: Random House, 1945) 13.

[22] Aquinas, Thomas, COMPENDIUM OF THEOLOGY, Part 1 Chapters 114-121, translator Cyril Vollert, S.J., (St. Louis & London: B. Herder Book Co., 1947) http://dhspriory.org/thomas/Compendium.htm#114

[23] Deagan, G., "St. Thomas and the Problem of Evil," *Universitas* 12 (Dec 2005): Centre for Thomistic Studies, Sydney, Australia. http://www.cts.org.au/2005/universitas12/probevil.html

[24] Singer, Tovias (2011) http://www.outreachjudaism.org/articles/who-is-satan.html.

25   Heschel, Abraham Joshua, *God in Search of Man: A Philosophy of Judaism* (New York: Farrar, Strauss and Giroux, 1955), 370.

26   Ibid, Singer

27   "Satan." *The Columbia Encyclopedia*, 6th ed., accessed on May 16, 2014, http://www.encyclopedia.com/doc/1E1-Satan.html.

28   Barnstone, Willis, ed., *The Book of the Secrets of Enoch (2 Enoch) Jewish Pseudepigrapha* (San Francisco: Harper & Row Publishers, 1984).

29   Frey-Rohn L., *Evil from the Psychological Point of View: Essays by Carl Kerenyi and Others* (Evanston, IL: Northwestern University Press 1967), 17.

30   Diamond, Stephen A., "The Psychology of Evil, Devils, Demons, and the Daimonic," in *Anger, Madness, and the Daimonic: The Psychological Genesis of Violence, Evil, and Creativity* (State University of New York Press, 1999), Kindle Electronic Edition: Location 1497 - 1510

31   Peck, M. Scott, *People of the Lie: The Hope for Healing Human Evil* (New York: Simon and Schuster, 1983), 42.

32   de Chardin, Teilhard, *The Phenomenon of Man* (New York: Harper and Row Publishers, Inc., 1959), 311–313.

CHAPTER 4

WHAT IS SIN?

Have mercy upon me, O God,
as befits Your faithfulness;
in keeping with Your abundant compassion,
blot out my transgressions.
Wash me thoroughly of my iniquity,
and purify me of my sin;
for I recognize my transgressions,
and am ever conscious of my sin.
Against You alone have I sinned,
and done what is evil in Your sight;
so You are just in Your sentence,
and right in Your judgment.
Indeed I was born with iniquity;
with sin my mother conceived me."

—Psalm 51:1–7

The Hebrew Bible's Notion of Sin

In the Jewish Scripture the general sense of the meaning of sin flows from violations of the Shema, the central prayer of Judaism, which is found in both the Hebrew Bible and in the Christian New Testament. Every observant Jew recites the following prayer three times per day: "Hear, O Israel! The Lord is our God, the Lord alone. You shall love the Lord your God with all your heart and with all your soul and with all your might." (Deuteronomy 6:4–5)

In the New Testament in response to a question as to which is the greatest commandment of all Jesus recites the Shema as follows: "This is the first; Listen, Israel, the Lord our God is the one, only Lord, and you must love the Lord your God with all your heart, with all your soul, with all your mind, and with all strength. The second is this: You must love your neighbor as yourself. There is no commandment greater than these." Mark 12:29-31. Note the second part of the command, i.e. to love one's neighbor and one's self. In the Shema is embedded the Decalogue (the Ten Commandments). The first three commandments stipulate the relationship between God and man. The following seven speak to the relationship between neighbors and by inference how we should respect and love ourselves. A violation of any part of these commandments is to do evil. It is to do evil against someone, particularly Yahweh. It is a transgression or violation of the covenant between Yahweh and his people. It shows contempt and infidelity to the divine Law. It is also an act of disobedience, immorality, idolatry, and apostasy. With respect to one's neighbor sin is to do evil against him or her, to give false witness, or to engage in adultery and fornication. It is also harshness and injustice against the weak, social or class exclusion or exploitation, or a failure to be a good neighbor. With respect to our selves it is a sin against our body as a Temple of the Holy Spirit. In a word, sin in Judaism is "to miss the mark" with respect to God, neighbor and self.

It was through the *transgression* of Adam and Eve that death and sin come into the world. God punishes them and evicts them from the garden, but in his compassion he makes garments for them to cover their shame. The immediate effect of their disobedience is seen in the stories of Cain and Abel, Noah and the flood, and the building of the Tower of Babel. God punishes Cain for killing his brother. He is to become a wanderer over the earth, yet God is again merciful and places a mark of some sort on him lest he be killed by whom he meets. This mark serves as a sign of God's care and protection. In the ancient world, to wander alone in the world is dangerous. The mark shows that Cain belongs to a tribe. Should anyone mistreat or kill Cain, he would be avenged by members of his tribe.

God looks upon mankind and is saddened by those whose evil doing was great and whose wickedness was widespread and vows to destroy all but one man and his immediate family. Noah and those who entered the ark survive a flood that destroys all life on earth. From Noah and his descendants a new creation is realized, and God enters into a covenant with his people. But the desire to become God continues.

The Tower of Babel completes the primal story. Here men build a tower "to make a name" for themselves. In other words, they build a tower to become God. God scatters these would-be builders over all the earth and confuses them by introducing diverse languages so that they could not understand each other. This last story ties all the previous stories together. In each story the pattern is the same. Man wants to become God. Sin and consequences follow. These are the primal stories. But there is more. A new chapter begins as mankind grows and fills the earth.

From a little known area in Mesopotamia God calls Abram, and brings him to a land called Canaan. There God enters into an agreement or covenant relationship with him. He promises to make Abram's descendants more numerous than the sands of the desert in exchange for their sole recognition of him as YHWH or their sovereign God. In time God changes Abram's name to Abraham and the name of his wife Sarai to Sarah. Abraham's progeny grow and prosper until the onset of a famine in Canaan. His grandson, Jacob, whose name had also been changed by God, to Israel, and his extended family journey to Egypt in search of food and find Joseph, a son he thought had been killed, the Governor of all Egypt. There they remain for a prolonged time. When a new Pharaoh came into power following the death of Joseph, the descendants of Jacob were placed in bondage, but God through his servant Moses calls them out of Egypt. While they are in the desert, God makes a new covenant with his people. He promises to make them his chosen people and to make of them a kingdom of Torah, if they obey and comply with the terms of this covenant. The entire people of Israel give their consent to its terms.

As his life draws to a close, Moses stands before his people and reminds them that each person can and must merit his or her own salvation. He tells them that obedience to Yahweh is neither too difficult nor too far off. Righteousness has been placed within their reach. He speaks these words:

> See I set before you this day life and prosperity, death and adversity. For I command you this day, to love the Lord your God, to walk in His ways, and to keep His commandments, his laws, and His rules, that you may thrive and increase, and that the Lord your God may bless you in the land you are about to enter and possess. But if your hear turns away and you give no heed and are lured into the worship and service of other gods, I declare to you this day that you shall certainly perish; you shall not long endure on the soil that you are crossing the Jordan to enter and possess. I call heaven and earth to witness against this day: I have put before you life and death, blessing and curse. Choose life—if you and your offspring would live—by loving your god, heeding His

commands, and holding fast to Him. For thereby you shall have life and shall long endure upon the soil that the Lord swore to your ancestors, Abraham, Isaac, and Jacob, to give to them. (Deuteronomy 30:15–20)

In Deuteronomy 31, we read where, after appointing Joshua as his successor, Moses writes down his teachings and instructs the Levites and admonishes his people to remain faithful to the teachings of the Torah and to return to the Lord with their hearts and souls. Nowhere is there a mention of the sin of Adam, but God does reveal to Moses that he knows that the Israelites will soon go astray to alien gods. They will break the covenant, yet he will not abandon them. God knows that the human condition – or the bane of our existence - involves a struggle between doing good and succumbing to evil.

Original Sin, a Hebrew Perspective

Turning to the sin of Adam and Eve, or what in Western Christianity has become known as *Original Sin,* nowhere in the Torah is it suggested that their descendants were complicit in their guilt or is there any reference to an *original sin.* What is noted is that Adam and Eve disobeyed their Creator and were duly punished. This was their sin and theirs alone. There is no specific doctrine comparable to Western Christianity regarding it. Nor is there any stated position about the inherent depravity of human nature. Nevertheless, the purpose of the Torah—the Law and the Prophets—is to present to us the nature of sin, our sinfulness and guilt, and its societal purposes (i.e., to show us how to "love God, our neighbor, and ourselves") and to encourage us to live righteously and to oppose injustice and oppression.

Sin in the New Testament

In Paul, we read that sin dwells in men and makes us slaves and most displeasing to God. In many of his epistles he lists many specific sinful acts, such as sexual immorality, injustice, greed, envy, murder, anger, slander, idolatry, adultery, jealousy, drunkenness, dirty talk, and the list goes on. (See Romans 1:26–31; 1 Corinthians 6:9–10; Galatians 5:19–21; Ephesians 5:3–5; and Colossians 3:5, 8.)

Paul also opined that Adam and Eve willfully disobeyed God's explicit command not to eat of the fruit of the tree, lest they die and hence, "it was through one man that sin came into the world, and through sin death, and thus death has spread through the whole human race because everyone has sinned" (Romans 5:12). He further suggested that just as through one man death came into the world, so through one man life will come to all. "As it was by one man that death came, so through one man has come the resurrection of the dead. Just as all die in Adam, so in Christ all will be brought to life" (1 Corinthians 15:21–22).

A decade after Paul's demise Matthew listed specific acts of sinfulness, many of which continue to have particular salience during the Lenten season.

> Then he will say to those on his left hand, "Go away from me with your curse upon you, to the eternal fire prepared for the devil and his angels. For I was hungry and you never gave me anything to drink, I was a stranger and you never made me welcome, lacking clothes and you never clothed me, sick and in prison and you never visited me." Then it will be their turn to ask, "Lord, when did we see you hungry or thirsty, a stranger or lacking clothes, sick or in prison, and did not come to your help?" Then he will answer, "In truth I tell you, in so far as you neglected to do this to one of the least of these, you neglected to do it to me." And they will go away to eternal punishment, and the upright to eternal life. (Matthew 25:41–46)

Sinful man thus offends against God and what is demanded by his and his neighbor's very being. It is a refusal to respond to his call to be who we are, to commit ourselves to his will, and to the history of salvation wherein God wishes to enter into us. It is refusal to respond to his summons of love. It comes from the free decisions we make within the deepest recesses of our being in our hearts and to which we give expression in our outward behavior, which is in conflict with the demands of morality, and in our inner attitudes and dispositions, which are nurtured by selfishness, pride, and the like. It is a decision made at the center of our "personness" to break away from the vital orientation of salvation a gamboling away of the life of grace.[1]

The Patristic Fathers

In the first four centuries of Christianity, church fathers in both the East (Greek) and West (Latin) more or less acknowledged Paul's teachings, particularly in Romans 5:12. However, the idea of an inheritance of sin or guilt—common in (later) Western tradition—was foreign to this perspective since in their view sin could only be a free, personal act. It was commonly accepted that human beings are blessed with free will and are neither depraved nor inherently sinful. At the same time all agreed that the world in which they lived was in many ways corrupt and sinful. Many like Irenaeus, who we met in the previous chapter, taught that the descendants of Adam somehow shared in the gravity or consequences of his sin but did not go so far as to allege that Adam's sin was the source of human sinfulness and immorality and that all human beings participate in his sin and share his guilt.

It was not until the third century that church fathers such as Tertullian, Cyprian, and Ambrose tended to agree that as a consequence of Adam's sin, mankind inherited corruption and mortality.[2] In summarizing the wisdom of other early fathers, such as Athanasius of Alexandria, Gregory Palamas, Cyril of Alexandria, and others, the Greek theologian John Karmiris[3] writes,

> The sin of the first man, together with all of its consequences and penalties, is transferred by means of natural heredity to the entire human race. Since every human being is a descendant of the first man "no one of us is free from the spot of sin, even if he should manage to live a completely sinless day" ... Original Sin not only constitutes 'an accident' of the soul, but its results, together with its penalties, are transplanted by natural heredity to the generations to come ... And thus, from one historical event of the first sin of the first born man, came the present situation of sin being imparted, together with all of the consequences thereof, to all natural descendants of Adam.

Augustine and Original Sin

By the fifth century Augustine, bishop of Hippo in present-day Libya, developed a distinct view of original sin as the result of a hotly debated controversy with an itinerant preacher and moralist named Pelagius. Pelagius believed that "neither the condition nor the guilt of original sin is inherited; rather, we all freely face the same choice between sin and salvation that Adam and Eve did." He claimed that humans have of themselves, without the necessary help of God's grace, the ability to lead morally good lives, and he denied both the importance of baptism and the teaching that God is the giver of all that is good. He further contended that the influence of Adam on other humans was merely a bad example.[4]

Augustine rebutted this argument with his contention that all Adam's descendants inherited the tendency to sin *and* the guilt of Adam and Eve's sin. These descendants were really present when Adam's committed original sin. Hence, all have sinned and are guilty, having inherited Adam's original guilt which was and continues to be transmitted by human propagation (sexual production) or *concupiscence* (in a metaphysical sense the privation of a good or a wound). The effect of the act of sexual intercourse is to severely wound Adam's descendants. An unfortunate consequence of Augustine's teaching is the assertion by the Reformers, i.e. Luther and Calvin, that man is utterly depraved in nature, lacks the freedom to do good, and cannot respond to the will of God without divine grace. The net effect is man's nature is so corrupt that he is incapable of exercising free will in the work of salvation.

One other unfortunate consequence of Augustine's teachings is his contention that unbaptized infants go to hell as a consequence of original sin. This teaching has held sway until the late twentieth century through the teaching of the existence of limbo. Only within the last decade has the Western Catholic church begun to downplay this teaching. Its catechism (1992) makes no mention of limbo but teaches that infants who die without baptism are entrusted by the church to the mercy of God under the principle that God desires the salvation of all mankind.

Contra-Augustinian Positions

A contemporary of Augustine named John Cassian did not go as far as Augustine in his observations. He did, however, agree that human nature had fallen, but he did not think it was totally bad. He further asserted that God's grace and not human free will is responsible for everything that pertains to salvation, even faith. He pointed out that people have moral freedom and have the option to choose to follow God. In his view only direct divine intervention or grace assures spiritual progress. Attributing the following remarks to John Cassian, Lauren Pristas[5] writes that "salvation is, from beginning to end, the effect of God's grace. It is fully divine. Salvation, however, is salvation of a rational creature who has sinned through free choice. Therefore, salvation necessarily includes both free human consent in grace and the gradual rehabilitation in grace of the faculty of free choice."

Thus, Cassian insists salvation is also fully human. Cassian's thinking has been criticized by the Western church as "semi-Pelagian." However, those in the Eastern churches accept him as fully orthodox, and his teachings have never been called into question or condemned by them.

Another contemporary of Augustine was John Chrysostom. While he acknowledged that human beings were made in the image and likeness of God, Chrysostom also recognized that because of original sin, corruptibility and death were visited upon not only Adam but also his descendants. Looking at the same passage from Romans 5:12, he concluded that although this sin weakened Adam and his descendants' ability to grow into God's likeness, it did not destroy their free will. This consequence notwithstanding, the real concern, according to Chrysostom, is the question of mortality. Sinfulness is simply a consequence of mortality. Other commentators on Rom 5:12 disagree with Augustine's interpretation. Many have contended that the Vulgate Latin translation of the Scriptures from which he worked was flawed in terms of its translation of the Greek phrase *"eph'ho"*, which actually means either *because, since, on condition that, with the result that,* or *so that,* but not *through* which implies that we inherited Adam's guilt as well as the consequences of his sin.[6] Thus the Latin translation of *"eph'ho" - in quo omnes peccaverunt -* ("in whom [i.e., in Adam] all men have sinned") is the source of Augustine's commentary on original sin and was used in the West to justify the assertion that we inherited Adam's guilt as well as the consequences of his sin.[7] The actual Greek text is accurately translated "death spread to all *because (or inasmuch as)* all have sinned."

The Reformers—Luther

I would be remiss not to mention at this point in our discussion the position of Martin Luther (1483–1546), a German monk, theologian, university professor, and church reformer whose ideas inspired the Protestant

Reformation. His reading of Scripture and exposure to the sins of his contemporaries led him to a belief in man's irresistible inclination to evil and sinfulness. He found that our first parents had egotistically and willfully chosen to turn away from God, and as a result they (and we) became sinful to the core. He asserted that we inherited the guilt of Adam and Eve and that from the moment of our conception we are in a state of sin. In this state our human nature is completely corrupt and depraved, and even Adam and Eve's inclination (concupiscence) to sin is passed down to us as original sin. As a result he overstated the effects of the fall of Adam and Eve and preached the radical sinfulness of our present human condition. Here is a quote from one of his commentaries on Romans and in which he defines original sin.[8]

> But what, then, is original sin? According to the Apostle it is not only the lack of a good quality in the will, nor merely the loss of man's righteousness and ability. It is rather the loss of all his powers of body and soul, of his whole outward and inward perfections. In addition to this, it is his inclination to all that is evil, his aversion against that which is good, his antipathy against light and wisdom, his love for error and darkness, his flight from and his loathing of good works, and his seeking after that which is sinful. Thus we read in Psalm 14:3: "They are all gone aside, they are all together become filthy; there is none that doeth good, no, not one"; and in Genesis 8:21: "The imagination of man's heart is evil from his youth." Actual sins essentially consist in this that they come from out of us, as the Lord says in Matthew 15:19: "Out of the heart proceed evil thoughts, murders, adulteries, fornications, thefts, false witness, blasphemies." But original enters into us; we do not commit it, but we suffer it. We are sinners because we are the sons of a sinner. A sinner can beget only a sinner, who is like him.

Orthodoxy and Ancestral Sin

Orthodox Christianity is in substantial disagreement with Augustine's portrayal of Adam and Eve. Citing the fathers (Irenaeus, Theophilus of Antioch, Ephraim the Syrian, Hilary of Poitiers, Maximus the Confessor, and others), orthodox theologians like Timothy Ware[9] insist that there is no biblical evidence that Adam and Eve, though possessing those natural qualities proper to man per se, were created with the infused attributes listed by Augustine. When God created Adam and Eve, he created them as perfect not so much in an actual as in a potential sense. They were children in a state of innocence and simplicity. They did not have at the onset a full understanding of their circumstances. They had to grow and come to completion in their likeness to God. They were sinless, at least until their act of disobedience. They were mortal but capable of achieving immortality through obedience. They were not perfect but able to sin.

Less certain than their Western counterparts, Eastern theologians admit that there is much about it that we do not really know. Like Augustine, they contend that humanity inherited the tendency to sin. Unlike Augustine, they deny that humanity inherited the guilt for Adam and Eve's sin. They posit that each person bears the guilt of his or her own sin and that the net result of this guilt is death. By the same token these theologians generally prefer to look at original sin from a spiritual perspective. Accordingly they submit that it is rooted in spiritual pride and disobedience. To that end Karmiris[10] writes,

> The Original Sin was a free transgression of our First Parents which grew out of egoism and boasting. Thus, through the envy and influence of Satan, directed against our First Parents, "the sin and transgression entered," and our First Parents transgressed the Law of God, motivated by a desire to be equal with God, or, as Chrysostom says, the "anticipation to become God"; man wanted to become independent from God, finding, by means of sin, divine knowledge, blessedness, and perfection.

Meyendorff[11] adds,

> The Greek patristic understanding of man never denies the unity of mankind or replaces it with a radical individualism. The Pauline doctrine of the two Adams [cf. 1 Cor 15:22], as well as the Platonic concept of the ideal man, leads Gregory of Nyssa to understand Genesis 1:27—"God created man in His own image"—to refer to the creation of mankind

as a whole [De opif hom 16; PG 44:185B]. It is obvious, therefore, that the sin of Adam must also be related to all men, just as salvation brought by Christ is salvation for all mankind; but neither original sin nor salvation can be realized in an individual's life without involving his personal and free responsibility ... A number of Byzantine authors, including [Patriarch] Photius, understood the *-eph ho-* to mean "because" [from Romans 5:12 "because all men sinned"] and saw nothing in the Pauline text beyond a moral similarity between Adam and other sinners, death being the normal retribution for sin. But there is also the consensus of the majority of Eastern Fathers, who interpret Romans 5:12 in close connection with 1 Corinthians 15:22—between Adam and his descendants there is a solidarity IN DEATH just as there is a solidarity IN LIFE between the risen Lord and the baptized....The sentence [of Romans 5:12] then may have a meaning which seems improbable to a reader trained in Augustine, but which is indeed the meaning which most Greek Fathers accepted: "As sin came into the world through one man and death through sin, so death spread to all men; and BECAUSE OF DEATH, all men have sinned."

It should be noted that this reading of Romans 5:12 points to death and sin as the consequences or *inheritance* of Adam's transgression. I might add the emergence of Satan as part of this equation. Meyendorff[12] in another place states that St. John Chrysostom "specifically denies the imputation of sin to the descendants of Adam."

What does this mean, "Because all have sinned" (Rom 5:12)? In that fall even those who did not eat of the tree— All did from the transgression of Adam ... For just as by the disobedience of one man the many were made sinners, so too by the obedience of One, the many will be made "just" (Rom 5:19) ... What does the word "sinners" mean here? It seems to me that it means liable to punishment and condemned to death.

Contemporary Views

Both Western and Eastern Christians believe that this sin—call it original or ancestral—separated humanity from God, making it susceptible to condemnation to eternal punishment. But with the coming of Jesus and his death on the cross, we were redeemed. We were reconciled with God. The gates of heaven and eternal life were once again available to those who believe.

At present contemporary Western theologians have shifted their views of original sin. Appreciating the substantial contributions of Augustine more than 1,500 years ago to cope with the problem of evil, they acknowledge that the tradition or original sin in the Western church has served to explain how God's creation was corrupted by human sin. This explanation has sufficed until the late eighteenth and early nineteenth centuries when the seeds of its undermining were planted with the discoveries in the various sciences, particularly geology, biology, genetics, and paleontology. Biblical scholars have found that Genesis has been misread and accepted in too literal a fashion. Theologians have come forth with differing perspectives. No less an authority as then Cardinal Joseph Ratzinger[13], who as head of the Vatican's Congregation of the Faith, admitted in 1985 that "the inability to understand 'original sin' and to make it understandable is really one of the most difficult problems in present day theology and pastoral ministry."

Although Karl Rahner[14] does not simply reject the idea of original sin as the sin of the first human being or human beings, he does assert that "in the Christian sense [it] in no way implies that the original personal act of freedom of the first person or persons is transmitted to us as our moral quality. In 'original' sin the sin of Adam is not imputed to us. Personal guilt from an original act of freedom cannot be transmitted for it's the existential no towards God or against him. And by its very nature this cannot be transmitted, just as the formal freedom of a subject cannot be transmitted." In a word, he rejects the existence of collective guilt as a result of this alleged sin having been transmitted to their descendants. He contends that this idea cannot be supported biblically or theologically. To him the issue is one of exercising one's freedom to sin or not to sin. Here is where each person is unique and solely responsible for his or her own acts.

Rahner goes on to say that "the biblical story about the sin of the first person or persons in no way has to be understood as an historical, eyewitness report. The portrayal of the sin of the first man is rather an aetiological or causal influence from the experience of man's existential situation in the history of salvation to what must have happened 'at the beginning' if the present situation of freedom actually is the way it is experienced, and if it is accepted as it is." If this is true, "then it is also clear that with regard to the visual representation of these events in the primeval beginnings of the human race, everything which cannot be arrived at by this aetiological influence from the present situation to its origin belong to the mode of representation and the mode of expression, but not to the content of the assertion." He concludes with the statement, "This assertion might be expressed per a myth—a completely legitimate mode of representation for man's ultimate experience."

Ratzinger joins the discussion by reminding us of the early Eastern fertility cults with which the early biblical writers had more than a passing acquaintance. In these cults the role of the Serpent was noteworthy. And so in the creation story just as in the fertility cults, the Serpent personified the lure of the subtle suggestion that if Eve ate of the fruit of the tree of life and death, she would become like God. She would "enjoy life in all its ecstasy." She would become immortal and no longer a mere creature. She would "be free to build her own world." She would "rise above the limitations imposed by good and evil." Ratzinger[15] writes,

> At the very heart of sin lies human beings' denial of their creatureliness, inasmuch as they refuse to accept the standard and the limitations that are implicit in it. They do not want to be creatures, do not want to be subject to a standard, do not want to be dependent. They consider their dependence on God's creative love to be an imposition from without. But that is what slavery is and from slavery one must free oneself. Thus, human beings themselves want to be God. When they do this, everything is thrown topsy-turvy. The relationship of human beings to themselves is altered, as well as their relationships to others. The other is a hindrance, a rival, a threat to the person who wants to be God. The relationship becomes one of mutual recrimination and struggle .... Finally, the world is altered in such a way as to become one of destruction and exploitation. Human beings who consider dependence on the highest love as slavery and who try to deny the truth about themselves which is their creatureliness, do not free themselves; they destroy truth and love.

He goes on to contend that they become "caricatures, pseudo-gods, slaves of their own abilities ... they live in untruth and unreality. Their lives are mere appearance; they stand under the sway of death."

But What Is Sin Today?

Sin is in essence a "renunciation of the truth." With Adam and Eve its history begins. Sin begets sin as the entire book of Genesis attests. The term *original sin* is an unfortunate description of this state of affairs. It is "a misleading and imprecise term." When it is all said and done, Adam and Eve violated their relationship with their Creator, with each other, and with creation. Sin is thus a "rejection of relationality because it wants to make the human being a god." Sin is a loss of relationship and a disturbance of relationship and not restricted to Adam and Eve alone. Sin touches others. It alters and damages the world and all of human relationship from the very beginning to the present moment. We are born into a sin-damaged world. What we call original sin goes well beyond the sin of two people at the dawn of history. It was the portal through which evil entered into the world and continues to play havoc with the human soul. But we know that God will prevail. Despite our depraved state we know that in each of us is a remnant of a divine spark that, if we choose, will burst forth to repair our relationship with God.[16]

We end this section with a reference to paragraphs 404 and 405 of Roman Catholicism's catechism, where we find the following:

> By yielding to the tempter, Adam and Eve committed a personal sin, but this sin affected the human nature that they would then transmit in a fallen state. It is a sin which will be transmitted by propagation to all man-kind, that is, by the transmission of a human nature deprived of original holiness and justice. And that is why original sin is called "sin" only in an analogical [similar] sense: it is a sin "contracted" and not "committed"—a state and not an act.
>
> Although it is proper to each individual, original sin does not have the character of a personal fault in any of Adams descendants. It is a deprivation of original holiness and justice, but human nature has not been totally corrupted; it is wounded in the natural powers proper to it;

subject to ignorance, suffering, and the dominion of death; and inclined to sin—an inclination to evil that is called "concupiscence."

For contemporary theologies of sin it is first and foremost a religious reality. It makes no sense apart from the reality and presence of God and our obligation in covenant to him expressed by "I will be your God and you will be my people" (Genesis 17:7). Sin is an infidelity and a failure of God's people to live up to their part of the covenant. Hence, sin is a willful refusal to be and do what God calls us to be and do. It is an offense against God. It is the substitution of some reality other than God. It is a placing of ourselves or another created thing where God should stand. For the biblical writers it is a form of idolatry of self. It is making ourselves God and taking upon ourselves his prerogatives.[17] In the Hebrew Bible sin speaks to the notion of a material transgression against the love of God or against some person. It is a gross ingratitude. In the New Testament sin is also an offense against God. The Greek word for sin, *amartia*, denotes a negative failure. It is like the marksman missing his target.

In philosophy sin is an evil human act, a misuse of liberty. It is a deprivation of some sort, a lack of correspondence with commonly held human values, a subtraction of something from reality. It is an assault on virtue, of a good. In theology sin is all of the above but more. It is an offense against either God or another person. It is a morally evil act that abuses the individual's power of free choice and disrupts his or her relationship with God.

The Gravity of Sin

The gravity of sin is dependent upon psychological, ethical, or personal factors. Psychological factors include the thoughts, feelings, attitudes, or other cognitive or affective characteristics of an individual that influence his or her behavior. It also includes several predispositions or tendencies of the individual, such as his or her aspirations, attitudes, emotions, motivations, propensities, perceptions for good or evil, or personality and value orientation. Ethical factors refer to patterns of behavior developed by education or environment. Education in this context refers to character formation and levels of maturity. Environment refers to parental and social influences, such as religious socialization.

The seriousness of sin arises from several sources among which are the degree to which a good is violated, whether or not the individual is aware of the wrong he or she is about to do, the actual making of a moral choice to do wrong, or whether or not there is an acceptable alternative to the sinful choice and/or one has to make a choice or a decision between two evils.

From another perspective the moral makeup of the individual is a factor in determining the culpability of the individual. If the individual is of weak rather than evil character, lacks will power, is strongly inclined to sensual pleasure, or is a congenital coward, his or her culpability is indeed serious. But if the individual sins with cold indifference and malice and has little to no remorse of conscience or any concern that his or her conduct is offensive to God or if the person is indifferent to or scorns the basic norms of morality, his or her culpability is much greater.

Another perspective of sin is to look at its degree of gravity, its object, and it consequences. Moral theology identifies two primary types of sin— mortal and venial. A mortal sin is defined as a sin against God and/or a person and is characterized by three elements. It concerns a grave matter, and it is committed with the full knowledge of the sinner, who gives deliberate consent to his or her action. Examples of mortal sin would include violations of the Ten Commandments, such as murder, lust, or theft. A venial sin is generally a sin against another person. It involves a deviation from the norm of right behavior and a relatively minor matter. It does not involve the great deliberation or full consent by the perpetrator, and it is more often than not committed out of weakness, surprise, or on the spur of the moment. Examples would include a so-called "white lie" that harms no one, stealing a very insignificant amount of money, or common vulgarity.

The consequences of mortal sin are such that the sinner becomes alienated from God and his gift of sanctifying grace. The threat of eternal damnation becomes very real unless he or she repents and God in his goodness and mercy is forgiving. Venial sin, on the other hand, weakens the sinner and disposes him or her to temptation and/or the actual committing of a mortal sin. It also impedes or increases the individual's progress in the exercise of virtue and the practice of moral good. Finally it deprives the sinner of grace and advances in the spiritual life. It is displeasing to God, but not in the same way as mortal sin is.

Redemption in Defeat: Reflections on the Wages of Sin

There is the story about a man who one day was out hiking in the mountains. He loved to venture out to the edge of cliffs so he could get the best views of the scenery; however, on this particular day he went out too far, and he fell over a cliff. With arms flailing in every direction he grabbed hold of a bush growing out of the cliff, thus breaking his fall. But now he was stuck. There was no way to get back to the top, and it was a long, long way to the bottom. If he fell, it was certain death on the jagged rocks far below. He caught his breath and yelled out, "Is anybody up there?" He waited a few moments, and all he heard was the sound of the wind blowing through the trees. So he yelled again, "Is there anybody up there?" And again his plea was met with silence. So he yelled a third time, "Is there anybody up there?" And a loud deep voice boomed back, "Yes." And the old boy asked, "Who are you?" The reply came, "I am God, your Creator." The man exclaimed, "Wow! What should I do?" And God said, "Let go!" The man thought for a moment, and then he cried out, "Is there anybody else up there?"

Paradoxically sometimes life is similar to falling off a cliff. We find ourselves confronting obstacles that we simply can't seem to overcome, or we fall in a proverbial hole from which we can't extricate ourselves. The more effort we expend, the deeper we find ourselves. Nothing seems to go right. We find ourselves in a dark, hard place. We are confused. We can't figure out how to put our lives back together again. Yet we keep trying to no avail. Even when the answer is in front of us, we keep looking in the wrong places. We refuse to admit to ourselves that we are powerless and that our lives have become unmanageable. I am reminded of a friend of mine who had lost it all—family, job, self-respect, and for a time his faith. He had hit rock bottom and was standing in a shower, stark naked, and screaming, "God! I give up. You're in charge." Shortly thereafter things started to turn around. His life got back on track.

He squarely faced the fact that he was not in charge, he was powerless, and his life had become unmanageable. Only then was he ready to come to grips with the fact that without God there was no way he was going to get out of the hole he had dug for himself over the years. Only then was he—like the old boy hanging from the twig on the side of the cliff—ready to get back to the top of the cliff. By confessing his shortcomings and giving up trying to control his life and calling on and trusting completely in God, he was able to gain control of his life. By admitting defeat, complete defeat, he was brought to safety.

Only with an acknowledgment and confession of our sins and shortcomings are we able to set into motion God's help to become who we really are and to see that life has meaning and is purposeful. In time we begin to realize that it is not through our efforts that we are rescued but through God's love and forgiveness. In time we begin to see the consequences of wallowing in sin. Unfortunately our culture has confused sin with legalistic arguments over right and wrong or over doing or not doing harm. Sin is an unpopular concept. It connotes unhealthy guilt and shame. Ask most people what sin is, and they would more than likely cite violations of the Ten Commandments. They would not realize that the authors of the Bible looked upon sin as a power able to move us toward unloving behavior.

The definition I prefer is that sin is "missing the mark." The mark is the standard of perfection set by God and lived by Jesus. Most of us prefer to live by our own standards. Few of us live up to Jesus' standard. Paul says in Romans 3:23, "All have sinned and fall short of the glory of God." It is clear then that we are all sinners. We need to understand this. We need to recognize our sins. It has been said that the only difference between us and those who sit in our nation's prison is the fact that they got caught. We may not have committed physical murder or grand larceny, but how many of us have *murdered* the good name of another by slander, lied, taken that which did not belong to us, cheated on an exam, or failed to feed the hungry, clothe the naked, or give drink to the thirsty, treated others with disdain, or put power ahead of justice?. The real question is this: Do we realize we have been guilty of these sins? Do we know the distance we have placed between us and God? "If we say, 'We have no sin,' we are deceiving ourselves and truth has no place in us; if we acknowledge our sins, he is trustworthy and upright, so that he will forgive our sins and will cleanse us from all evil. If we say, 'We have never sinned,' we make him a liar, and his word has no place in us." (1 John 1:8–10).

Another way of looking at sin is by looking at the sinner as one whose life is ruled by selfishness. Whenever I inordinately choose to do what is best for me, it is conceivable that selfishness is operating in my life. Whenever I say, "I am going to do my thing," I have sinned because I have made myself king of my life instead of God. I have denied God his rightful place as ruler and Lord of my life and exalted myself in his place. I have committed a sin of selfishness. According to Scripture, when we love ourselves, money, or pleasure more than

God, we are guilty of selfishness. We have not only ignored God, the God who made us, but also enthroned ourselves as the *gods* of our own lives.

Often when we see things we have done that are wrong, we tend to compare ourselves with other people we know who are worse than we are in order to settle our consciences. This may help us to feel better, but it does nothing to change our guilty condition before God. Some people imagine that God grades on the curve or weighs our good deeds against our bad deeds and therefore will not punish us, even though we have grievously sinned. Both of these concepts are wrong. Isaiah 64:5 says, "We have all been like unclean things and our upright deeds like filthy rags. We wither, all of us, like leaves, and all our misdeeds carry us off like the wind."

When we break God's laws in either our actions or our thoughts, we are guilty of rebellion against God's authority over us. We are guilty of fighting God. When we selfishly choose our own desires and ways instead of God's, we thus honor ourselves above God and are guilty of playing God. We are being selfish. And our guilt before God is very great. However, it does not end with us. There are consequences to us and to others.

Until we become consciously committed to living in the Spirit, selfishness will rule our hearts. For addicts in recovery, this truth is obvious. It is the drinking or gambling or excessive eating or the desire to control others or whatever that rules the heart. In beginning to examine your hearts for evidence of selfishness, ask yourself, "To what am I inordinately attached? What upsets me when I am denied it?"

Most of us, when reflecting on these questions, will find that our selfishness is directed toward one or more of five passions—pleasure, power, status, security, or esteem. There are legitimate ways to meet these needs, but selfishness makes them the very centers of meaning and value. People can live for years, selfishly pursuing these passions. In the end, however, none of these bring happiness, for they are conditional achievements. They can be taken away at any time. Empty though they are, the world holds them out as roads to human fulfillment, and many travel these roads.

Happily God has created us in such a manner that we cannot find true happiness apart from living in the Spirit. As St. Augustine puts it, "Thou has created us for thyself, O Lord, and our hearts will not rest until they rest in thee."

It would be wonderful if we could live this truth from the beginning of our lives until the end. Most of us, however, travel the selfish road for a while, flirting superficially with the spiritual life but never surrendering our selfish centers until we grow tired of them. The selfish road leads to broken relationships and inner emptiness. Whatever material gains we make are bracketed by anxiety, for the economy could fail and leave us with nothing.

Paradoxically it is the unhappiness of our selfish ways that can lead us to commit our lives to God in earnest. Some must go through considerable pain before they come around; others learn by observing the consequences of selfishness experienced by others. But none among us is immune to the insidious powers of sin, and none among us has escaped from selfish tendencies.

It is not coincidence that the first beatitude taught by Jesus is this: "How blessed are the poor in spirit; the kingdom of heaven is theirs" (Matthew 5:3). Who are these poor in spirit? They are the people who know their need for God, people who have learned that *their way* does not bring true happiness. They are those who have been beaten up by life through social injustice, addiction, divorce, or other problems. Through these experiences they learn their inability to control things. There are also those who struggle with the immensity of their selfishness and their need for the Spirit to help them overcome this selfishness. The critical importance of poverty of spirit is that until we embrace it, the Spirit will do little to help us. If we are not poor in spirit, then we are rich in our sense of power and self-importance. We are like the *healthy* people in the Gospels whom Christ could not cure because they did not believe they were sick.

We are all sick. We were created to know love, peace of mind, creative enterprise, and harmony with the earth and other creatures. But deep down inside most of us are filled with fear, and we use selfish *fixes* to inoculate us against this fear. The fear, however, cannot go away until we allow the Spirit entrance into our hearts.

The best way to cultivate poverty of spirit is to practice honesty. This is difficult, for it means we must get in touch with the dark side of our nature as well as our true strengths. We examine our center to see what we are living for. We note the consequences to ourselves and others that come from this center. We pay attention to our thinking process and trace our thoughts to our deepest desires. We acknowledge our selfishness, and we see how fear motivates us. Reflecting in this way, we begin to bring the darkness in our hearts into the light where it can be healed. This process can be painful, but it is a sweet pain. There is within it new life that amplifies life's meaning.

Remember that old boy we left hanging on to the bush? Every single one of us is hanging on to an old, scraggly bush that clings precariously to the side of a cliff. But we have to let go and trust God. That is what faith is all about. Unless we admit that we are powerless without God in our lives, life has no meaning.

Yes, Many of Us Love the Darkness More than We Love the Light.

Many of our religious leaders and pastors often are of little to no help in bringing us into the light. They feed us pabulum rather than the Word of God. They are more concerned with buildings than building communities of lovers of God. They work themselves to death and wonder in the end why they have little sense of accomplishment. They shy away from telling us what we need to hear rather than what we want to hear. They have watered down the gospels. They have abandoned their role as preachers and teachers for other roles. They and the rest of us are afraid to come into the light lest our evil deeds are exposed. Each of us wears a mask of self-delusion because we fear knowing our true selves and who we really are in relation to this light. We fear appearing naked before our brothers and sisters. We prefer the safety of our sins. We embrace darkness. We reject Jesus, the Light.

Jesus is the light. He came into the world because his father loved us, not because he wanted to condemn us. He gave us his very Son so that we might have life, life that is everlasting. "He that follows me shall not walk in darkness, but shall have the light of life" (John 8:12). And this light promises hope.

Victor Frankl[18] in his book about the horrors of the Nazi concentration camps writes of several prisoners who seemed to cope fairly well despite the inhumane and incredibly cruel treatment by the camp guards and other personnel. One man in particular stood out. He was always upbeat, even though many around him simply gave up, wasted away, and died. This man was very strong. He often talked about when he would get out of the camp, and he looked forward to being united with his wife and family. It so happened that this man received word that his wife had died in another concentration camp. Overnight he, too, died. Why? Frankl surmised that as long as he had hope, this man would survive without food despite unbearable hardships. But when this hope—this light shining in the darkness—was extinguished, his dream of being united with his wife was dashed.

In Jesus hope is alive. In these days of Lent, let us stop denying sin and come out of the darkness. Listen and hearken to his call to repentance and forgiveness. Let us seek to reconcile ourselves with God by confessing our sins and participating in the Eucharistic meal. Let us confront our secret failings and lay them at the feet of Jesus. Let us learn to live in the light, choose our real selves and not the phony facades we present to our neighbors. Let us live by the truth and learn of Jesus from the Scriptures, from the teachings from the pulpit, and from one another. Come into the light and live.

The light that was thought to have been extinguished on Good Friday burns ever-so-brightly in the person of Jesus the Christ at his resurrection. This light overcomes the darkness. All we have to do is to follow its path home.

Summary: Prelude to Salvation History

The preceding three chapters are certainly not meant to be an exhaustive study of the theology of Christianity's seminal thinkers. It is intended to provide the reader with a starting point on his or her Lenten journey. In the liturgy of the Easter Vigil Mass the very first reading after the Exultet[19] is the story of the creation. It is the story of our beginnings as God's people. It is the story of sin and grace, which underscores so much of our Judeo-Christian heritage. Accordingly it is of the utmost importance that we *listen* to Genesis 1 and 2 with the "ear of our heart." Not only will these paragraphs hopefully bring you into contact not only with great literature, but they will also provide you with an idea of the foundational concepts upon which our heritage rests, albeit not without considerable commentary, scholastic elaboration, wide-reaching exchanges in order to safeguard key concepts of the natural and supernatural life and principles of spirituality that find their roots in the creation story about sin and the promise of restoration. In addition these paragraphs will explain how Augustine and his interlocutors throughout the centuries have constructed the very basis of the ethical, ecclesial, and sacramental system of our Christian faith.

Endnotes

[1] Schoonenberg, Piet, "Sin and Guilt," *Encyclopedia of Theology: The Concise Sacramentum Mundi*, edited by Karl Rahner (New York: Seabury, 1975), 1579–586.

[2] Latourette, Kenneth Scott, *A History of Christianity* (New York: Harper & Brothers: Publisher, 1953), 177.

3   Karmiris, John, A Synopsis of the Dogmatic Theology of the Orthodox Catholic Church, translated from the Greek by the Reverend George Dimopoulos (Scranton, PA: Christian Orthodox Edition, 1973), 35–36.

4   DeFrancisco, James, Original Sin and Ancestral Sin: Comparative Doctrines published for Miltha Ministries at www.aramaicbibleperspectives.com/uploads/ABP - ORIGINAL SIN OR ANCESTRAL SIN.pdf (2007).

5   Pristas, Lauren, *The Theological Anthropology of John Cassian*, unpublished PhD dissertation (Boston: Boston College, 1993).

6   DeFrancisco, Original Sin and Ancestral Sin

7   Ibid.

8   Luther, Martin, *Commentary on Romans*, translated by Theodore Mueller (Grand Rapids, MI: Kriegel Publications, 1976), 95.

9   Ware, Timothy, *The Orthodox Church* (London: Penguin, 1997), 218–224.

10   Karmiris. A Synopsis of the Dogmatic Theology of the Orthodox Catholic Church

11   Meyendorff, John, Byzantine Theology: Historical Trends and Doctrinal Themes (New York: Fordham University Press, 1974), 143–145.

12   Ibid.

13   Ratzinger, Joseph Cardinal with Vittorio Messori, *The Ratzinger Report* (San Francisco: Ignatius Press, 1985), 70.

14   Rahner, Karl, *Foundations of Christian Faith: An Introduction to the Idea of Christianity* (New York: The Seabury Press, 1978), 111–114.

15   Ratzinger, Joseph, *In the Beginning— A Catholic Understanding of the Story of Creation and the Fall,* (Grand Rapids, MI: Wm. B. Eerdmans Publishing Co., 1986), 70.

16   Ibid, 73.

17   O'Connell, Timothy E., *Principles for a Catholic Morality* (New York: The Seabury Press, 1978), 67–82.

18   Frankl, Victor, *Man's Search for Meaning,* (New York: Washington Square Press, 1959).

19   The Easter Proclamation or hymn sung generally by a deacon during and after the procession into the church of the paschal candle during the Easter Vigil before the beginning of the Liturgy of the Word principally in the Roman Catholic Rite of the Mass and in Anglican and Lutheran churches.

CHAPTER 5

THE HOLY TRINITY, THE INCARNATION, AND THE ONSET OF OUR REDEMPTION

The Holy Trinity: The Core of Christianity

One day while he was pondering the mystery of the Trinity, St. Augustine found himself walking on a beach at Hippo, which is in modern-day Libya. He came upon a little boy digging sand and putting it into a bottomless pail. Augustine asked the child what he was doing. "Trying to put all the sand of the world into this bucket," the child replied. "Why, that is impossible," said Augustine. "And so too is it impossible for you to understand the Trinity," replied the child as he vanished in thin air.

Whether or not this story is true, it underscores the difficulty in understanding this, the central doctrine of Christianity. It is truly a mystery, one that has caused considerable consternation among the great minds of both the Eastern and Western churches. As difficult complex, at times incomprehensible as this mystery is, let us try to at least grasp a few essentials. Please be warned that I don't promise this to be an easy read.

Coined in the third century by Tertullian, an early church father, the doctrine of the Trinity has developed along different paths in the East and West.

In both the East and West there is but one God indivisible in essence, which is divine, but three persons—Father, Son, and Holy Spirit—united in their diversity yet distinct in personal characteristics. The Father, the first person of the Trinity, is unbegotten, having his source and origin solely in himself. The Son, the second person of the Trinity and equal to and co-eternal with the Father, is begotten from all eternity from the Father. The third person of the Trinity is the Holy Spirit. At this point there is a marked divergence between East and West Christendom. The First General Council of Nicea in 325 CE initially expressed the teachings of the universal church in what has become known as the Nicean Creed, which says, "[We believe] in the Holy Spirit, the Lord and Giver of life, who proceeds from the Father, who together with the Father and the Son is worshipped and glorified, who has spoken through the prophets."

In the Third Council of Toledo (589 CE) the words "and the son" were inserted in the creed. This is the *Filioque*, which asserts that the Holy Spirit proceeds from the Father and the Son. Herein is a significant point of contention between the Eastern (Greek) and Western (Latin) churches.

The Eastern Church's fundamental position with respect to the Trinity is that God the Father is one. It defines the relationship of God the Father to the Son and the Holy Spirit in the light of this one God and Father. Hence, it follows that the Holy Spirit proceeds solely from the Father. Like the Son, his source and origin is found in the Father, but his relationship to the father is different from that of the Son. He is not begotten but proceeds from all eternity from the Father. In a word, the Son is begotten of (or from) the Father, and the Holy Spirit (the Paraclete) proceeds (issues) from the Father. The New Jerusalem Bible seems to recognize this fundamental position of the Eastern Church: "When the Paraclete comes, whom I shall send to you from the Father, the Spirit of truth who issues from the Father, he will be my witness." (John 15:26).

However, the Western church, principally in the person of Augustine, took a different perspective. Instead of beginning with the one God and Father, he concentrated on the one nature or substance of God—that which he thought was common to the three persons. He and subsequent Latin theologians concentrated on the nature of God as logically prior to the persons within the Godhead. Personality was viewed as the final complement of God's nature. Hence, God's nature is one, and he is known to us as the one God before he can be known as three persons. This perspective holds that there exists one God in three divine persons—the Father, the Son, and the Holy Spirit. Put another way, this doctrine teaches that within the Godhead there are three persons but one nature (i.e., God the Father, God the Son, and God the Holy Spirit). Each person is fully God yet distinct from one another. Each is united through a mutual indwelling. This essentially Augustinian perspective can be summarized in the following:

- "The Father, and the Son, and the Holy Spirit intimate a divine unity of one and the same substance in an indivisible equality; and therefore they are not three Gods, but one God: although the Father has begotten the Son, and so He who is the Father is not the Son; and the Son is begotten by the Father, and so He who is the Son is not the Father; and the Holy Spirit is neither the Father nor the Son, but only the Spirit of the Father *and* of the Son, Himself also co-equal with the Father and the Son." [1]

- The divine nature is prior to the personalities. God is simply the Trinity, not God the Father. [2]
- Every external operation of God is due to the whole Trinity and cannot be attributed to one person alone. [3]
- "Thus the Father and the Son and the Holy Spirit, and each of these by Himself, is God, and at the same time they are all one God; and each of them by himself is a complete substance, and yet they are all one substance." [4]

According to St. Augustine, the Son proceeds from the Father as an act of the intellect. On the other hand, the Holy Spirit proceeds as an act of divine will. It proceeds from both the Father and the Son through the love by which God loves himself. As mentioned previously, this viewpoint found its way into the Nicene Creed in 589 CE during the Third Council of Toledo. It was ratified by the Eleventh Council of Toledo in 675 CE. [5] It was there that it was promulgated that the Holy Spirit is God, one and equal with God the Father and God the Son. It was of one substance and one nature "not begotten or created but proceeding from both," and it was the Spirit of both the Father and the Son. The Holy Spirit is thus a result of the mutual love of the Father for the Son and of the Son for the Father and proceeds from both the Father and the Son. This precise formula over the centuries has presented an obstacle toward reunification of the Western and Eastern Church, which most refer to as the Filioque controversy.

The Eastern or Orthodox Church interprets Augustine's representation of the Trinity as a double procession of the Spirit. They are willing on occasion to concede that the Spirit proceeds from the Father through the Son, but they hold firmly that he does not proceed from the Son, whom they believe is begotten eternally and came into this world through natural birth of the Virgin and lived among us.

Eastern theologians also agree with the West that the Spirit is sent by the Son and hence is rightly called the Spirit of the Son just as he is the Spirit of the Father. The scriptural justification for this position is found in John 15:26, which says, "When the Paraclete comes, whom I shall send to you from the Father, the Spirit of truth who issues from the Father, he will be my witness." This position is clearly at odds with the Augustinian position. Mindful of this reading, orthodox theologians also argue that just as the Son is the wisdom and power by which God is wise and powerful, so the Spirit is the holiness or sanctity by which he is holy. This concept of Spirit is understood in light of John 10:22, where Christ breathes on the apostles and confers on them the Holy Spirit. Hence, the Holy Spirit is the breath of Christ, breathed by him on the apostles and on us, dwelling in us as sanctifying grace.

This difference over the doctrine of the Filioque clause was partially addressed by the Latin church in 1995 homily by Benedict XVI in the presence of the Ecumenical Patriarch Bartholomew I, expressed a desire that "the traditional doctrine of the Filioque, present in the liturgical version of the Latin Credo, [be clarified] in order to highlight its full harmony with what the Ecumenical Council of Constantinople of 381 confesses in its creed: the Father as the source of the whole Trinity, the one origin both of the Son and of the Holy Spirit." He stated that "The doctrine of the Filioque must be understood and presented by the Catholic Church in such a way that it cannot appear to contradict the Monarchy of the Father nor the fact that he is the sole origin of the Spirit." He thereby acknowledged that the Filioque of the Latin Church is, in fact, "situated in a theological and linguistic context" different from that of the Eastern Orthodox churches.[6]

The Incarnation and the Onset of Our Redemption

> We believe in one Lord, Jesus Christ,
> the only son of God,
> eternally begotten of the father,
> God from God, Light from Light,
> true God, from true God,
> begotten, not made,
> of one Being with the Father.
> Through him all things were made.
> For us men and for our salvation
> he came down from heaven:

by the power of the Holy Spirit
he became incarnate from the Virgin Mary,
and was made man.

—Nicene-Constantinopolitan Creed

Who, being in the form of God, did not count equality
with God
something to be grasped.
But he emptied himself, taking the form of a slave,
becoming as human beings are;
and being in every way like a human being, he was humbler yet,
even to accepting death, death on a cross.

—Philippians 2:6–8

The doctrine of the Incarnation is inseparable from the doctrine of the Trinity. Together they constitute the very center of the Christian message and its understanding of salvation history.

In chapter 2, we read where God promises us a Savior, a Messiah, one who will restore our status as his heirs and adopted sons and daughters. With the Incarnation salvation history begins. God the Father sent his only Son, notwithstanding his heavenly status, in accordance with the promise he made in Genesis 3:15, "I will put enmity between you and the woman, and between your offspring and hers; They shall strike at your head and you will strike their heel."

In the fullness of time God begets a Son. Born of a woman, his Word is incarnated as human flesh through the agency of the Holy Spirit. In the God-man Jesus, God's promise in the garden is realized. Another way of stating this mystery is that the triune God communicates itself to us in the person of the second person of the Trinity, who becomes human flesh and blood like us. The Incarnation is the moment for which all creation has awaited, staring from that fateful moment in the garden and going to the paradoxical moment in which God and man meet in Jesus. It is when "God entered fully and unconditionally into human life … God en-fleshed, en-manned, and othered himself totally in Jesus so that in experiencing the man Jesus the apostles also experienced God as personally present in their midst."[7]

He vows to return to us the supernatural grace our ancestors lost in the Garden of Eden. This grace will enable us to once again become immortal in spirit, even though we will still be subject to bodily death as a penalty for the sin of our ancestral parents, Adam and Eve. The principle elements of this doctrine as itemized by Neuner and Dupris with appropriate references include the following[8]:

- "Christ is truly God, eternally begotten from the Father."
- "He is truly man, born in time from the Virgin Mary."
- "The two natures, divine and human are united in the person of the Son of God the second person of the Holy Trinity."
- "The divine Son-ship of Christ excludes his being an adopted son of God."
- "Christ brings the fullness of God's revelation."
- "Mediator between God and human beings, he has saved everyone through the sacrifice of his cross."
- "He has satisfied and merited for all."
- "By his resurrection he has become for all the source of a new life."
- "The Paschal Mystery is the supreme revelation of God's love."

Hence, the Incarnation becomes the central fact of Christianity and its theological foundation. God the Father sends his Son into the world to become man and to dwell among us. The Son empties himself or divests himself of his divine glory, assumes the status of a slave, and becomes like a man in all things except sin. The Word of God becomes flesh, and through his death and the ignominy of the cross, he redeems us, thus ushering in the age of the Holy Spirit. In the words of the old spiritual, "He came for to die." He became the long-awaited Messiah and Savior. To this the church teaches, and Scripture attests. Paul is explicit in 1Timothy 1:15, where he writes, "Christ Jesus came into the world to save sinners." John 3:17 summarizes this teaching with the following: "God sent his son into the world not to judge the world, but so that through him the world might be saved." Later in John 17:4, John suggests that another purpose of the incarnation is to give glory to God: "I have glorified you on earth by finishing the work that you gave me to do."

This work of redemption consists in freeing mankind from sin and its attendant evils (i.e., servitude to Satan and the bondage of death). In a word, by his sacrificial death on the cross Jesus restores mankind to its original relationship to God and atones for the sin of Adam and Eve. During Lent we remember why he came, and we renew our faith in his everlasting love.

The General Council of Chalcedon in AD 451[9] captures the essence of this mystery and its basic boundaries. According to this council, Jesus Christ is one divine person in two natures (divine and human). This attestation continues to be orthodox doctrine for all of Christendom. Jesus Christ is both God and man. Here is the actual creedal statement of the council:

> We all with one voice confess our Lord Jesus Christ to be one and the same Son, perfect in divinity and humanity, truly God and truly human, consisting of a rational soul and a body, being of one substance with the Father in relation to his divinity, and being of one substance with us in relation to his humanity, and is like us in all things apart from sin. He was begotten of the Father before time in relation to his divinity, and in these recent days was born from the Virgin Mary, the *Theotokos* [God-bearer], for us and for our salvation. In relation to the humanity he is one and the same Christ, the Son, the Lord, the Only-begotten, who is to be acknowledged in two natures, without confusion, without change, without division, and without separation. The distinction of natures is in no way abolished on account of this union, but rather the characteristic property of each nature is preserved, and concurring into one Person and one subsistence, not as if Christ were parted or divided into two persons, but remains one and the same Son and Only-begotten God, Word, Lord, Jesus Christ; even as the Prophets from the beginning spoke concerning him, and our Lord Jesus Christ instructed us, and the Creed of the Fathers was handed down to us.

Today we know of his birth, ministry, death, and resurrection. However, that was not the case in the years immediately following his resurrection. During his ministry and the interval between his death and resurrection and the appearance of the Pauline corpus and the gospels, his followers increasingly came to see him as not only human but also somehow divine. At first he was seen as the Messiah (Mark 8:29) and even the Son of God (Matthew 16:16).

Yet, as Luke Timothy Johnson[10] writes, "Such titles could scarcely have been intended to say that Jesus had a uniquely ontological relationship with God." He lists other titles by which Jesus' contemporaries described him—prophet, King, Son of Man, and Savior—each of which could be traceable to the "symbolism of the Torah and cultural and political realities of first century Palestinian Jewish life." In none of these appellations was there a reference to Jesus as a participant in the divine life.

Despite his claims, ministry, or exorcisms, neither his opponents nor his disciples saw Jesus for who he was. In the minds of his opponents the harsh reality of the crucifixion gave ample evidence that he was a failure, a disappointment, that he was not the Messiah. If anything, he was a false prophet to these people. To them and indeed to all Jews it was unthinkable that the long-awaited Messiah was to be crucified as a common criminal. Even in light of the empty tomb and his several appearances, the disciples were confused, riddled with doubt, beset with disbelief. It was only after the experience of his resurrection sank into their consciousness did the disciples begin to surmise Jesus' unique relationship with God. It took a long time to come to grips with this new reality. The Jesus they knew had really been brought back from the dead.

The earliest Christians experienced Jesus the man through the teachings of his immediate disciples and the apostles. Two generations after his resurrection, writings about Jesus begin to appear, first in the early epistles or letters of Paul (AD 50 or 51–63) and then around 67–70 CE in the gospel of Mark, the first of the evangelists. Mark was followed by the gospels of Matthew and Luke, which appeared in the late 70s CE. John's gospel did not appear until somewhere between the years 85 and 105 of the Common Era. Still later other writers appeared in the second and third century, such as Ignatius, Polycarp, Irenaeus, Clement, and the Cappadocian Fathers, Basil the Great, Gregory of Nyssa, and Gregory of Nazianzus.

It was not until the fourth century and after several centuries of divisive polemics or internecine disputes and sustained and critical reflection that the church solidified its belief that Jesus was indeed the Christ—both human and divine. Here is a summary of the words of the creed that emanated from the church councils of Nicea and Constantinople in 322–325 CE and the aforementioned Council of Chalcedon in 451 CE: "Jesus is the Son of God the Father, born of the Virgin Mary by power of the Holy Spirit!"

This second of the core tenets of Christianity speaks to the fulfillment of God's promise in the garden. A Savior has come, and through the mystery of his death on the cross and his resurrection, he restores us to our original likeness to the Creator as his heirs—sons and daughters—by adoption. It gives meaning to our Lenten journey from the desert to the resurrection.

Endnotes

1. Augustine, *On the Holy Trinity*, Translated Rev. Arthur West Haddan, 1887, in The complete Works of Saint Augustine, 2013 Kindle Electronic Edition, Book 1, Chapter 4, Paragraph 7 Location 105498 of 216397

2. Ibid, Book V Chapters 8 – 10, Location 108810 to 108880 of 216397

3. Ibid

4. Augustine, *On Christian Doctrine*, Edited by Philip Shaff, Translated by James F. Shaw, 1887, in The Complete Works of Saint Augustine, 2013 Kindle Electronic Edition, Chapter 5. Location 24488 of 216397

5. Eleventh Council of Toledo, AD 673–675, www.ewtn.com/library/councils/Toledo, Accessed March 2014

6. pontifical Council for Promoting Christian Unity, "The Greek and Latin Traditions Regarding the Procession of the Holy Spirit" L'Osservatore Romano, September 20. 1995, Weekly Edition in English http://www.ewtn.com/library/curia/pccufilq.htm (Accessed August 18, 2014)

7. Lane, Dermot A., *The Reality of Jesus* (New York: Paulist Press, 1975), 133.

8. Neuner, J, and J. Dupois, *The Christian Faith in the Doctrinal Documents of the Catholic Faith*, edited by Jacques Dupuis (Bangalore, India: Theological Publications in India, 2001), 216–217.

9. General Council of Chalcedon in AD 451, as cited in Alister E. McGrath, *An Introduction to Christianity* (Cambridge: Blackwell, 1997), 131–132.

10. Johnson, Luke Timothy, *The Creed" What Christians Believe and Why It Matters* (New York: Image Book, Doubleday, 2003), 105

Part 2

Preparations

CHAPTER 6

ASH WEDNESDAY COME: FOLLOW ME THESE FORTY DAYS

For dust you are, and to dust you shall return.

—Genesis 3:19

"Yet even now," says the Lord—
"Turn back to me, with all your hears,
And with fasting, weeping, and lamenting—
Rend your hearts
Rather than your garments
And turn back to the Lord, your God.
For He is gracious and compassionate,
Slow to anger, abounding in kindness."

—Joel 2:12–13

Have mercy on me, O God, as befits your faithfulness,
in keeping with your abundant compassion,
blot out my transgressions
wash me thoroughly from my iniquity, and
purify me of my sins.

—Psalm 51:3–4

But when you give alms, your left hand must not know what
your right is doing; your almsgiving must be secret, and your
Father who sees all that is done in secret will reward you.

—Matthew 6:3–4

But when you fast, put scent on your head and wash your
face, so that no one will know you are fasting except your
Father who sees all that is done in secret; and your Father
who sees all that is done in secret will reward you.

—Matthew 6:17–18

shes symbolize mourning, mortality, and penance. Throughout the Bible we find instances of individuals putting on sackcloth and ashes as a sign of one or all of these sentiments. In the face of pending danger the prophet Jeremiah calls for the Israelites to repent. "My poor people put on sackcloth and strew dust on yourselves! Mourn, as for an only child" (Jeremiah 6:26).

Job repented in sackcloth and ashes (Job 42:6). Perhaps the best-known example of repentance in the Hebrew Scriptures is the story of the prophet Jonah, who after much hesitancy and not without a little sullenness finally obeyed God's command to proclaim the eventual destruction of the city of Nineveh (Jonah 3:6). To Jonah's surprise the people of Nineveh believed him and "proclaimed a fast, and great and small alike put on sackcloth. When the news reached the king of Nineveh, he rose from the throne, took off his robe, put on sackcloth, and sat in ashes."

Mordecai (Esther 4:1) tore his clothes and put on sackcloth and ashes when he was told of the decree by King Ahasuerus to kill all of the Jewish people in the Persian Empire. Daniel pleaded to God to rescue Israel from Darius, king of the Chaldeans, by saying, "I turned my face to the Lord God, devoting myself to prayer and supplication in fasting, in sackcloth, and in ashes" (Daniel 9:3).

There are many other such examples throughout the Hebrew Scriptures.

In the New Testament both Matthew (Matthew 11:21) and Luke (Luke 10:13) have Jesus reproaching several towns that had not received the disciples he had sent to proclaim the good news. "Alas to you, Chorazin! Alas to you, Bethsaida! If the miracles worked in you had taken place in Tyre and Sidon, they would have reformed in sackcloth and ashes long ago."

As we begin the forty day penitential season of Lent, the church reminds us (with the sign of a cross traced on our foreheads with ashes) that we are mortal and we are going to die and return to the dust from whence we came. The cross also reminds us that we are sinners and are called to turn away from our sins and to rededicate ourselves to the God who became man so that we might become gods and regain the status that we lost in the garden of Eden. Jesus came, suffered, died, and rose from the dead to restore and transform us into his likeness so that we might "become, as he is, divinely human" (Merton, 2004). Jesus has much to say to us during these forty days. During these days he calls us to give alms, fast, and pray in secret. He also calls us to discipleship to take up our crosses and follow him. Lent is a time of preparation, renewal, metanoia or turning from our sinful ways, and purification. It is a time to remember that we came from the earth and to the earth we will return, or as the minister recites as he or she places ashes on our forehead, "Remember man that you are dust, and unto dust you shall return." But there is more. Lent is the remembrance of that first sin committed by our forbearers, Adam and Eve, and the promise of God that he would not abandon their progeny. He would send us his very own Son.

During these next forty days God wants us to detach ourselves from earthly matters and return to him. He wants us to recognize and confess our sins. He calls us to do penance, to realize genuine sorrow, to pray for forgiveness and the strength to take concrete steps to turn away from these sins and to change our lives, even if we have to start anew each day.

God wants us, as St. Benedict tells us, "to listen with the ear of our hearts" to the teachings of his Son, Jesus. Like Moses with the wandering Hebrews at the foot of Mt. Sinai, Jesus teaches that we should love the Father with our whole hearts, our whole souls, our whole minds, and our whole strength. We should also love our brothers and sisters just as we love ourselves. If we live out this teaching, our lives will be transformed, or as Eusebius puts it, "all things will be set aright." Lent is the season to realize this transformation by sharing our "bread with the hungry, taking the wretched poor into your homes, when you see the naked, clothe him," binding up the wounds of the afflicted (Isaiah 58:7). This transformation is also realized by our prayers, contrition, and fasting—not simply depriving ourselves of a simple delicacy but removing from our presence "oppression, false accusation and malicious speech" (Isaiah 58:9). And so this Lent, let us enter into the grounds of our very being and find God by giving alms, fasting, and praying in a spirit of love and gratitude for his many graces.

Giving Alms

Remember the story of the "widow's mite" (Luke 21:1-4), where those who were well off gave from their surplus but the widow gave all that she had? Jesus observed that her gift was the greater and indeed pleasing to the Father because, though in poverty, she gave her all. During Lent Jesus calls each of us to give to or assist those in need. We all know of people who are experiencing hard times because of illness, old age, unemployment, or the aftereffects of natural disasters or catastrophes, including floods, forest fires, earthquakes, hurricanes, war, famine, or epidemics. Those who have many possessions are enjoined by most every religion—Jewish, Christian, Muslim, Hindu, and others—to practice almsgiving by contributing to the welfare of those in need.

The early church realized the importance of this obligation. We read in the Acts of the Apostles and in the epistles of the ministry of deacons and deaconesses who were responsible for the collection and distribution of clothing, food, money, and other needed items for the welfare of the faithful. This was the beginning of a worldwide system of charity and stewardship that is with us even today.

Moral theologians generally recognize three categories of need. When our neighbor lacks what is essential for life or when imminent peril threatens his or her life, the need is extreme. When our neighbor is denied help that would prevent serious harm to his or her family's economic well-being, the need is serious or pressing. When our neighbor faces considerable obstacles in securing what is necessary for life, the need is common or ordinary. Scripture and tradition underscore these three categories and places upon all Christians the obligation of almsgiving. Where there is imminent peril, significant loss, extreme poverty, or illness, given our socioeconomic status, we are required to come to the assistance of our neighbor with alms or some other form of help. Not to do so involves a serious transgression. This does not mean that we are required to take extraordinary measures to assist such a person. With respect to responding to ordinary troubles confronting those in need, one is not obliged to answer every call but to be ready to give alms according to what he or she deems appropriate to the situation and his or her economic wherewithal.

In giving alms one should be discreet, humble, and cheerful. One should give in secret and with a prayerful spirit. One could give alms as an individual or via an organization, such as the church, organized charities, or other institutions established by governments.

> I ask you, how can God's love survive in a man
> who has enough of this world's goods
> yet closes his heart to his brother
> when he sees him in need?
> Little children
> let us love in deed and in truth
> and not merely talk about it.
> Happy the man who is compassionate and thoughtful.
> His memory will be cherished forever.
>
> (1 John 3:17–18)

How can we give alms in this day and age despite the fact that we are in tough economic times? There is always someone worse off than we are. Perhaps the old practice of tithing is something we should consider. This is not generally something that Roman Catholics practice, although they are expected to support their parish, church-sponsored charities, and diocesan causes. Orthodox Catholics are similarly expected to support their local parish, priest, and parish-sponsored charities. But for many Protestants tithing is normal and expected.

Perhaps we can identify a worthy cause in our community to which we can contribute on a consistent basis? Or maybe we could volunteer to help out at a local charity or social action program. Examples might include working at a local soup kitchen, a women's abuse network, or a youth-oriented program like the Boys & Girls clubs in most communities. Remember, however, Jesus' admonition is to give alms in secret.

Fasting

How about fasting, which is closely tied to almsgiving? Isaiah says it best,

> This is the fast I desire:
> To unlock the fetters of wickedness,
> And untie the cords of the yoke
> To let the oppressed go free,
> To break off every yoke.
> It is to share your bread with the hungry,
> And to take the wretched poor into your home;
> When you see the naked, to clothe him,
> And not to ignore your own kin.
> Then shall your light burst through like the dawn
> And your healing spring up quickly;
> Your Vindicator shall march before you,
> The Presence of the Lord shall be your rear guard.
> Then, when you call, the Lord will answer;
> When you cry, He will say: Here I am. (Isaiah 58:6–8)

How is Jesus calling you to fast? I submit that he is calling you and me to do more than give up chocolates. If we accept Isaiah's suggestion, how well do we address those practices of charity toward our neighbor that we know as the corporal works of mercy? I bring your attention to Jesus' parable found in Matthew 25:34,

> Then the King will say to those on his right hand, "Come, you whom my Father has blessed, take as your heritage the kingdom prepared for you since the foundation of the world. For I was hungry and you gave me food, I was thirsty and you gave me drink, I was a stranger and you made me welcome, lacking clothes and you clothed me, sick and you visited me in prison and you came to see me." Then the upright will say to him in reply, "Lord, when did we see you hungry and feed you, or thirsty and give you drink? When did we see you a stranger and make you welcome, lacking clothes and clothe you? When did we find you sick or in prison and go to see you?" and the King will answer, "in truth I tell you, in so far as you did this to one of the least of these brothers of mine, you did it to me."

Both Isaiah and Jesus are in effect telling us that fasting is much more than the voluntary refraining or abstaining from food or drink during a given period of time. Within the context of spirituality, fasting is a powerful spiritual discipline. Unfortunately it is also one of the most neglected of spiritual disciplines.

According to Jewish law, Yom Kippur, the Day of Atonement, was the only day in the year in which fasting (abstaining from food and drink) was prescribed for all Jews. It was and is a solemn day of repentance. Today Jews hold public fasts for occasions of public mourning and in times of natural disasters. They also hold private days of fasting for personal devotional reasons or for God's blessings on an important occasion or task. Other people of faith also hold fasting in high regard (e.g., the Muslims and Ramadan).

However, for Christians, fasting is more than abstaining from food. Just as with other faith traditions, fasting focuses on spiritual growth and giving glory to God. It is a way to further our relationship to God. It encourages humility. It is a way to focus on what is important, namely God.

In Mathew 9:10–15, Jesus and his disciples are at a dinner party given by Levi (Matthew), a tax collector whom the Lord had just called to be one of his disciples. It appeared that everyone but the Pharisees was having a pretty good time. They were offended that Jesus and his followers were eating with tax collectors and sinners. So they asked him why his disciples did not fast as they and their forefathers had been taught to do. In reality, the scribes and Pharisees are implying that Jesus is not the religious person he claims to be. Interestingly Jesus invokes the image of a wedding, in which he is the bridegroom. He asks, "How can his guests fast while the groom is with them?" This is a time of joy, of happiness, of laughter, of music and dancing. It is a wedding feast. The invited guests are those who are family and friends of the bride and groom.

Scripture frequently compares the kingdom of God to a bridal banquet. In the Hebrew Bible the prophets, particularly Hosea and Isaiah, depict the relationship between Israel and Yahweh as a marriage covenant. Often unfaithful, Israel is the bride and Yahweh the bridegroom. Here in Mathew 9:15, Jesus is appropriating a designation that belongs to Yahweh alone. With this metaphor Jesus is announcing the fact that in his person the kingdom of God has come into the world. He is suggesting that he is the Messiah and that in his coming as the bridegroom, the eschatological festival begins. When he is taken away—a reference to his passion and death—then it is appropriate to fast.

What then does fasting mean? It is the cry to God of a hurting individual for strength and healing. It is a humble plea for mercy and help because we either lost our way or can no longer face up to our problems. It is loosening the chains of injustice, freeing the oppressed, feeding the hungry, providing for the poor, sheltering the homeless, clothing the naked, visiting the imprisoned and the sick, and comforting the afflicted. In a word, it is focusing on others rather than ourselves.

Fasting is sharing in and entering more deeply into the central mysteries of our Christian faith, Jesus' passion, death, and resurrection. It is a way to detach ourselves from the extraneous elements in life and cling more firmly to Christ himself. It is a way to clear away the detriment that clouds our judgment and shows us how much we really need God and how much our brothers and sisters need us. It is about a radical shift in our lifestyles, a move away from the excesses of modern life and anything that comes between us and God. It involves action and risk.

Lent is not so much about us and our spiritual practices as it is about Jesus and our relationship with him and our brothers and sisters. It is about us assimilating and living the vision and values of Jesus. It is not about giving up chocolate or our favorite foods. It is about fasting from our personal habits and patterns, which may be keeping us from God, such as anger, resentment, criticism, selfishness, not loving ourselves, indifference, or apathy. It is about reaching out to others, thus setting them free of their oppressions and being set free by them. It's about being partners with Jesus.

Unfortunately many of us fast in the hope that God will give us something or change our circumstances to our advantage. The deal is that if we fast, God will answer even if what we ask for is not right with him or according to his purposes. If he does not give us the answer we are looking for or if he responds in a way that is not to our advantage, he is patently unfair. Others make a show of fasting, hoping to draw attention to our holiness and godliness. We seek to appear pious. Jesus commented upon this way of fasting in Matthew 6:16, "When you are fasting, do not put on a gloomy look as the hypocrites do: they go about looking unsightly to let people know they are fasting. In truth I tell you, they have had their reward."

In a later passage he condemns those who display their piety while at the same time exploit or take advantage of their employees or brothers and sisters by laying a heavy burden on them. "They tie up heavy burdens and lay them on people's shoulders, but will they lift a finger to move them? Not they! Everything they do is done to attract attention" (Matthew 23:4–5). God does not help those who oppress others. Instead, seeing that they are motivated by sin, wickedness, and deceit, he judges them. Those of whom I speak are masters of manipulation, false humility, self-importance, adulation, and lies. We speak the right words, but our souls are darkened by sin in its many manifestations. How many of us are in this camp? How many of us put up an elaborate front, a show with no substance, no change of heart, and no sense of reality. Is it any wonder that Isaiah in his day and the honest preacher in our day would deny that this is not the fasting of which God would find acceptable?

Other than those who wrote the Scriptures, perhaps no one has quite equaled John Cassian's (AD 360–435) description of fasting.[1] He writes,

> When the Apostle said, "Make no provision to fulfill the desires of the flesh" (Romans 13:14), he was not forbidding us to provide for the needs of life; he was warning us against self-indulgence. Moreover, by itself abstinence from food does not contribute to perfect purity of soul unless the other virtues are active as well. Humility, for example, practiced through obedience in our work and through bodily

hardship, is a great help. If we avoid avarice not only by having no money, but also by not wanting to have any, this leads us towards purity of soul. Freedom from anger, from dejection, self-esteem and pride also contributes to purity of soul in general, while self-control and fasting are especially important for bringing about that specific purity of soul which comes through restraint and moderation. No one whose stomach is full can fight mentally against the demon of unchastity. Our initial struggle therefore must be to gain control of our stomach and to bring our body into subjection not only through fasting but also through vigils, labors and spiritual reading, and through concentrating our heart on fear of Gehenna (Hell) and on longing for the kingdom of heaven.

A Call to Discipleship

Lent is also a call to discipleship, a call to die so that we might live. To die? Yes, to die to ourselves and to become who we are meant to be. This not only involves prayer, but it also involves going out to serve others.

A few years ago I gave a talk to a student group at our local university. I was specifically asked to address the question how to live the gospel as a college student. I began by quoting a few passages from Scripture, particularly Isaiah 58:6–11 and Matthew 25:31–45. Each of these passages reminds us to see Jesus in others. We are told that whatsoever we do to the least of Jesus' brothers and sisters, we do also to him. This implies that whoever we meet on our earthly journey is a manifestation of Jesus. Before I venture further into this talk, let me recount a very recent experience of mine.

Sometime ago on my way to the office I saw a man in a wheelchair wheeling himself along the side of the road. He had an upper torso but no legs. It looked as if he was without the middle of his body, which gave rise to a question. How does he eliminate waste? I glanced at his face. He was hard-looking, even mean-looking, yet determined to get where he was going. I wondered how he got to be in this condition. What kind of life he led? Did he have a skill or an education? How did he get in and out of bed? The questions were multiple. But one thing was certain. Despite losing his legs and part of his body, he is still a person beloved by God. But does he love himself? Does he look upon his *condition* as a stumbling block to his relationship with God? Does he have a caretaker or someone who loves him, who cherishes him as a son, a wife? What are his living conditions? Does he realize that he is beloved and cherished by the only reality that matters, God? I cannot imagine what is in this man's heart. I can only pray for him. And this I must do. But there is a lesson here that is germane to our discussion of discipleship.

Jesus clearly tells us that to put his words into practice calls for making a connection between our faith and compassion, religion and justice, worship and ministry, the love of God and love of our neighbor. These are but a few of the demands and obligations of discipleship. But you ask how to *operationalize* these demands and obligations.

Recall the corporal and spiritual works of mercy or charity that we discussed in an earlier chapter. By way of review they include Jesus' admonition to feed the hungry, give drink to the thirsty, clothe the naked, visit those in prison, visit the sick, shelter the homeless, and bury the dead. They also include admonishing the sinner, instructing the ignorant, counseling the doubtful, comforting the sorrowful, bearing wrongs patiently, forgiving injuries willingly, and praying for the living and the dead. To many of us they seem to involve extraordinary activities or to be directed at strangers. Nothing could be further from the truth. They include ordinary, everyday activities and involve our relationship with our families, friends, and acquaintances. Let me suggest a few ways.

Work in a soup kitchen. Get involved with the local food bank or Meals on Wheels or contribute financially to their operations. This activity obviously goes in the category of feeding the hungry and giving drink to the thirsty.

Giving a drink to the thirsty could also give rise to thoughts about preserving the environment, particularly as it relates to clean water, chemicals polluting rivers and lakes, industry contributing to acid rain falling over parklands hundreds of miles away, and wetlands losing ground to developers and urban sprawl.

As for sheltering the homeless, how about volunteering to be a Habitat for Humanity volunteer or working in a shelter for the homeless or helping elderly people paint their homes, repair their household appliances, wash their windows, scrub or vacuum their floors, etc. You get the idea.

Look in your closet. What do you have that you have not worn in years, probably never will wear? Why are you holding on to these clothes? Could someone else wear them? In your home communities there are several thrift shops that will gladly take these items and distribute them to the needy.

If you are a bit antsy about visiting a prison, how about babysitting for a mother or a grandmother who is confined to a "prison of four walls" in order to give them a free afternoon or evening to get their hair fixed or to go shopping? Or how about babysitting for a mother who must travel a great distance to see her spouse or sibling or child who is imprisoned? At home, how about volunteering to take care of your younger brothers and sisters so that your parents can have a free evening to go out to supper, a movie, or a play?

I have to mention here the many church ministries to local and state prisons. Visiting prisoners can take many forms—writing letters, helping them continue their education while in prison, training them for jobs, bringing tape recorders and children's books to mothers in prison so their children back home can hear their mothers read them bedtime stories and say, "I love you, Mommy." There is also the political task of watching pending legislation relating to prisons, capital punishment, etc. Read Sister Helen Prejean's *Dead Man Walking* to get a feel for this ministry.

Visiting the sick takes on many forms. It can be as simple as visiting an infirm neighbor in his home or visiting a friend in the hospital. Frequently parishes look for people to take Holy Communion to the infirm or to those in hospital, hospice, or nursing home. Spending time with the sick can be very fulfilling. One does not have to say very much. Just being there is often of comfort.

Volunteering to help with the RCIA program or Sunday school is certainly a Christian activity that we can include in the category of instructing the ignorant. But why can't we label tutoring fellow students in mathematics or some other subject or helping your siblings with their homework in a similar way? A student's primary vocation is that of being a student. Helping another fulfill a vocation can be seen as a Christian act of service just as truly as going to Appalachia to serve or helping with Habitat for Humanity.

As an example of counseling the doubtful, consider the fact that every person, young or old, at times has self-doubt or feelings of inadequacy, uncertainty, disappointment, and disillusionment. We need reassurance. In such times a sincere compliment, a warm hug, an affectionate touch, an attentive and sympathetic ear, a pat on the back, and/or a shared meal can do much to alleviate the painful experience. We all need others—friends with whom we can talk about our feelings, our joys and disappointments, our successes and failures, our plans? Why not see such actions as the type that Jesus would commend?

Extending sympathy and help to someone who has lost a loved one obviously fits the category of comforting the sorrowful, and most people would readily classify such actions as Christian or religious. But family life offers many opportunities for easing pain and sorrow. Do we tend to overlook such actions as also Christian and religious?

How do we admonish the sinner as Jesus did? Our Christian faith tells us that we are all sinners, that Christ died for us, and that God loves us as we are. We should begin by acknowledging that we are sinners and seek God's forgiveness and blessings lest we see the splinter in our brother or sister's eye and not the beam in our own. We need to experience forgiveness ourselves. We need to learn to love the sinner and to not be harsh as we lovingly pray that the person will see his or her error. Some years ago a father shared with me the pain he experienced when one of his unmarried daughters told him that she was pregnant. He told me that he didn't know what to say. He just gave her a big warm hug. I assured him that he probably had done the best thing for her. Hugs speak more loudly than words, and they speak on the feeling level. Certainly this action imitating the example of the heavenly Abba (Daddy) as portrayed in the parable of the prodigal son should be regarded as something Jesus would praise.

These are but a few of the things we might want to consider in these beginnings days of Lent These are a few examples of practices we might want to consider making a part of our Christian lives.

But Lent is about more than *practices*. It is also about soul work, our soul work. During this season we need to encounter and recognize our *selves*. We have to work through life's *crust*. In the words of Jung, that is our shadows— those features of ourselves that we or society/family/culture/church and others have pushed down into the depths of our psyches, specifically our personal unconscious. The shadow reveals to us who we are, warts and all, those impulsive, wounded, sad, or isolated parts of ourselves that we generally try to ignore or deny.[2] As the cover of Connie Zweig's book *Romancing the Shadow* puts it, "Beneath the social mask we wear every day, we have a hidden shadow side: an impulsive, wounded, sad, or isolated part that we generally try to ignore."[3]

Lent is the ideal time to discover this side of us, to meet our dark side, accepting it for what it is, learning to use its productive energies in productive ways. Drawing again on Zweig and Wolf in addressing this side of our being, we conceivably will find a "pathway to healing and an authentic life." Zweig and Wolf call this "shadow work." It involves bringing to light what lies in the dark recesses of our psyche, acknowledging and defusing negative emotions and revisiting forbidden thoughts or feelings. It involves coming to grips with, accepting and addressing our real selves and faults as well as taking steps to cultivate compassion for those who we have come to dislike or betrayed. We might even find in this endeavor new and creative strengths with which to meet life's vicissitudes and purposes[4].

It is to this effort that we turn during this Lent. Prayerfully we will see our individual faults for what they are, acknowledge the sinful acts we have committed now and yesterday, yet atone for them by mining for them the gold of self-forgiveness through confession, penance, atonement, and metanoia (i.e., turning away from them and toward the Christ within us).

"How do you do this?" you may ask. How does one align one's self with Christ? I suggest the keys are humility, discernment, obedience, "conversatio" (fidelity to a life dedicated to God's will), and contemplation, all of which we have spoken in an earlier chapter. One does not attempt to realize each of these steps sequentially, but each day or moment calls for the exercise of one or several others. Benedict's ladder of humility expresses it well. The sides of the ladder represent the body and soul. We ascend the ladder through humility, losing the weight of self-importance (e.g., pride, self-aggrandizement, an extreme or prolonged anger in response to criticism, self-promotion, lack of compassion, personal jealousies, and other failings). We descend by *exaltation* of these characteristics. As we ascend the ladder of humility, we begin to be able to discern God's will, sensing what is right for us. This is not necessarily the most obvious. Here we get outside of ourselves.

We practice and realize discernment through prayer, lectio (sacred reading and meditation), and in "community." This means different things to each of us depending on our circumstances. Prayer in this context could be private or corporate as in attending church services or liturgies such as the Mass. Lectio, or in Latin - Lectio Divina, is the practice of praying or meditating through the medium of scripture or other sacred writings with the intention of entering into a deeper relationship with God. It is not intended to promote the intellectual study of such writings. For me as a married man with grown children, my immediate community is my wife, children, grandchildren, extended family, church, etc. Discernment[5] is being sensitive to one's interior movements. These movements relate to one's thoughts, imaginings, emotions, inclinations, desires, feelings, attractions or repulsions. It includes reflecting and understanding where they come from and where they conceivably could lead one.

Obedience comes from the Latin word *obadere*, which means "to listen." The presumption is that one is awake and able to listen to the other, to ourselves in meditation, and of course, to God in contemplation when we are silent before him. Here silence—or rather solitude, silence, and prayer—are all important. Obedience is not about jumping through hoops at someone's command. It goes hand in hand with discernment. One other point is appropriate here. Joseph Campbell often said to his students, "Follow your bliss; there is where you should be." And so it is with us. Listen deeply. Where there is passion or bliss, there is probably the will of God at play. Another point is the watershed moment when one breaks free from structure and realizes that all of creation and not just the church is the place of spirituality. Real responsibility can only develop in freedom. One learns to manage structure, not to be managed by it.

"Conversatio" to the Benedictine or Cistercian is an openness to a change of manners, an ongoing, dynamic, and lifelong fidelity to transformational growth in spirituality, morals, and interactions (or lifelong conversation) with my brothers and sisters, whether or not they are monastics. That is to say that although conversatio has particular relevance for the Benedictine or Cistercian, as a lay Cistercian, it is also relevant to the life of every Christian or the seekers of spiritual growth.

Prayer is "a state of standing before God ... turning the mind and thoughts towards God ... standing before God with the mind in the heart."

Finally there's contemplation. This is the deep-down demeanor that results from growth of the above. One need not be in a monastery to be a contemplative. It speaks to being "still, mindful, and peaceful." It opens us to the transcendental. It keeps us grounded and faithful to whatever God is calling us to.

All of this adds up to how to live the gospel as an adult who sees the importance of developing a spiritual life, acknowledging our good and bad points, those times when we were in the state of grace and those times when we were not, our good and holy deeds and behaviors, and our many sins. In acknowledging it all, we begin to see the blessings God bestows on us, even though we are in sin. It also gives us an opportunity to express our sorrow and beg our Father's forgiveness like the prodigal son.

But there is more.

Thomas Merton was asked what he most wanted out of life. He replied that he wanted to be a good Catholic. His friend Bob Lax responded that that was the wrong answer. Merton should have responded, "To be a saint," for that is why we are created. We have but to state it in word, deed, thought, and soul. After that we have but to leave it to God. He will do the rest. Only then can we step into our truth and see ourselves as we really are. The only admonition I offer is that all that is in this chapter takes a lifetime. If you are fortunate enough to realize even a fraction, don't worry. Our quest for sainthood continues on the other side.

Conclusion

In the beginning of this chapter we observed that Jesus calls us during these forty days of Lent to discipleship in order to take up our crosses and follow him, specifically to give alms, fast and pray in secret. We reviewed three aspects of Lent—the giving of alms, fasting, and the essential forms of prayer, including vocal, meditation, and contemplation. We also looked at several concrete practices that would enrich our Lenten journey. In later chapters we will turn to prayer, specifically *Lectio Divina*, Centering Prayer, the official prayer of the universal church, (i.e., the Liturgy of the Hours, the Jesus Prayer, and the prayer given to us by our Lord). But first there are several other topics that need to be covered. Suffice it to say that at this point we are poised to focus on the fundamental purposes of Lent as a time of preparation, renewal, and metanoia when we can turn away from our sinful ways.

Endnotes

[1]   Cassian, John, *On the Eight Vices on Control of the Stomach* (London: Faber and Faber Limited, 1979), 74.

[2]   Zweig, Connie, and Steven Wolf, *Romancing the Shadow: A Guide to Soul Work for a Vital, Authentic Life* (New York: Random House Ballantine Publishing Group, 1997).

[3]   Ibid

[4]   Ibid

[5]   For an interesting overview of discernment see English, S.J. John J., *Spiritual Freedom, From an Experience of the Ignatian Exercises to the Art of Spiritual Guidance*, 2nd Edition (Chicago, ILL: Loyola Press, 1995) 111-128; 174-194

CHAPTER 7

THE FIRST WEEK JESUS CONFRONTS SATAN

Heaven opened and the Holy Spirit descended on him
in a physical form, like a dove.
And a voice came from heaven,
"You are my Son; today have I fathered you."
—Luke 3:21–22

Filled with the Holy Spirit, Jesus left the Jordan
and was led by the Spirit into the desert,
for forty days being put to the test by the devil.
—Luke 4:1

And at once the Spirit drove him into the desert
and he remained there for forty days, and was put to the
test by Satan.
He was with the wild animals, and the angels looked after him.
—Mark 1:12–13

This pericope for the first Sunday of Lent conveys a sense of immediacy, almost urgency. Jesus has just been baptized by John the Baptist in the River Jordan. Right after his baptism that same Spirit, which had descended like a dove on him, now impels Jesus or drives him into the desert.

This desert is probably between Jerusalem and the Dead Sea. It is thirty-five miles in one direction and fifteen miles in the other. Its landscape is one of extremes with rolling dunes, deep valleys or canyons, crumbling wind-formed rock formations, dry creek beds, sparse vegetation, harsh sunlight, snakes, lizards, hawks, sun-bleached bones of animals or human remains, a wasteland. It is barren with little to no sign of water or vegetation. What one notices about the desert is its immensity and how desolate and frightening it is by day and night. By day it is incredibly bright with multiple hues of khaki sand or soil, and grayish brown craggy large outcrops of shale. At night the sky is pitch-black, and the noise is heightened by the sound of the wind, which is like that of a howling coyote or wild dog.

Here one's senses are heightened. It's as if you can see forever and hear mysterious sounds. Day or night, puffs of swirling sand morph into full-throated sandstorms that are unmerciful and blinding, penetrating into the orifices of the body. The smell of carrion, one's sweat and body odor, and dry-baked earth assault the senses. One feels and tastes desert grit and dust, the bitter taste of insects that somehow get into one's mouth. The unbearable heat of the day causes the raising of one's body temperature, portending dehydration, sun stroke, and sometimes death. The wind and the freezing cold at night triggers cracked lips, frostbite, hypothermia, or mental confusion. Walking on rocks, gritty sand, and hard-packed ground causes numbness in one's legs and more pain. If one is hungry, there is only wild game, rabbits, or rats. The solitude is almost eerie. The silence is absolutely deafening in its roar. It is a time to listen to the rhythms of your body and the still, small voice of God. It is also a time to remember other deserts where people live in fear or destitution, forgotten in slums, in prisons, or in danger to limb and/or life. Just as Satan came to Christ in the Sinai, so too does he come into places such as these. Indeed it is a desolate, frightening, and lonely land that ends at a steep cliff below which is the Dead Sea.

The Jews of this period believed that wild beasts and wicked spirits ruled the desert. For them it was the habitat of evil spirits. It was a place of temptation and spiritual struggle. The Canaanites of early Scripture feared the presence of a god named Mot (a word that also means *death*), who held sway over the heat and barren summers when rain ceased and signs of life were scarce. Jesus was also driven into this desert by the Spirit so that he might make preparation for his ministry in Galilee and Judea. Jesus' forced drive into the desert by the Holy Spirit recalls his ancestor's long desert experience.

It was during their long desert pilgrimage when they encountered and yielded to multiple temptations. It was in the desert that the Hebrews of the first covenant dwelled for forty years before they entered the Promised Land. Here God gave them the Decalogue. It was here also where the prophets would suggest they return whenever they fell into sin and their love and faithfulness to God faltered. It was here where they were to rediscover who they were and to what God had called them. Both Elijah and John the Baptist were people of the desert. It is in the desert that after forty days of fasting and intense communication with his Father, Jesus meets the Devil, with whom he engages in battle.

The Devil is the embodiment of evil, the tempter and spiritual enemy of mankind. An adversary of God, he is known by several names—Satan, Lucifer, or Beelzebub—and he is often depicted as a snake or serpent. He is the same Serpent who tricked Adam and Eve in the garden of Eden.

According to an ancient myth, Adam was believed to be like one of the angels. There is another old myth—probably stemming from Babylonian mythology and referred to in Isaiah 14:12—that all the angels were commanded by Michael, an archangel, to pay homage to the image of God. All bowed before Adam except Lucifer, who, in punishment for his pride and rebellion, was hurled from his heavenly heights to the depth of the abyss, hell. His place was reserved for Adam. Lucifer, renamed Satan, became man's enemy, and it is he who in many guises sets out to seduce him. The book of Wisdom states that "God created man for immortality, but through the envy of Satan death entered the world."

Jesus is the new Adam. The Devil knows full well who Jesus is. Hence, his scheme is to strike first. It is conceivable that this is the most important event in the life and work of Jesus. It is his initiation as the fully divine Son of God and the fully human offspring of *the woman*, whom we know is Mary, the Mother of God. As a man, he is about to undertake (in obedience to the Father) the work for which he came into this world. But first he had to confront the Prince of the World.

For forty days Jesus remained in the desert and engaged in spiritual combat with Satan. In the Middle East this simply connotes a long time. Mark's emphasis is on the testing or trial of Jesus. It does not appear that he is forced against his will. Perhaps he is beginning to come to grips with his messianic mission. Or perhaps he simply recognizes that his acceptance of this mission made this conflict essential to his preparation for it. Notwithstanding, it is in the desert that Jesus gives evidence of his true character. Mally[1] tells us, "The notions of testing or temptation are connected with the view that a state of war existed in the world between good and evil powers, in which the believer was constantly exposed to the devil's attacks. Unlike Matthew and Luke, Mark does not indicate the nature of Jesus' temptation, or even that it may have been occasioned by hunger."

Mally adds that although the exact details are unknown, this testing is generally thought of as a titanic struggle with the powers of evil. It is in some ways a testing of Jesus' resolve and purpose as well as a declaration by Jesus of his authority over evil and a statement that he is truly the Son of God.

Of all the evangelists Mark is the only one to mention wild animals. Scholars are not of one mind with respect to the significance of the presence of wild animals or wild beasts. Some suggest that they could symbolize the beginning of the messianic age, a nod to the garden of Eden and Adam's mandate to govern the earth (Genesis 1:26–28). Others suggest that they could symbolize the prevalence of the evil and the satanic hostility with which Jesus had to contend (Psalm 22:11–21; Ezekiel 34:5, 8, 25).

Mark also mentions that angels looked after Jesus. We do not know, however, whether the angels ministered to Jesus during or after the struggle. Although Mark does not tell us the outcome of this struggle, there is a strong implication of Satan's defeat as spelled out in Jesus' exorcisms of demons or other battles with unclean spirits that would characterize a significant portion of his ministry.

Mathew and Luke speak to three specific temptations. In almost identical language both evangelists tell us that the Spirit led Jesus "into the desert to be put to the test by the devil" and that "he fasted forty days and forty nights" (Mathew 4:1–2).

The First Temptation

Luke 4:2–3 says, "During that time he ate nothing and at the end he was hungry. Then the devil said to him, 'If you are the Son of God, tell this stone to turn into a loaf.' But Jesus replied, 'Scripture says: Human beings live not on bread alone.'"

Mathew 4:4 adds, "But on every word that comes from the mouth of God."

In the Judean desert then and even today there are stones shaped to look like small loaves of bread. They are everywhere. There are other stones that look like melons. The natives call them Elijah's melons. To a very hungry man given to hallucinations, they look very real. For someone with Jesus' gifts he could have used his powers to turn these stones into bread and to make people believe in him. There were plenty of hungry people in Israel. The crowds would flock to him. But Jesus did not fall for this ploy of the Devil. He did not come simply to make life better for people. He came to make better men and women. What is more Jesus knew that it was to his Father that he owed his obedience, not the Devil. His answer is foreshadowed in Deuteronomy 8:3, which says, "He subjected you to the hardship of hunger and then gave you manna to eat, which neither you nor your fathers had ever known, in order to teach you that man does not live on bread alone, but that man may live on anything that the Lord decrees."

In this first temptation Jesus does not deny the very human need for food or pleasure, but putting human life in perspective, he underscores Moses' assertion that when one is dependent on material things and not on God, we are more susceptible to temptation and sin.

The Second Temptation

Luke 4:5–8 says, "Then leading him to a height, the devil showed him in a moment of time all the kingdoms of the world and said to him, 'I will give you all this power and their splendor, for it has been handed over to me, for me to give it to anyone I choose. Do homage, then, to me, and it shall all be yours.' But Jesus answered him, 'scripture says: you must do homage to the Lord your God, him alone you must serve.'"

What is the Devil up to now? He is offering the elixir of political power and wealth. But first Jesus must worship the Devil. Jesus saw this ruse for what it was. If Jesus accepted his offer, he would be turning his back on his Father. Just as Yahweh had promised the Hebrews that they would enter the Promised Land only if they trusted him alone, Jesus knew full well that as His Son, he was bound by his duty to trust in his Father alone. His answer is reflective of Moses' admonitions. "The Lord your God is the one to whom you must do homage, him alone you must serve" (Deuteronomy 6:13). "Do not put the Lord your God to the test" (Deuteronomy 6:16). "You must revere the Lord your God: only Him shall you worship, to Him shall you hold fast, and by His name shall you swear" (Deuteronomy 10:20).

This second temptation continues even to this day. All too often we have succumbed to the lust for power. We have individually and collectively sought to accumulate power and dominance in the marketplace, in government, and in our daily dealings with our neighbor. In the myopic pursuit of money, temporal goods, and power, we have neglected the poor, the education of our children, our infrastructure, and the well-being of our planet. We have overlooked the maltreatment and discrimination of our brothers and sisters in our pursuit of special privileges at the expense of everyone else, crony capitalism, political gain, and ideological purity. We have passed tax laws that protect and benefit the wealthy and shackle moderate-income citizens. We have substituted the invisible hand of the market for the hand of God in governance, in social welfare, even in the church. Those of us who call ourselves people of the Book are no stranger to using politics to gain temporal power. The Devil is in our synagogues, temples, churches, and mosques just as he is in every other aspect of our lives.

The Third Temptation

Luke 4:9–12 says, "Then he led him to Jerusalem and set him on the parapet of the temple, 'If you are Son of God,' he said to him, 'throw yourself down from here, for scripture says: He has given his angels orders about you to guard you, and again: 'They will carry you in their arms in case you trip over a stone.' But Jesus answered him, Scripture says: Do not put the Lord your God to the test.'"

These passages are taken from Psalm 91:11–12. The Devil knew them well. It was a clever ruse. He must have known that the other two temptations would not work, but surely this one would. Surely these quotations would make his suggestion acceptable. Jesus really did trust his Father.

But Jesus knew what the Devil was up to. He knew that people wanted to see miracles, signs that he was from God. If he could impress them, they would more easily believe and accept him as the Messiah, the Son of God. But Jesus also knew that his Father did not want this. Hence, his response, which comes from Deuteronomy 6:16. Jesus would not show his power like this. His responsibility was to choose the cross. With that the Devil leaves Jesus.

The Desert, Silence, Solitude, and Prayer

Imagine Lent as our desert into which we are driven by the same Spirit. In this desolate environment the solitude and silence are palpable. Absent are the noises of our everyday lives. Let us look at how one man handled this experience.

St. Anthony, the father of monasticism, is one of our best guides to solitude. Born about 251 CE, Anthony was eighteen years old when he heard the gospel passage in church, "Go sell what you have and give to the poor and then follow me" (Matthew 19:21). It seemed to Anthony that these words were meant for him. In time he went into the desert, where he remained for twenty years. After a short period of time with a holy man from whom he learned the basic principles of spirituality (i.e., fasting and prayer), he ventured deeper into the desert. During the course of several years he underwent unimaginable temptations of the flesh, attacks by demons, lurid thoughts, confusion, boredom, and discouragement. But he also learned how to endure and counter these trials by combining manual work and prayers. After twenty years he emerged from solitude and reentered society, a changed and new man, whole in body, mind, and soul, having surrendered unconditionally to Jesus Christ. For Anthony solitude was a period of great struggle but also one of kenosis, purification, and transformation. It was the place where God molded Anthony in his own image and freed him from the compulsions of the world.[2]

Nouwen[3] calls solitude the "furnace of transformation." It is the place where we disengage ourselves from a society that entangles us with its delusions. It is where we struggle against what in us is false and sheer fantasy. It is where we like Anthony experience cravings of the flesh, greed, power, and fame and find ourselves to be "naked, vulnerable, weak sinful, deprived, broken—nothing." Solitude is being alone with God. Jesus himself implored his disciples to leave behind the cares of the world and withdraw into the peace and silence of the desert to pray "in a deserted place and rest awhile" (Mark 6:31). It could conceivably be one of the richest and most blessed periods on one's spiritual lives. It is in the solitude or loneliness of the desert that God finds us, and in silence we listen to his voice. In solitude our trues selves begin to emerge, and we find ourselves remade in the image and likeness of God. Our old selves die. Our delusions and fantasies are shattered. We become new men and women. We experience the Christ within and realize that he has been with us through all this interior strife. He lives within us. He is your true self.

We need to enter the desert frequently and sit awhile in the gentle presence of this Christ in silence. We need to become people of solitude, balanced, gentle, caring, and Christlike. But there is more.

Closely connected with solitude is silence. Nouwen adds that silence completes and intensifies solitude. It is what makes solitude a reality. In Proverbs 10:19, we read, "Where there is much talking, there is no lack of transgressions." In Proverbs 17:28, it is found, "Even a fool, if he keeps silent, is deemed wise." James 3:2 goes even further by stating, "Someone who does not trip up in speech has reached perfection and is able to keep the whole body on a tight rein." And in Matthew 12:36, we hear Jesus saying that "for every unformed word people utter they will answer on Judgment Day, since it is by your words you will be justified, and by your words condemned." Silence—interior and exterior—has always been a mainstay of monastic life and the preparation of religious men and women for their ministries and the furtherance of their spiritual lives. In fact, the founders of every religious order or congregation have insisted on the observance of silence as an essential rule of their charism, even those devoted to active ministries, such as service to the poor or infirm, teaching, and other more or less nonspiritual occupations. Silence has always been considered as indispensable in the maintenance of a prayerful life. It is in silence that we hear God, speak with him, and ponder in our hearts the thoughts that he has placed deep within.

In *The Screwtape Letters*, C. S. Lewis[4] has the Devil say,

> Music and silence—how I detest them both! How thankful we should be that ever since our father (that is Lucifer) entered hell no square inch of infernal space and no moment of infernal time has been surrendered to either of those abominable forces, but all has been occupied by, Noise—Noise, the grand dynamism, the audible expression of all that is exultant, ruthless and virile—Noise which alone defends us from silly qualms, despairing scruples and impossible desires. We will make the whole universe a noise in the end. We have already made great strides in this direction as regards the earth. The melodies and silences of heaven will be shouted down in the end.

How accurate a description this is of our city streets with the deafening rumble of the subway, trucks, and automobiles, the sound of construction activities or airplanes overhead, and the blaring of cacophonies emanating from storefronts and boom boxes. It is no wonder that once we are inside our homes and apartments, we seek a moment of silence or cherish the quiet moments in the country. We need to somehow recover our psychological equilibrium.

To be able to be with God fully, we need silence, peace, and solitude. Only then can we recover our spiritual equilibrium to reflect, ponder, meditate, and contemplate. Only then are we open to hearing the voice of God and absorbing his wisdom. Only then will we grow in the love and knowledge of Christ. Only then can we welcome the stirrings of Holy Spirit. Psalm 46:10

says it all, "Be still and know that I am God." A meditation on this reveals the following:

- Silence is necessary to come to the knowledge of God and to acknowledge that he is God.
- With God, silence finds its highest value and meaning.
- Silence in this context finds its highest value and meaning.
- Silence becomes restorative and redemptive.
- Silence becomes an act of worship.
- Silence opens us up to receiving the fullness of God into our souls.
- Being still enables us to be attentive and connected to one another.
- Being still enables me to know myself at a deeper level.
- It is only in silence that we find the Christ within and know that he really loves us.
- Silence works to prevent evil and strengthen our resolve to cast our evil tendencies at the feet of Christ.
- Silence is an aid in the practice of good by placing a guard on our tongue.
- Silence involves self-denial and restraint.

The Christian spiritual tradition teaches us that the practice of silence is the prerequisite for coming to know God. The most basic spiritual practice is learning how to be silent. Practicing silence is an act of faith precisely because one cannot know for certain that anything is to be gained from it. It might be a waste of that most precious commodity—time. Yet each of us is on a journey. During that journey we will—if we have not already—spend some time in the desert. St. John of the Cross calls it the dark night of the soul, in which we are alone with our feelings of desolateness. It is part of God's plan, and in retrospect it is a blessed experience. During this period we grow to maturity. Hopefully we come to grips with the work God wants us to do and the person God wants us to be. In this desert our faith and trust in God are tested. We find the strength to embrace our cross and undertake with confidence what God has willed for us.

The Message to Us

On Ash Wednesday we meditated on almsgiving, prayer, and fasting. On that same day we marveled at the large number of Christians who received ashes as a symbol of this period of mortification. Perhaps we have begun to turn our thoughts to the needy, the hungry, the thirsty, the sick, etc. Many of us might have taken to frequent if not daily worship and community prayer. It is fitting that this first week of Lent concentrates on striving to overcome our temptations and to choose Christ. St. Peter tells us, "Keep sober and alert because your enemy the devil is on the prowl like a roaring lion looking for someone to devour. Stand up to him, strong in faith" (1 Peter 5:8–9).

Jesus' desert experience raises several important questions for us. Here I will repeat the following questions I recently heard in the homily of a priest I do not know: "What are some of the desert experiences I have experienced in my life? What desert experience am I living through right now? When and how do I find moments of contemplation in the midst of a busy life? How have I lived in the midst of my own desert wilderness? Have I been courageous and persistent in fighting with the demons? How have I resisted transforming my own deserts into places of abundant life?"

During this Lent, let us realize how privileged we are to be with Jesus in prayer, Scripture, and liturgy. Let us understand that he has been tested in every way, not unlike us. He knows how hard it is to maintain a vibrant spiritual life. Go to him. He is a compassionate Lord and is present to us even in the midst of temptation and sinfulness. Welcome to the desert.

And so it is with us. Consider the desert as a place or a retreat where we, too, are tested, grow into the persons we were meant to be, and discover that God is with, that he is in us, that he cares for us, and that he will give us strength to withstand those who would tempt us. Let us listen to our inner voices, remember our many blessings, examine our motives, and write our worries in the sand. And thank God we have not had to engage in anything like Jesus' cosmic struggle with the angel of darkness.

Endnotes

[1] Mally, Edward J., "The Gospel According to Mark," *The Jerome Biblical Commentary*, in *The Jerome Biblical Commentary*. Ed, Raymond E. Brown, S.S., Joseph A. Fitzmyer, S.J., Roland E. Murphy, O.Carm. (Englewood Cliff, NJ: Prentice Hall, Inc., 1968) 25

[2] St. Athanasius, *St. Antony of the Desert* (Rockford, IL: TAN Books and Publishers, 1995).

[3] Nouwen, Henri, *The Way of the Heart* (New York: Ballantine Books, Random House, 1981), 13.

[4] Lewis, C. S., *The Screwtape Letters* in The Complete C. S. Lewis Signature Classics (San Francisco: HarperSanFrancisco, 2002) 170.

CHAPTER 8

JESUS IS CALLING ALL SINNERS WHAT IS MY RESPONSE?

See, I set before you this day life and prosperity, death and
adversity.
For I command you this day to love the Lord your God, to
walk in His ways,
and to keep His commandments, His laws, and His rules,
that you may thrive and increase, and that the Lord your
God may bless you—
But if your heart turns away and you give no heed,
and are lured into the worship and service of other gods,
I declare to you this day that you shall certainly perish—
I have put before you life and death, blessing and curse.
Choose life ... by loving the Lord your God, heeding His
commands,
and holding fast to Him.

—Deuteronomy 30:15–20

He said, The Son of Man is destined to suffer grievously,
to be rejected by the elders and chief priests and scribes
and to be put to death, and be raised up on the third day.
Then speaking to all he said, If anyone wants to be a follower
of mine, let him renounce himself
and take up his cross every day and follow me.
For anyone who wants to save his life will lose it;
but anyone who loses his life for my sake, that man will save it.
What gain, then, is it for a man to have won the whole world
and have lost or ruined his very self?

—Luke 9:22–23

I n this chapter we are reminded that during Lent we are particularly called to a new life. In the previous pericope Moses offers the Israelites a choice between life and death. He urges them to choose life. The choice is between life in the covenant and life outside the covenant. From this perspective biological existence and even prosperity if not in the covenant constitutes death. The reference to love and walking in his ways means to act loyally and to honor the commitments of the covenant. Those commitments are to love God, our neighbors, and ourselves.

In Luke's gospel, Jesus lays down the conditions of service for those who would follow him. To be his disciple we must not only keep the listed commitments but also answer his call to leave all and follow him even if it costs us our lives. He calls us to discipleship. As the German pastor Dietrich Bonhoeffer[1] writes, "When Christ calls a man, he bids him come and die." At the beginning of Lent Jesus calls us to take up our cross every day and follow him even to Golgotha and certain physical death.

Jesus knew of what he was speaking in equating the cross with discipleship. To be his disciple means to choose the way of the cross rather than the way of the world, the flesh, or the Devil. To be his disciple means to deny yourself and bear the cross for Jesus' sake. Only then will we realize the scriptural passage, "My yoke is sweet and my burden light" (Matthew 11:30). Only then will we realize that bearing our cross is not a tragedy but the fruit of an exclusive allegiance to Jesus Christ, not an accident but a necessity and an essential part of the Christian life. Only when we are totally committed to discipleship can we begin to experience the meaning of the cross as rejection, shame, and suffering. In a word, shouldering our cross means abandoning the attachments of the world, surrendering ourselves to Jesus, dying to our own will, throwing off the old man, and putting on the new man.[2]

The call to discipleship by way of the cross means suffering, rejection, and death, but it also means new life, joy, and the assurance of Christ's presence and fellowship. The disciple must allow nothing to come between Christ and himself, neither the law, personal piety, the world, nor church leaders for whom this commitment is simply an emotional uplift that makes no costly demands or who preach that forgiveness does not require repentance, that communion does not require confession, or that the measure of religion is prosperity, happiness, or self-aggrandizement.

When Jesus was still a youth in Nazareth, he could not have but witnessed several crucifixions. He must have been appalled at the cruelty and viciousness of justice. Yet he selects the metaphor of the cross to teach us that to answer his call means to be prepared to face even death out of loyalty for him, to be ready to endure every hardship for his sake. Only then are our lives saved. To live to self is to die. To die to self is to live in Jesus.

And so the question is this: How much do I want to follow Jesus? How much do I want to commit myself to him? Am I willing to deny myself to the point of turning my back on the comforts of home, family, career, and the pursuit of pleasure and possessions? Can I say no to myself that I might have a personal relationship with Jesus, whom I can't see with my naked eye? Can I abandon myself to the point of giving it all up, renouncing all that I hold precious to follow a Jewish carpenter and itinerant preacher who in the eyes of his contemporaries was an abject failure, being nailed to a cross as a common criminal? Dare I submit myself to the jeers and taunts of my colleagues who will think I have gone off the deep end?

To follow Jesus is to deny myself completely, to embrace the death of myself, and to lose myself for his sake so that I might save myself. This calls for struggle. This is my cross. To take up my struggle is to live a life that is consonant with what Jesus is calling me to do. This view of the cross is very different from the perception of most people who think of it as a burden (e.g., a hapless and strained marriage, a miserable job, a pain-filled physical ailment, or a cantankerous colleague). This is in reality self-pitying pride. This is not what Jesus meant when he said, "Take up your cross every day and follow me" (Luke 9:23).

Yes, the cross of which Jesus speaks still represents torture, ridicule, disgrace, death to self, a call to absolute surrender, and a willingness to die in following Jesus. But it also speaks to atonement, forgiveness, grace, and love. We gain everything by losing all. "Anyone who wants to save his life will lose it, but anyone who loses his life for my sake, will save it. What benefit is it to anyone to win the whole world and forfeit or lose his very self?" (Luke 9:23–25).

Am I up to this call? Can I bear rejection from kith and kin? Can I stand up to life's trials and tribulations? How about the many sacrifices that will be demanded of me?

The third and fourth pericopes listed above extend this call. On their surface these gospel passages are about the call and conversion of Levi, perhaps a descendent of the tribe of Levi and identified in Mark 2:14 as the son of Alphaeus. Levi was later to be known as Matthew, one of the twelve apostles.

Now Levi was a tax collector. His job was to collect taxes on behalf of Rome, a hated foreign occupier of Palestine. Because they represented

Rome, tax collectors were despised and shunned. In Jewish society they were considered robbers, thieves, renegades, and traitors. Whatever amount of money they collected over and above what the Romans exacted, they got to keep. Usually tax collectors became quite wealthy.

Palestine was a police state, and residents did not have many civil rights unless they were citizens of Rome. All a tax collector at that time had to do to extract money from a person was to threaten to report him to the soldiers of Herod or Rome. Entering a house to dine with such a person rendered the faithful Jew spiritually and ceremonially unclean, according to the Pharisees. They were to be avoided at all costs by respectable society. Nevertheless, many tax collectors did have friends, such as Gentiles who lived in the community or Jewish sinners who failed to abide by standard rules of purity. Apostate Jews or excommunicated members of a synagogue were considered sinners along with those who were notorious sinners, robbers, evildoers, and adulterers.

Mark tells us that as he was walking along the shore of the sea of Galilee, Jesus passed a small tax office or customs house and simply said to the man inside, "Follow me." Levi immediately gets up and follows Jesus, leaving behind his money tables and joining Jesus' retinue. Think about this. Jesus speaks with and personally calls this despised, hated, ostracized, ostensibly sinful man to follow him, to be accepted by him, and to be unconditionally loved by him. Luke 5:28 records, "And he left everything, and rose and followed him."

Levi invites Jesus to dine with him as a guest in his home that very night. Jesus accepts. Levi makes preparations for a great banquet and invites a large crowd of tax collectors and others, many of whom are social pariahs. Jesus arrives and is quite comfortable. Indeed he seems to be enjoying himself, meeting people who were probably afraid to approach him before this event. He eats and drinks heartily. He embraces Levi and his friends with much warmth and friendship. Even Peter, Andrew, James, and John—who like most good Jews despised him and who as fishermen were more than likely victimized by him—warmed up to Levi because of Jesus' acceptance of him.

But the Pharisees and scribes could not believe what they were seeing. They were enraged. To them Jesus did something intolerable. He had gone to the home of someone where one could never be sure that the dietary laws would be observed. "Why do you eat and drink with tax collectors and sinners?" they ask. The teachers of the law of Moses and their followers are scandalized. How could this man claim to be the Messiah? How could such a man associate himself with criminals such as these? If he was truly the Messiah, surely he would avoid such people who violated God's law and were social and religious outcasts. It is as if they are accusing Jesus of being an accomplice of criminals and approving of their behavior. Levi's guests are stunned at the venom behind this question. But Jesus chooses to respond directly. "It is not the healthy who need a doctor, but the sick. I have not come to call the righteous, but sinners to repentance" (Luke 5:31–32).

What the Pharisees and the scribes fail to see is that although sinners invite Jesus to be their guest at dinner, Jesus invites them—by repentance—to become his guests at the eschatological banquet. By his presence Jesus transforms their banquet into his own.

The Pharisees and the scribes also fail to see that pride is their undoing. In their smugness they fail to see Jesus as the physician who comforts troubled souls. They are unaware that he is calling even them to repentance. They could not see that this call is open to all people of high and low estate. Jesus has come for all, for we are all sick and we are all sinners. No one is good except God alone. We must all confess our sins and seek God's mercy and forgiveness in order to have life and to be saved. There is no reason for the Pharisees and scribes to think that they are justified under their particular concept of the law. All of us need God every day. He doesn't care what others think about us or how others value us. He loves us even if there are those who consider us outcasts and unworthy of their love. His mission is to the poor, the sick, the oppressed, and the brokenhearted.

Jesus rebukes the Pharisees and scribes. He addresses their smug self-righteousness. They imagine themselves to be strong and well and not sinners. They cannot see that they are every bit as sick as these tax collectors and the other guests.

There is a message here for us as well. Our society, our church, and we ourselves are sinners. We are among the sick. We are nowhere near as strong and well as we sometimes think we are. And so we ask, "Come, Lord Jesus, blessed physician, penetrate to the depths of my soul and cure me of the sickness of hypocrisy and pride." With the psalmist I cry,

> Have mercy upon me, O God,
> as befits your faithfulness;
> in keeping with your abundant compassion,
> blot out my transgressions
> Wash me thoroughly of my iniquity
> and purify me of my sin;

for I recognize my transgressions
and am ever conscious of my sin
Against you alone have I sinned,
and done what is evil in your sight
so you are just in your judgment.
Indeed I was born with iniquity;
with sin my mother conceived me. (Psalm 51:3–7)

Jesus has come to call me, a sinner. He is calling me to repentance regardless of my sins and weaknesses. Why do I delay?

Jesus is concerned about me and those like me who have sinned through our own fault. Jesus is concerned about those of us who are lame and broken, those who are desperate and feel forgotten. He has great compassion for us and will heal us and bind up our wounds. He will make us well again. But first we must acknowledge the fact that we are sinners. Like Levi, we must not be afraid to respond to his call and return to Father God, no longer fearful of his wrath, for he loves us. He knows who are and what we have done. And his mercy and forgiveness is certain. He came for us, not the virtuous.

Okay, but let's try to look at this from the perspectives of the Pharisee and scribe. Imagine your parish priest or minister being seen frequently in your city's red-light district. Wouldn't this give rise to a measure of scandal? Would you not feel compelled to ask him why he has been going into this area? If you saw him there eating and drinking with prostitutes and their consorts, wouldn't you become very concerned about his character or at least his judgment? Would you not question his fitness to administer the sacraments or to proclaim the Word of God from the pulpit? I suspect you would. So let's not be so hard on the Pharisees and scribes. For the purposes of Luke's message, they serve as a useful foil. By the way, what are *you* doing in that area in the first place?

Why indeed does Jesus dine with sinners and tax collectors, the reprobate and the depraved, the unclean and the vile, you and me? In the parlance of young men and women of today, it is where the action is. A doctor seeks to treat sick people. For the doctor this is where the action is. For Jesus and those whom he calls to follow in his footsteps, the action is to seek to serve the needy, the lost, the lonely, the suffering, and the sinner, all those who feel estranged from God and their brothers and sisters because of their conditions and situations.

Jesus seeks to heal the whole person, body, mind, and spirit. Jesus seeks to restore the sick to wholeness. It is up to those who claim to be disciples of Jesus to make the first move to go to them, to give them sustenance, and to give witness of God's love for them. Jesus did not say wait for them to come to you and preach the good news. He said that he came to call sinners, not the upright. Ironically the Pharisees and the scribes were also among the sinners, but they did not know it. They were too proud to admit it. Jesus was also calling them to wholeness, to metanoia, a turning to their better angels and to repentance. Their redemption was also at hand.

Carroll Stuhlmueller[3] offers an interesting gloss on this pericope. He suggests that while sinners invite Jesus to be their guest at dinner, Jesus in turn invites them—by repentance—to become his guests at the eschatological banquet. Hence, this meal has a sacred dimension. It is in anticipation of the meals Jesus will share with his own people in the kingdom that is to come.

Conclusion

Every night the media revels in exposing the sins and missteps of public figures from Hollywood to Wall Street to the corridors of governments. They make millions and entertain millions more by denouncing and humiliating wrongdoers. Of course this is done from positions of moral rectitude. And many of us to whom the media directs its message share in a common sentiment of moral outrage. But be careful. Carl Jung tells us that by seeing in others all the things we hate and despise, it is most likely that we are looking into a mirror at ourselves. And so it is with our gospel story today. Let he or she who would criticize the Pharisee or scribe take note.

Are you up to this call? His call does not allow for the halfhearted or those who are not willing to pay the cost. Sometime it will mean the loss of face, friends, family, reputation, career, and possessions, and in some instances it may even cost your life. Are you willing to take up your cross and follow Jesus? He is looking for a few good men and women. The pay is low. The conditions of employment are often perilous with the threat to life, limb, and comfort. Can you muster the strength? During this Lent, can you commit to Jesus and take up your cross daily? Are you willing to lose your life for his sake so that you might save it?

Endnotes

[1]   Bonhoeffer, Dietrich, *The Cost of Discipleship* (New York: Macmillan Publishing Co., 1963).

[2]   Ibid.

[3]   Stuhlmueller, C.P. The Gospel According to Luke, *The Jerome Biblical Commentary*, vol. 2, 134. Editors, Brown, Raymond, et al

PART 3

THE DESSERT

CHAPTER 9

FOUR QUESTIONS: WHERE? WHAT? WHO? WHY?

For me to become a saint means to be myself.
Therefore the problem of sanctity
and salvation is in fact the problem of finding out who I am
and of discovering my true self.
Trees and animals have no problem.
God makes them what they are without consulting them,
and they are perfectly satisfied.
With us it is different. God leaves us free to become whatever
we like.
We can be ourselves or not, as we please. We are at liberty
to be real or to be unreal.
We may be true or false, the choice is ours. We may wear
now one mask and now another, and never, if we so desire
appear with our own true face.
But we cannot make choices with impunity. Causes have effects,
and if we lie to ourselves and to others,
then we cannot expect to find truth and reality whenever we
happen to want them.
If we have chosen the way of falsity we must not be surprised
that truth eludes us
when we finally come to need it.
We are called to share with God in creating our true identity.
—Thomas Merton, *New Seeds of Contemplation*

Before embarking on our actual Lenten journey and with the assumption that we are really serious, this section offers a process that will prepare us for the journey. This is where the rubber meets the road. Now is the time to begin. To travel the road in front of us is to do more than give up chocolate for Lent or to attend daily Mass, even though the latter is certainly appropriate. To this end I propose four initial questions.

1. Where am I?
2. What am I?
3. Who am I?
4. Why am I?

These questions are among the most important questions we as humans can ask ourselves. Their ultimate purpose is to come to grips with the meaning of our individual lives. This has been the purpose of every man, woman, and child of every race, culture, and age for thousands of years. All religious texts address these questions, and they form the major themes of writings from antiquity up to the present time. How we answer these questions holds the key to how we live our lives and our direction as people.

The first question, "Where am I?" seeks to take a bird's-eye view of our location in the scheme of life. This is the most basic of the four questions. It stems from a very simple statement we have all heard at one time or another, "You can't know where you are going unless you know where you are." The second question, "What am I?" can be answered from several perspectives, such as biological, behavioral, psychological, or spiritually. In other words, I am a living human being that behaves in a certain way within a particular sociocultural milieu, and I consist of a psyche (Jung) and a spiritual connection with a higher power outside of myself. My psyche includes my biological, mental, and spiritual aspects. The third question, "Who am I? presents its own set of problems. It is perhaps the most difficult of all the questions. While it speaks to who I am in terms of Jung's *self*, it goes beyond Jung to address who I am in terms of my relationship to God. I am a creature made in his image yet a sinner who is prone to missing the mark because of my fallen human nature. Still I am a child of God. The answer to the final question, "Why am I?" is directly traceable to how you answered the preceding questions. It speaks to another question, namely "What is my calling? To what is God calling me?"

Where Am I?

It is imperative that each of us knows our story. Where and to whom were we born? What are our earliest memories? Who were our significant others?

What milestones do we recall as children, students, young adults, and now grown men and women. What about landing our first jobs, getting married, and becoming parents or grandparents, etc.? What other events, individuals, family rituals, or rites of passages have helped to define us as well as foster or inhibit our growth? What other experiences have provided your life with a sense of direction or threatened it? What are some of the earliest memories of spirituality? What did it look like then and now? Who were the people who influenced you one way or the other? Who are they now? What significant spiritual struggles have you had to confront? What memories would you rather forget? Our overriding question becomes this: "What is my story, and what does it mean to me?"

One way to construct our story is to put together what Curry and Dailey[1] call a time line which records "critical events, defining moments, and other growth facilitating or growth inhibiting experiences." In the context of this chapter the time line should also capture "developmental milestones, spiritual events, spiritual challenges and other changes." It should enable us to surface our biases and spiritual assumptions and bring to light changes in our spiritual practices, beliefs, and values. It might also help us discover new spiritual energies. Finally the time line provides us with the material with which to address the other four questions.

One way to capture the essence of one's story is to not only draw a time line of your personal journey by using words, pictures, or symbols, but to also share it with someone close to you. To construct a spiritual time line, you will need construction paper, graphing paper, or plain white paper, crayons, markers, and/or colored paper. If you are creative, you might want to design a collage with photographs, clip pages from magazines, or paint or draw items or symbols to embellish your time line.

Start by dividing your current age into thirds. Let the first third be the period from youth through young adulthood, the second third midlife, and the final third the period that best represents where you are presently. For each third of your life choose three to five significant experiences or traumatic events, illnesses, major transitions, positive or negative milestones, or decisions that influenced your spiritual life or relationship with God. Include the people who influenced you at each stage. Start with the earliest memories you have of growing up and move forward to the present. If possible, record the actual date. Let the memories flow, even those that are hard to face or still hurt or give rise to old fears and angers. Take your time doing this time line. Live with it for several days. Design it so that from time to time you can revisit, update it, and include your dreams, hopes, aspirations, and future goals. This way it becomes a living document that grows over the course of your life. After all, this is all about you and where you have been or where you are at any given point in time.

One thing to take away from this exercise is the observation that you are not where you were yesterday despite your best efforts or strategies. This is food for thought.

What Am I?

The second question is "What am I?" This is a harder question than first meets the eye. You and I are flesh and blood. We share much with inanimate matter and sentient creatures, many of which find their way to our kitchen tables. We identify ourselves as human beings to differentiate ourselves from other animate creatures. Revisiting our time line, we cannot help but see that we occupy many roles. We are daughters and sons, brothers and sisters, students and playmates. We are students, friends, citizens, spouses, parents, employers or employees, and members of faith traditions. We are recipients of talents, abilities, and skills. We possess distinct personalities and cognitive, physical, and emotional attributes. And yet we know we are more. Even when taken together all these descriptors and the ones mentioned earlier do not really satisfy this question.

If we rephrase the question to read "What is man?" we might begin to come up with a better answer. Martin Luther King, Jr.,[2] writes,

> There are some people that believe "man is little more than an animal" and there are those "who would lift man almost to the position of a God." There are then those who would "combine the truths of both" and see in "man a strange dualism, something of a dichotomy." They find that "there are depths in man that go down to the lowest hell, and heights that reach the highest heaven." He cites, "Thou hast made him a little lower than angels, and crowned him with glory and honor."

Carl Jung (1875–1961), the Swiss psychologist, looked at man in terms of *psyche*, a Greek word that initially referred to the ideas of body, soul, self, and mind. He postulated that the *psyche* consisted of the totality of man as a biological reality with a physical body, a psychological reality in terms of his *personal consciousness* and *personal unconsciousness* existing within the *collective unconsciousness*, which he shares with other men. Man's third dimension or reality is that he is an embodied meaning seeking spiritual being. Each of these realities possesses distinct characteristics, but when one reality is out of sorts, the others are affected in some way. In other words, when we are physically ill, our psychological and/or spiritual reality is affected in some way. Jung focused on establishing and fostering a relationship between each of these realities. He opined that such a relationship enriches the person. Without this relationship he thought that unconscious processes could weaken and even jeopardize one's personality. Let's look at each component of the psyche.[3]

Personal Conscious

According to Jung, the personal conscious consists of the *persona* and the *ego*. The persona is the public face or mask we present to the world. It includes our social roles, professions, the kind and style of clothes we wear, and the affectations, personalities, and attitudes we adopt to impress other people. The persona has both negative and positive aspects. An inflated persona is where the individual sees himself only in terms of his or her perceived social role or superficial façade. Conversely the persona can also be construed as positive, as it protects the ego and the psyche from adverse social and cultural forces. It can be crucial to our personality development as the ego gradually comes to identify with it.

The ego is the complex of ideas that constitutes the center of our field of consciousness and is one of the major archetypes of the personality. It provides a sense of consistency and direction in our conscious lives. The ego arises from the personal unconscious, yet within it are no unconscious elements, only conscious contents derived from personal experience. As the ego identifies with the persona, the individual starts to believe that he or she is what they pretend to be, and others begin to erroneously equate that with who he or she is. More often than not this process is harmful, particularly in the case of minority group members and other social outsiders who have adopted certain personas for protection against cultural prejudice and social rejection. Jung has suggested that such individuals are likely to have problems in the long run with learning who they really are during the process of individuation, which we shall discuss later in this essay.

Finally the persona and the ego are not the central elements of the psyche, only the conscious elements. The other half is the personal unconscious.

Personal Unconscious

The personal unconscious is the aspect of the psyche that does not generally rise to the level of the personal conscious and appears in overt behavior or in dreams. It is the source of original thoughts, creative ideas, and meaningful symbols. It consists of the shadow, complexes, the contra-sexual images (the *anima* and the *animus*), and the self.

The *shadow* is the dark side of our personality that contains the animal (and sexual) instincts—the amoral remnant of our instinctual animal past. It is those parts of our personalities that have been repressed as incompatible with the ego ideal as determined by our families of origin, significant others, economic status, sociocultural environment, religion, and the resultant psychological interactions with these selves. As the ego is developed, certain *wrongs* or *bads* are repressed in us, while certain *rights* and *goods* are reinforced. The net result is the creation of a *false self* or a *disowned self*. Jung referred to it as that long bag we drag behind us and into which we toss everything we refuse to acknowledge about ourselves. But the rejected parts of ourselves never go away. We project our shadows upon other people and cultures where the other person's or culture's shadow always seem more apparent, more sinister, or even more golden than our own. In our dreams our personal shadow shows up as a person of the same gender as the dreamer. It is as if we are looking in a mirror and see a reflection of our real selves. This may be a flattering reflection or its opposite. No matter, we are looking at who we really are, good or bad. There is a message here, a message to which we may have to attend.

Complexes are unconscious clusters of emotionally laden thoughts that result in a disproportionate influence on behavior. Jung[4] writes,

> I understand the complex as consisting of two factors. First, there is a nuclear element which acts as a magnet, and second, there is a cluster of associations that are attracted to the nucleus. I see the nuclear element itself as made

up of two components. One is determined by experience, and so is causally related to the environment. The other is determined by the disposition of the individual in question, and is innate; its foundation is basic to the structure of the psyche. When the disposition of the individual at some point confronts an experiential situation which can in no way be handled, a psychic trauma occurs.

Jung suggests that this nuclear element is characterized by its "feeling tone" or the intensity of the emotion or energy involved. The greater the intensity or volatility, the more likely everyday experiences are drawn into the complex. Examples of these clusters are the mother or father complex and an inferiority/superiority complex.

Jung also identified what he called our contra-sexual images (the *anima* and *animus* or female and male roles and urges). The animus—from the Greek word for *spirit*—is the male archetype in women. It is experienced as a projection upon a male. It predisposes the woman to understand the nature of a man, serves as the compensatory rational inner face of the sentimental female persona, and is experienced as a masculine voice within the psyche, thereby expanding the woman's sphere of consciousness. In the dreams of women men represent the woman's *soul*. It shows up in a woman's propensity to become opinionated or pushy. The task of the woman is to integrate the male *logos* (thinking).

The female archetype in men is the anima—from the Greek word for *soul*. It is experienced as a projection upon a woman. It predisposes the man to understand the nature of a woman, serves as the compensatory sentimental inner face of the rational male persona, and is experienced as a feminine voice within the psyche, thereby expanding the man's sphere of consciousness. In the dreams of men women represent the man's *soul*. It shows up in a man's mood swings. Men must integrate the feminine *eros* (feeling).

Jung concludes his treatment of the anima and animus by pointing out that their intra-psychic function is to provide the individual with new ways of functioning, challenge one to live life with greater gusto, and move the individual to a greater and more comprehensive understanding of his or her *self*.

This *self* is the center or totality of one's personality—or as Jung says, "the regulating center of the psyche and facilitator of individuation. Specifically, the Self is the gateway to 'Who we are.' It is the ordering, structure loving principle within the psyche." It gives meaning and purpose to our lives and enables us to sort out the gold within our shadows by enabling the person to reconnect with his or her ego and become thereby whole in terms of right action and conviction and becoming authentic, knowing who we are, becoming who we are, and finally coming to terms with the God within. In a word, we become individuated, which Jung defines as "becoming a single, homogeneous being" (i.e., who we are in our uniqueness and as fully actualized).

The Collective Unconscious

Before we leave this section, we must remember that what we are is also influenced by what Jung called the *collective unconscious*, that psychic substrata of the unconscious, universal themes, memories, myths, instinctual patterns, structures, and experiences of the human race. Although it is also a storehouse of "latent predispositions to apprehend the world in particular ways," it is the deepest and most inaccessible layer of the psyche.

It consists for the most part of an unlimited number of *archetypes*—stories, myths, themes, visual symbols, or primal energies that exist in our psyches and form the unconscious. An archetype is an inherited predisposition to respond to or perceive certain aspects of the world. Some are readily understood while others bring subliminal messages that are there to help trigger one's memory of why one is here and the truth behind the illusion of reality. Archetypes can often convey messages that verbal and written information cannot.

Who Am I?

Who are you? As implied previously, one way to find out is to explore Jung's concept of the self.[5]

> As an empirical concept, the Self designates the whole range of psychic phenomena in humans. It expresses the unity of the personality as a whole … It encompasses both the experience-able and the inexperience-able (or the not-yet experienced). Insofar as psychic totality, consisting of both conscious and unconscious contents, is a postulate, it is a transcendental concept, for it presupposes the existence

of unconscious factors on empirical grounds, and thus characterizes an entity that can be described only in part, but for the other part, remains at present unknowable and illimitable.

It is here where we learn the answer to the question "Who am I."

"Know thyself." These words were chiseled above the entrance to the temple of Apollo at Delphi, the site in ancient Greece of the sacred oracle. It was customary for people to visit the oracle to ascertain their destinies or what specific courses of action they should take in given situations. However, in our case in this instance the very suggestion, "Know thyself," is what we seek. It is sufficient unto itself. Put another way, what it advises is that we know who we are. This is the most fundamental question of our lives. Its answer is our personal truth. Upon it the answer to the other three questions depends. It goes well beyond our personal beliefs, spiritual or otherwise. It is a question that is deeply rooted in our being. It points to what Jung calls the self, the core of our being.

Self, in this context, means the God within us. The self contains one's totality of personality. This totality includes the shadow and gives meaning and purpose to life and a connection to something larger than our egos. According to Jung the purpose of becoming an individual or individuation is reconciliation with the self, when the person hears its voice and obeys it in terms of right action and conviction, even when it appears to go counter to collective codes of behavior or urgings of the ego. Only when this reconciliation is realized does one become authentic.

Scripture tells us the same thing. You are more than a body. You are also spirit, a soul. Looking at your time line, you see that you are also your past. This includes your experiences from birth to the present, the impressions others have left on you and you have left on them, and your relationships and seminal moments. It also consists of the present, meaning your thoughts and feeling of the moment. Finally your time line points toward your future, namely your dreams, plans, and wishes. The bottom line, however, is that to come to terms with this takes a long and at times difficult and winding path. The reality is that no one can give you the answer, not even religion. Only one thing is certain. You are unique. There is no one else quite like you. You are on a journey to becoming that does not end with your physical death. Who you will be tomorrow is a mystery. All you can really do is connect with an inner truth that tells you who you are.

Listen to your heart. Observe your feelings, thoughts, reflections, reactions, and actions. DeMello[6] tells us to "wake up!" Connect with the love within. Embrace the many roles you are called to assume, but not too tightly.

So who am I? I am a biological creature that also happens to possess a psyche that consists of my body, my personal conscious, and a personal unconscious. I also am affected by what Jung calls the collective unconscious.

But still I am more. I am also in relation with others of my own kind and with a higher power. I am a child of God. How do I know this? Perhaps the story of Moses and the burning bush might have within it a hint. We read that while he was tending his father-in-law's flock, there appeared to him a burning bush from which the voice of God called out his name. Moses answered, "Here I am." The voice instructed him to remove his sandals, "for the place on which you stand is holy ground." Then the voice identified himself as "the God of your father, the God of Abraham, the God of Isaac, and the God of Jacob." God went on to say that he was concerned about the plight of his people, the Israelites, and had heard their cry. He continued, "Come therefore, I will send you to Pharaoh, and you shall free My people, the Israelites, from Egypt." Moses asked two questions. The first was, "Who am I that I should go to Pharaoh and free the Israelites from Egypt?" God responded that He would be with Moses.

Moses asked a second question, "What is Your name? When I come to the Israelites and say to them, 'The God of your fathers has sent me to you,' and they ask me, 'What is his name?' what shall I say to them?" God's response was "Ehyeh-Asher-Ehyeh," which is often translated from the Hebrew to mean "I Am that I Am," "I Am who I Am," or "I Will Be What I Will Be." Talmud scholars posit that this last translation is probably the best. In effect, what God is saying is that his nature will become evident from his actions.

This last sentence points us to our possible answer to this question, "Who am I?" Only the one who asks of us the question gets to hear the answer. Who we are will be evident—at least to God—from our actions. It is in living the life of the Spirit that the question is answered. It is more than a question of self-discovery. It is a question that refers to our inner being. It is a question that can be accessed only through an examination of our past and our present experiences and relationships with our neighbors and our God. It calls for what Jung would call doing our shadow work and coming to grips with our complexes.

By shadow work I mean facing the repressed or denied part of ourselves. These include the hurts, fears, anger, and what we have done in our past and are ashamed of. They are the parts of our personalities that our parents, teachers, society, church, or other external entities have told us are unacceptable or inappropriate. Statements like "Little boys don't cry" or "little girls don't play with trucks" may feed these shadows. Maybe we were ridiculed because of our color, our race, or our behavior that failed to comport to someone else's ideas of what was proper. Excessive and self-centered grief over the death of a loved one often turns into anger and bitterness against a God who would let such a thing happen. And so we suppress these things that society and significant others have denigrated and the hurts and moments of grief we have suffered. But nonetheless, they color our very demeanor as we find ways to compensate for them (i.e., creating bogus pasts and adopting equally false personas or turning our backs on our faith and once deeply held convictions and finding novel religious practices or belief systems that cover a perceived void yet fuel additional woes).

As we learned to repress these unacceptable qualities about ourselves, we threw them into sacks that we have been carrying around our whole lives. In shadow work we take steps to look at those parts of ourselves that we have stuffed into these sacks. These may be positive or negative. Whatever they are, they are parts of ourselves that have split off from our true personalities. The reality is that not acknowledging them keeps us from being who we really are or want to be. But we must be careful in examining its contents. Though there are several parts of ourselves that are pure gold, there are also parts of ourselves that are what religion calls sins or moral defects that require metanoia or a turning to God for repentance and forgiveness.

This is easier said than done. The question is this: How do we go about recognizing or examining our shadows? One way is to notice what we dislike in another person of our same gender. What is it about that person that annoys you and makes your blood boil? There is a significant possibility that what you see in that person is a projection of you. That person is a mirror that reflects your traits, your faults, and your shadows. Conversely notice what you really like or admire in another person of your same gender. What is it about that person that you like? Why do you look up to him or her? The chances are you are projecting onto that person qualities that you possess either because of many of the reasons cited in the preceding paragraph or because of a sense of false modesty you have disavowed. Jung called these our "golden" shadows.

Another way to identify our shadows is to notice what and when we disregard our consciences, when we commit sin, no matter how trivial. We know we should not be spending time with unsavory persons who facilitate the occasions of sins we know are wrong and dangerous. Such examples include excessive drinking or carousing or taking what does not belong to us. It also includes spending more time with these persons than we spend with our spouses and children or pursuing questionable relationships with someone other than our spouses. If these behaviors become regular, it is a sign the shadow is running the show.

There are many ways to deal with our shadows. But they all begin with recognizing our shadows for what they are, part of who we are. We can seek professional help from therapists, or we can work with spiritual directors who have facilities for dream work. In either case a safe container is built wherein you are helped to process your shadow. Outside pressures are set aside so you can see clearly in a safe environment. For example, in a dream group you notice how everyone agrees to withhold judgment, to look at their own prejudices and faults, and to refrain from giving advice. Every participant learns to appreciate the many paths to wholeness, release, and peace.

When it is all said and done, shadow work is only one path to learning who we are. It can be learned by understanding our complexes and our personality patterns. As regards the latter, Jung has provided the rudiments of what has become known as the Keirsey or Myers-Briggs test, which determines whether we are extrovert or introvert, intuitive or sensing, thinking or feeling, perceiving or judging types. Another is the Enneagram. Together they give us a helpful profile of our talents and other God-given talents that make us the unique people we are. Of course, neither of these instruments replace the simple reality of prayerfully listening to the voice of the God within.

Who we are can also be learned through the impressions we have left with others and they have left on us, our dreams, and our deep desires. It really is a quest to find our truth, to be who we are. It takes a lifetime. No one can give you the answer because you are unique, one of a kind. You must find it yourself. Your journey to knowing who you are is ongoing. You are not today the person you will be tomorrow. And when you reach that tomorrow, you will still not be the person you will be another tomorrow. You might have a guide, but the reality is that all he or she can do is accompany you on your journey to your inner truth and prayerfully channel the Holy Spirit. Moreover, the journey does not end on this plane of existence. It will take you into your next stage or state of being. So in addition to knowing your Myers-Brig and/or Enneagram, listen to your head or heart or gut. Know your feelings, thoughts, reactions, and actions. Be aware. Be conscious.

But there is more. Not only are our shadows part of who we are, so too are our complexes. In Jung's system, complexes like the shadows are located in our personal unconscious. They are emotion-laden themes from our past lives. For example, if one of your parents during your childhood was overbearing or cruel or extremely needy, more concerned about his or her sense of well-being than yours, this reality would influence your life in profound ways. Even as an adult, you will experience deep and troubling feelings or emotions at the memory of how you were treated. You will find it difficult to be around your parents should they still be alive. Hence, a complex in Jungian terms is a grouping or systems of related individual and unique thoughts and emotions tied together by a psychologically powerful event or life experience. A complex often manifests itself in dreams or fantasies or as a provocation bought about by an unusual reaction to an event or experience or as a reaction to what Jung calls archetypes, deep-seated, inherited, and primitive psychic patterns and images derived from the collective unconscious that enter the personal unconscious as preexistent forms through the complex, shadow, and anima/animus.

There is still more. Who am I in terms of my relationship to God? Christianity tells me I am a creature made in God's image yet a sinner who is prone to missing the mark because of my fallen human nature. Still I am a child of God. My task is to square the previously outlined with this assertion.

Tony DeMello,[7] ever the master storyteller, tells a story of a dying woman who is in a coma. She suddenly has a feeling that she is taken up to heaven and stands before the judgment seat.

"Who are you?" a voice says to her.

"I'm the wife of the mayor," she replies.

"I did not ask whose wife you are but who you are."

"I'm the mother of four children."

"I did not ask whose mother you are but who you are."

"I'm a schoolteacher."

"I did not ask what your profession is but who you are."

And so it goes. No matter what she replies, she cannot seem to give a satisfactory answer to the question, "Who are you?"

"I'm a Christian."

"I did not ask what your religion is but who you are."

"I'm the one who went to church every day and always helped the poor and needy."

"I did not ask what you did but who you are."

She evidently failed the examination, for she was sent back to earth. When she recovered from her illness, she was determined to find out who she was. And that made all the difference.

Why Am I?

Why am I here? This is another fundamental question. Why am I here on earth? Where did I come from? What am I worth? Do I have any intrinsic value? Do I serve a purpose? What is my calling? These are all fundamental questions. They are life's *big questions*. How you answer these questions determines how you see the world and how you treat the world. Because you are a part of the world, how you see the world also determines how you see and treat yourself. So it's important that we resolve these fundamental questions. And it's important that we discover the honest truth. Wrong answers to important questions aren't helpful.

In large measure the answer to this question depends on how we answered the previous question, "Who am I?" In this question we live our day-to-day lives, struggling between good and evil, love, joy, and misery, happiness and suffering, fulfillment and discontent. Who I say I am points to why I am where I am. It presupposes certain assumptions, including the certainty that God not only exists but he is a loving, caring God who loves me with an abiding love. This certitude is fundamental. This assumption assures me that as a creature of God I have a purpose, a destiny. My life is meaningful. I am bound by several immutable laws among which are the Ten Commandments, which were given on Mount Horeb by God to Moses and summed up in the Great Commandment or the Hebrew Shema.

And so what is my answer to this all-important question, "Why am I?" The German philosopher Nietzsche is reputed to have said, "He who has the *why* to live can bear almost any *how*." This quote gives rise to several ancillary questions. Am I oriented toward my future, my goals, my hopes, my destiny, and my purpose? As a Christian, I know that I was created through the agency of my parents in God's image to know and love him and to husband and preserve all creation in his name and in thanksgiving for his goodness. I was also created to serve his purposes and to join him in glory, where "in the mystery of the incarnate Word" my mystery as a human person is illuminated in true light and where I reproduce the image of Jesus the Christ, the Son of God, who is the perfect "image of the invisible God."[8]

The way for me to learn how God wills that I serve his purposes is to take appropriate steps to discover my talents, natural skills, passions, and gifts. I am also called upon to live a moral life, choosing to do what is right and just and to avoid that which is wrong and evil. I am accountable for my moral decisions. I exist to give glory to God and am responsible for being all that I can be, given my God-given talents and abilities and the opportunities or inclinations he has granted me. Finally *why* also speaks to trust and hope—trust that God loves me and as St. Paul says, "he will never send me more than he and I cannot deal with," as well as hope that no matter the circumstances, God's plans for me are for good. I trust and hope in him, but I realize that I must do my part. Thus begins my Lenten work. Now that I know the *why*, the *how* follows.

Endnotes

[1]   Curry, Jennifer R. and Stephanie Dailey, *Exploring Spirituality Across the Lifespan with Timelines: Developmental Milestones, Defining Moments, Changing Beliefs and Practices Argosy University* http://www.aservic.org/wp-content/uploads/2011/12/Module-9 (Accessed 2012)

[2]   King, Jr., Martin Luther, "What is Man?" in *The Measure of a Man* (Philadelphia: Fortress Press, 1959).

[3]   For further explanations of each component of the psyche, see Samuels Andrew, Bani Shorter and Fred Plaut's *A Critical Dictionary of Jungian Analysis* (New York: Routledge & Kegan Paul, 1986).

[4]   Jung, C. G. *A Review of the Complex Theory: The Structure and Dynamics of the Psyche* (Princeton, NJ: Princeton University Press, 1960), 92–104.

[5]   Jung, C. G., *Psychological Types* in Bollingen Series, (Princeton, NJ: Princeton University Press, 1971), 460.

[6]   DeMello, Anthony, *Awareness: The Perils and Opportunities of Reality* (New York: Image Book, a division of Doubleday, 1990), 5.

[7]   DeMello, Anthony, *Taking Flight: A Book of Story Meditations* (New York: Image Book, a division of Doubleday, 1988), 140.

[8]   US Conference of Catholic Bishops, *Compendium of the Catechism of the Catholic Church*, Chapter 1, Paragraph 67 (Washington, DC: USCCB Publishing, 2006), 24.

CHAPTER 10

THE FIRST THREE STEPS
TO SPIRITUAL WHOLENESS
BEGINNING THE PURGATIVE WAY

Examine me, O God, and know my mind; probe me and
know my thoughts.
See if I have vexatious ways and guide me in ways everlasting.
—Psalm 139:23–24

Happy is he whose transgression is forgiven, whose sin is
covered over.
Happy, the man who the Lord does not hold guilty, and in
whose spirit there is no deceit.
As long as I said nothing my limbs wasted away from my
anguished roaring all day long.
For night and day your hand lay heavy on me
My vigor waned as in the summer drought.
Then I acknowledged y sin to You, I did not cover up my guilt;
I resolved, "I will confess my transgressions to the Lord,"
And you forgive the guilt of my sin.
—Psalm 32

This chapter sets the stage for the real work, the nuts and bolts of a
meaningful Lent. I warn you that from this point onward the going
is going to get tough. This chapter and particularly those that follow
it are not for the faint of heart or those for whom Lent is simply another period
in the church's liturgical year. Here I introduce a process based in large part
on the time-proven twelve-step program of Alcoholic Anonymous (AA).[1] This
is strong but effective medicine for those of us who realize we are sinners and
that we are held captive by our individual sins and those of the society in
which we live. Here I speak of the desert.

The two major themes of the Lenten season are penance and spiritual renewal. As we prepare to renew our baptismal promises at Easter, it is appropriate that we take stock of those parts of our lives of which we are less than proud. What behaviors do we need to acknowledge as misdeeds or areas of our lives where we missed the mark? The wisdom of the twelve-step program forces us to look at our personal demons and addictive behavior and to take steps to acquire with God's help spiritual sobriety and in many cases a whole new way of living. This program is not some magic formula. It does not promise an instant cure. It demands commitment, prayer, and much courage. If you are willing to travel the narrow way of the twelve steps with God at your side, you will experience reconciliation, renewal, and the joys and peace of resurrection. So let us begin. But first a few words about the history of the twelve-step program are in order.

It all started June 10, 1935, when two improbable and incorrigible alcoholics named William Griffith Wilson (Bill W.) and Dr. Robert Holbrook Smith (Dr. Bob) founded a program we now know as AA. Actually the idea for the program was conceived by Bill W. while he was in a hospital during the preceding December because of his excessive drinking. While he was in the hospital, he ostensibly had a spiritual experience that removed his desire to drink. From December through June while he developed the rudiments of his program, he tried to persuade other alcoholics he knew to stop drinking but to no avail—that is, until he met Dr. Bob, his first convert. Within four years Wilson and Smith published a book titled *Alcoholics Anonymous*[2] (1939), which presented a twelve-step spirituality-based program of recovery from alcohol.

Several sources influenced the development of this program. Wilson and Smith write that while they were trying to attract followers to their program, they attended several meetings in New York of the British-based Oxford Group movement, where they met Sam Shoemaker, from whom they "absorbed most of the Twelve Steps of Alcoholics Anonymous, steps that express the heart of A.A.'s way of life." Wilson later recalled, "The early A.A. got its ideas of self-examination, acknowledgment of character defects, restitution for harm done, and working with others straight from the Oxford Group and directly from Sam Shoemaker, their former leader in America, and from nowhere else."

Based on what they learned from Shoemaker, Wilson and Smith launched Alcoholic Anonymous, a weekly gathering of alcoholics who subscribed to a set of six steps. These included:

1. an admission of powerlessness over alcohol;
2. an inventory and acknowledgment of one's moral defects or sins;

3. the confession to another person (in confidence) of one's shortcomings;
4. the making of restitutions to all those harmed by one's drinking;
5. taking every opportunity to help other alcoholics, with no thought of reward or prestige; and
6. praying to God or to whatever higher power one subscribes for the power to practice these precepts.

Over time Wilson revised and expanded these six steps until they took their present form, which includes:

1. admitting our powerlessness with respect to sin;
2. trusting in a higher power;
3. centering in God;
4. knowing ourselves;
5. admitting our wrongs;
6. eliminating character defects;
7. letting go, letting God;
8. making peace in relationships;
9. making amends and forgiveness;
10. living one day at a time;
11. meeting God through prayer; and
12. walking the walk.

Lodged within these twelve steps is a veritable plan for spiritual wholeness. Herein is an outline for our Lenten journey to spiritual sobriety. For many of us—this includes the author of this book—there is much ground to cover. But we are not alone. Our partner on this journey is none other than Jesus himself. We have but to call and lean on him and listen to him with our hearts. Let us start today to begin the process of saving our lives.

Steps 1 through 6 are particularly relevant to the first purpose of Lent, namely penance, while the remaining steps are pertinent to developing a spiritual life. The first six steps are comparable in several ways to the traditional approach to spiritual development known as the purgative way; however, steps 7 through 10 are similar to the illuminative way and steps 11 and 12 are helpful with respect to the unitive way, where we seek union with God.

Let us attend to these twelve steps to spiritual wholeness by beginning to see who we really are and to acknowledge our inability to see, name, or own our sin. Here is where shadow work begins (i.e., looking inside ourselves to confront where we are poor, radically broken, and in need of healing). Wake up. See, hear, touch, feel, and be with our poverty of spirit and blindness.

Just as the alcoholic stands bowed in front of his fellow alcoholics, so too must we stand in front of our fellow brother and sister sinners and acknowledge that we are not in charge, our lives are powerless, and we are sinners. This is when I must stand before you and say, "Hello, I am Milton. I'm a sinner, and these are my sins." In effect, we do this each time we go to confession. At the beginning of the liturgy of the Mass we also publicly acknowledge our sins and the fact that we are sinners. We do this when we stand before our brothers and sisters in our respective congregations when we acknowledge that we have sinned, at times grievously against God and our neighbors. This is no time to stand in denial and to keep trying to control my feelings or anyone else's. Only when I take responsibility for my sins, stop playing games, and be honest about my reality will I begin my journey. Only when I stop lying and weaving illusions and stewing in meaningless guilt fostered by others, even my church, will I be able to build my truth. Only when I get tired of being tired and sick of being sick because of my lies and wrongdoings will I be able to break out of my chains of debilitation. Only when I surrender will I begin my journey to live in God's Spirit.

The Purgative Way

I am taking a certain liberty with Tanquerey's description[3] of the purgative way as "the spirituality of beginners." He writes that these beginners are those individuals who are generally free of serious sin. I am not necessarily including in this account those of us who are guilty of what the church calls mortal (grave) but rather those of us who are guilty of venial (less serious) sin. I contend that most of us are *beginners* in the spiritual life.

The first three steps of this journey set the stage. Here is where we actually admit that we are powerless in the face of sin, that our lives have become unmanageable and without meaning. The harder we try to dig ourselves out of our hole, the deeper in misery we find ourselves. We have hit rock bottom and have no place to go to assuage our misery. During Lent we are thrown a lifeline. But there is a catch. Do we believe that God can make us whole if we turn our will and our lives over to Him? If our answer is yes, then "let go and let God" work in our hearts to transform us.

Step 1: We Admit Our Powerlessness with Respect to Sin.

We have seen that evil and sin are very real. This is true on both the individual and the collective level. Carl Jung speaks of the reality of evil and sin when he writes about the shadow. For individuals it is the ego that controls and keeps this shadow in check. Most people try to wear an innocent face, a persona for the benefit of others. They dare not display in public the dark or sinful side of their individual conscious personality.

Shadow work—which has been mentioned in an earlier chapter—is essential in this context. The shadow is the part of the self that is unacceptable—at least that is what we were taught by society, family, significant others, and a whole host of other people and organizations. Here we are taught right and wrong and either/or, and it is here where we develop our complexes when we know in the deepest recesses of our being that we are being denied or denying parts of ourselves that make up our reality and our ingenuity. Here in our hearts we know we are being phony, hypocrites, and everything else we hate in other people. But our reaction is to deny this. Instead as John Welch[4] points out, "Those things which we cannot abide in ourselves we project upon others. If I do not admit my shadow side, I will unconsciously find another who will carry my shadow for me. Once this projection is made, then I need not be upset with myself. My problems are now outside and I can fight them "out there" rather than within the real arena, myself."

Jung[5] adds, "We still attribute to the other fellow all the evil and inferior qualities that we do not like to recognize in ourselves, and therefore have to criticize and attack him"

On the other hand, society as a collective also has its dark and sinful side or shadow, which it tries to keep in check by suppressing unacceptable behaviors. It is instructive to spend some time acknowledging this reality, considering that it impinges upon our individual behavior and attitudes and is also the result of multiple individual projections, our own included.

Every time we open a newspaper or watch the evening news, we see the effects of this shadow projection. We see it in literature. We see it in such classic tales of Grendl and Beowulf, Shakespeare's *Macbeth* and *Hamlet*, Mephistopheles and Faust, Darth Vader and Luke Skywalker, and Captain Ahab and the white whale. We see it on YouTube, Facebook, Twitter, etc. We see it on our city streets, the homeless sleeping in doorways, young girls standing under streetlights and waiting for the next John, and X-rated neon-lit shops. We hear its plaintiff cry in neighborhoods, cities, and suburbs where women are abused, children are hungry, and men are without jobs or dignity. We see it in the local bank and other financial institutions where money is being embezzled. We see it in corrupt, power-hungry politicians and courts where a parody of justice is meted out. We really see it in the eyes of those who people our jails and prisons. We see it in a government that makes a virtue of secrecy and shadowy operations that function with minimum to no accountability through faceless bureaucrats. And we see it in an invading army in a foreign land, the sale of arms to mad, power-hungry leaders, the pollution of rivers and streams and oceans with oil spills and other deadly chemicals. We see it in the poisoning of our food with invisible pesticides and the activities of global giants like Monsanto and their genetically modified seeds.

While most of us enjoy some of the blessings of the good life, many of our brothers and sisters live lives of unbearable hardship. We have a tendency to want to put them out of sight. In time they become the object of negative group projections and the collective shadow takes the form of scapegoating, racism, or enemy-making. Where there is racism (the belief in the inherent superiority of one race over all others and thereby the right to dominance), the collective shadow is at play. Where there is sexism (the belief in the inherent superiority of one sex over the other and thereby the right to dominance), the collective shadow is at play. And so it is with ageism, homophobia, elitism, and classism—the collective is also at play in these. It also shows itself

- in an uncontrolled power drive for knowledge and domination of nature (expressed in the amorality of the sciences and the unregulated marriage of business and technology);
- in a fast-paced, dehumanized workplace (expressed by the apathy of an alienated workforce and the hubris of success);
- in the maximization of business growth and progress;
- in a materialistic hedonism (expressed in conspicuous consumption, exploitative advertising, waste, and rampant pollution);
- in a desire to control our innately uncontrollable intimate lives (expressed in personal exploitation, manipulation of others, and abuse of women and children); and
- in our ever-present fear of death (expressed in an obsession with health and fitness, diet, drugs, and longevity at any price).

The collective shadow is present throughout the width and breath of our society. We see it at every level of politics throughout history. In the United States the shadow has been alive and well during the war between free and slave-holding states, during the Civil Rights Movement, and the times whenever there has been major social, economic, and political transitions. In the last century and in the early days of this century, we have seen the evils of nationalism, Nazism, communism, fascism, totalitarianism, wars to further economic exploitation, the morbid and sick anti-Muslim tirades we hear on our airways, the increasing insidiousness of new levels of criminal activity, the encroachment of powerful and rich interests into the political process, the growth of extreme idealism and hypocrisy, the rise of a plutocracy at the expense of a rapidly contracting middle class, and the growing of a large number of people living under the poverty level. The list goes on.

Whenever one group, one society, or one nation is convinced of its own moral goodness and righteousness, the shadow is lurking. This shadow is more than happy to oblige by assigning blame and responsibility to the other person or group—in other words, anything to keep it from attaching to oneself or one's group. So when media or cable news offers up scandals to excite, surprise, and titillate, the reason the public is so gripped and so held under its spell is that this person or group has become the carrier of the population's own darkness. It seems that indeed "the world has become a stage for the collective shadow."

What is happening is that we tend to project onto *the other* our inadequacies or issues rather than recognize or deal with it in ourselves. In other words, we project our own worst nightmares that we have dutifully repressed under lock and key. The more tightly the shadow material is repressed, the darker and more dangerous it becomes. The cycle then continues, and this shadow material gets projected onto another group or individual. New scapegoats are born; new enemies constructed. And it is always without fail projected onto someone or something else. One cannot avoid this or do away with it through willpower. It always comes back to bite.

This is how entire populations of people are made into enemies. This is also what props up racial, religious, and ethnic suspicion and hatred. Whenever one feels oneself or one's group is superior to another, one is engaged in shadow projection. This *other* becomes the *scapegoat* to carry away the sins of the father. The so-called sins are never carried away. They just go underground where they breed more hatred and shadow material. It sets up a vicious cycle.

Like a society, each community also has its built-in taboos, its forbidden arenas. The shadow exists beyond the personal level. Communities also have shadows. Families and towns have collective shadows. This is a shadow that is shared by everyone. This type of shadow is particularly potent because many different people feed it. The community shadow contains all that is rejected by the community's conscious awareness, those feelings and actions that are seen as too threatening to its self-image. In an upright, Christian, conservative community this may mean getting drunk or marrying someone of another faith or choosing a gay relationship. In a liberal, atheistic community it may mean thinking that everything is relative and one person's perspective is as good as another's as long as neither tries to impose his or her thinking on another. In our society wife battering and child abuse used to be hidden away in the family shadow. Today they have emerged in epidemic proportions into the light of day. The shadow being projected is always in glaring contrast to the community's presumed ideals. This holds true for individuals and families as well as communities. Whenever one group, one community, one society, or one nation is convinced of its own moral goodness and righteousness, the shadow is lurking. This shadow is more than happy to oblige by assigning blame and responsibility to the *other* person or group.

Is it any wonder why sin is so overpowering? Notwithstanding our desire to keep our individual and collective dark sides in check, we know that there are times when sin overpowers our best efforts. *The AA Big Book* opines that somehow our "so-called willpower becomes non-existent. We are unable, at certain times, to bring to our consciousness with sufficient force the memory of the suffering and humiliation of even a week or a month ago." We continue to fall into our sinful ways. We are pressured not only by our individual wrongful desires but also by a collectivity that glorifies sin and adds its own pressures. Although there is much we can do with respect to our collective shadows and it is good to know them for what they are, our immediate emphasis is on the individual plane. Step 1 is crucial. It is the first step to freedom. Admitting the truth of my sinfulness and my incapacity to deal with it is substance of this first step. It is essential to becoming once again a whole person—the person that God initially created.

The worse sin is for us to try to be who we are not, to assume personas that conflict with who God created us to be. During Lent your task (and my task) is to take a good long look at these phony persons we have become and acknowledge the *bricks* with which we have constructed our false selves. We need to see ourselves as God really sees us, warts and all. This also means we need to recognize those malignant forces and powers within us that bespeak the work of Satan as he tempts us to do what we know we should not do. By the same token we need to listen to those admonitions that urge us to avoid evil and to do good. In short, Lent is the time look at and acknowledge our shortcomings, radically turn our lives around, and respond to God's desire to be true to ourselves, to be real, and to be who he created, no more, no less.

But reality tells us that not until we hit rock bottom and admit complete defeat in the face of our sins are we really prepared to undergo the rigors of the desert by going into that long and heavy bag of sins (or shadow material) we carry behind us. We should feel the pain and stress our sins cause us personally and within our families and with others in our immediate social, business, or professional circles. Examples of this pain and stress are addictive behaviors like alcoholism, which can cause unhappiness within our families, divorce, unemployment, bankruptcy, the loss of our homes, debilitating or terminal illnesses, and even death. Other examples include a sense that we are not in control of our own lives, feelings of dismay and anger, and the realization that our lies are coming back to haunt us. Still other examples of the ravages of sin include our secret shames—those things we would secretly love to do but for the fear of embarrassment or how it would impact our personas. These secret shames include illicit desires, compulsive behaviors, or addictions.

We cannot but notice the existence of these shadow projections when we find ourselves saying things we wish we had not uttered, such as cruel or sadistic statements or jokes at another's expense or off-color remarks. As we grow into middle age, we experience what has been called the dark night of the soul, which gives rise to multiple questions such as the following: To what am I summoned? Or what is it I regret having done or not done with my life? Finally we notice these hurtful moments whenever we reach for something to assuage our pain, such as work, food, sex, alcohol, or dependent relationships as salves. We see these patterns of powerlessness, shame, guilt, and low self-esteem when we are alone, in traffic, or during sleepless nights. We know that only God can help us. The shadow can sabotage the better angels of one's nature. But the good news is that once we recognize these patterns for what they are and admit our powerlessness and inability to manage our lives, we have taken the first step to meeting and dealing with our shadows, recovering, and growing spiritually.

Step 2: I Have Come to Believe that a Power Greater than Me Can Restore Me to Sanity.

The second step tells us that there is "a power greater than ourselves that can restore us to sanity." We do not have to allow the insanity of others to drive us insane.

In his very infinite, wonderful mind God designed this thing called man. Not only did he design it, but he also created and formed it from dust. Then he literally gave it breath – he breathed on man - saying to him very clearly and very powerfully that life comes from God. He created a person, a very unique person, one of a kind, YOU. And he looked upon you and loved you and all men and women with an abiding love.

He intended that life be immortal. In theological parlance we know that when God created man and woman, he endowed them not only with those natural gifts required by their nature but also with what are called preternatural gifts, which made them exempt from bodily, mental, and spiritual infirmities. That is to say that he made man and woman immortal, free from death, pain and suffering, from strong intense sexual desires, and ignorance. They were made sinless. They were crowned lord and lady of the earth. God also conferred on man and woman other gifts in the realm of the supernatural, wherein they became his adopted sons and daughters and heirs and a partakers of his divine nature. This is life as God intended. He intended it to be purposeful and fulfilling. These are whom he walked with "at the breezy time of the day." (Genesis 3:8)

Tragically what unfolded in the Garden of Eden is a tale of man and woman throwing away what God had given. He had told them not to eat of the Tree of the Knowledge of Good and Evil. He warned them of the consequences—sin and death. But they ignore God's warning, disobeying his commands. Listen again to the punishment they bring on themselves. "He drove the man [and woman]out, and stationed east of the garden of Eden the cherubim and the fiery every-turning sword, to guard the way to the tree of life" (Genesis 3: 24).

God steps in and drives Adam and Eve from the garden and brings upon them a judgment of death. Man and woman forfeited much by this act of disobedience. I think it is interesting to note in this context that not only does sin separate us from God but it separates us from life as God intended it to be—that is, life with God in the Garden of Eden. Apart from God there is no meaning in life.

Do we try to find meaning? Do we continue to strive to understand life? Does man still try to find and create a meaning for life? Yes, absolutely! But what most people call life is a poor substitute. Like Paul each of us "know of nothing good living in me—in my natural self, that is—for though the will to do what is good is in me, the power to do it is not" (Romans 7:18).

But all is not lost. There is a Power that can restore our sanity. That Power is God. He sent us his only Son and his Holy Spirit to that end. But first let's look at the insanity that has become the bane of our existence. Then we will look at what we can do to begin the process of becoming whole once again.

Pride, the Root of our Insanity

When we reference *insanity* in this step, we are in reality speaking of pride. *Webster* defines pride as "inordinate self-esteem, conceit, proud and disdainful behavior or treatment of others." It is frequently manifested by ostentatious displays of one's possessions or talents. In the context of this chapter pride is the desire to be all-powerful gods knowing good and evil and being sufficient unto ourselves (i.e., being our own law, our own strength, and our own virtue). The prideful person denies a need for God, thinking he can go it alone in all things and finding in himself the beginning and end of all his or her actions. This was the sin of Lucifer and of Adam in the garden. It is the excessive desire or love of one's self and excellence. The prideful person loves himself or herself more than God. This is the insanity at the root of one's failure or inability to deal with one's addictions or spirituality.

Pride is mortally sinful when we deliberately seek our own good apart from God—that is, when we positively exclude him or when we regard the goods we have as being strictly the result of our own merits. The culmination of pride is contempt of and for God or of his representatives. Left unchecked, pride is the cause of most every sin. It is the most difficult of sins to see in ourselves.

When we are self-righteous, we are being proud. When we combine our self-righteousness with unnatural piety, we are being proud. Generally we are blind to our own condition, but ready to pass judgment on everyone else. Our very abhorrence of sin is traced less to a love of God than love of our own moral uprightness. Our horror at the sins of others is really a pharisaical pleasure at the thought that we are not as these adulterers and thieves.

Pride is an insidious vice. It insinuates itself even into our best actions, if we do not take proper precautions. There is nothing we cannot be proud of, not even of our progress in humility. In everything we do, pride is liable to appear. Pride brought down Lucifer. It caused the sin of Adam. In Dante's *Divina Comedia* the deepest region of the inferno or hell is reserved for the proud. Pride was the sin of Adam, who desired to be as a god knowing good and evil. Nivard Kinsella[6] notes,

> Pride was the sin of Adam, pride is a repetition of that scene in the garden. We would be as gods—we would be sufficient unto ourselves, we would be our own law, our own strength, our own virtue, we would do without God. Perhaps it may not appear quite as openly as that but what else is it at root? Pride is the excessive desire of our own excellence ... We tend to misunderstand that freedom which is God's greatest gift to us, and to regard it as complete autonomy. As though we were completely sufficient unto ourselves, and could find in ourselves the beginning and end of all our actions. What else in fact are we doing when we refer any good to ourselves, or when we ignore God and commit sin?

Pride's sister, vanity, differs from pride in that it seeks to be known to others. Its sinfulness lies in wanting to be either praised for something we do not possess or for something that is not praiseworthy or praised by persons whose praise is not worth having. Now don't get me wrong. It is not sinful to want to be praised or to be glad when one is praised, provided the reason for the praise is adequate and the pleasure we take in it is proportionate and detached. In fact, psychologists tell us that praise is appropriate in motivating others. But vanity is extremely dangerous. It can lead to boasting, being a show-off, misdirected ambition, disobedience to legitimate authority, resentment, hypocrisy, belligerency, and many other evils. It can even enter the heart of a professed Christian so that the person becomes vain because of his or her spirituality. In sum, pride and vanity lead to insanity.

Humility - the Antidote to Pride

The truth is that our every act is colored either by pride or humility. Both pride and humility have many possible ramification and many facets. Humility's practice may lead a man to deprecate praise, to evade the limelight, to be tolerant and kind toward another, to speak of his or her unworthiness, and/or to smile at a rebuff or a slight or even at what appears to be a disaster. Yet humility is in and of itself none of these things. It is something very simple. It is a realization of our creature-ness—a true knowledge of ourselves in relation to God. We are his creatures. We were created in his image through the agency of our fathers and mothers.

It should also be noted that excessive humility is not a virtue. When one is overly obsequious or given to unwarranted servility or the undue influence of another person, these propensities might serve to excite pride in others and may become an occasion for their sins of tyranny, arbitrariness, arrogance, or other vices and evil acts. What is humility in the context of this Step?

Humility is the foundation virtue of the spiritual person. If you seek God, you must first learn to be humble. As James writes, "God opposes the proud, but he accords his favor to the humble" (James 4:6). It is a virtue that is necessary for salvation. "Shoulder my yoke and learn from me, for I am gentle and humble in heart" (Matthew 11:29). Humility is generally distasteful to modern men and women. It is strong meat. In this day of freedom and independence, doing your own thing, being your own person, self-discovery, and development, humility is not a sought-after personal quality.

Initiative, drive, and aggressiveness are the qualities this generation most admires. This is good. Far too many think that humility is opposed to all these qualities. They think it is opposed to all legitimate self-expression and initiative. Nothing could be further from the truth. Humility assumes maturity and integration of personality, free will, well-balanced common sense, perspective and proportion, and a true mastery of judgment and intellect. It is a virtue of the strong, not the servile. It is only for the well-balanced mature man or woman and not for the spiritually weak.

Humility is not only difficult to grasp intellectually but also a difficult virtue to acquire. Those who have it are usually unaware that they have it. The very realization that you are lacking it is a sign that you possess it in some small degree. You may have it and have few of its outward signs.

On the other hand you may appear humble without really being so. It is easily confused with weakness, timidity, or a particular kind of temperament. If we ourselves happen to possess it, we may have fears about it because of disturbing affinities we imagine it to have with inferiority complexes and self-depreciation.

So What Is Humility?

Humility is the opposite of pride. It is a disposition of our will that enables us to see ourselves as we really are in relationship to God and our neighbor. In relationship to God it is a realization of our creature-ness. It is an attitude and act of a creature in the presence of its maker. We see ourselves as totally dependent on his power and his love for our very existence. We live continually in the palm of his hand. Without him we could not be. It is his breath that keeps us alive.

We recognize that he is the source of our natural gifts and graces. The very word is derived from the Latin *humilitas*, whose root is *humus* or the ground or dirt beneath us from which we were created and unto which we shall return. As a virtue, humility is a quality by which people keep themselves within their own bounds, not reaching out to things above, beneath, or beyond those boundaries within which God has placed them. In relationship to our neighbor humility is a recognition and acknowledgment of the good in him or her. In relation to nature and the environment we see ourselves as fellow creatures and custodians rather than exploiters of the planet. We acknowledge that when we abrogate or abuse these relationships, we are sinners.

St. Benedict,[7] the founder of Western monasticism, speaks to the virtue of humility in chapter 7 of his *Rule*. Although written primarily for monks, much of Benedict's observations are salient, timely, and appropriate in the context of our Lenten reflections. To that end we benefit mightily from taking note of what he has to say. He begins by directing our attention to Luke 14:11 and 18:14. "Whoever exalts himself shall be humbled, and whoever humbles himself shall be exalted." Benedict illustrates this point with an image of a ladder. The sides of the ladder are our bodies and souls "into which our divine vocation has fitted the various steps of humility." As we exalt ourselves or revel in the praise others heap upon us, we descend this ladder. As we humble ourselves, we ascend the ladder.

> If we want to reach the highest summit of humility, if we desire to attain speedily that exaltation in heaven to which we climb by the humility of this present life, then by our ascending actions we must set up that ladder on which Jacob in a dream saw angels descending and ascending (Gen 28:12). Without doubt, this descent and ascent can signify only that we descend by exaltation and ascend by humility.

Now the ladder erected is our life on earth, and if we humble our hearts the Lord will raise it to heaven. We may call our body and soul the sides of this ladder, into which our divine vocation has fitted the various steps of humility and discipline as we ascend.

Benedict then describes each rung of the ladder to humility. He writes that the first step is to keep the "fear of God always before [our] eyes" (Psalm 35:2) and to never forget it, constantly remembering God's commandments, guarding ourself against "sin and the vices of thought and tongue, of hand or foot, of self-will or bodily desire."[8] Benedict cautions his monks to remember that God knows every thought and desire and what is on our hearts and minds.

I believe Benedict is here speaking of God's awesomeness; he is not suggesting that we dread God. It is that reverence and sense of awe we have for someone who is far beyond our understanding but whom we know sees us and loves us as our Father. It is an all-pervading attitude, a habitual disposition of mind and will that looks upon God as infinitely adorable and in doing so loses sight of everything else. When I do something wrong or commit a sin, I hasten to seek his forgiveness so that I can be made whole in my relationship with him. I love him, but I fear him. There is a healthy tension when the child is in awe of his father's strength, his authority, and his ability to punish my wrongdoing. Notwithstanding, I still love him, and I revere him. But I am not afraid of him. He is my Father. I am his son.

The second rung of the ladder of humility teaches us "that a man loves not his own will nor takes pleasure in the satisfaction of his desires." Instead he must comport with Jesus' saying, "I have come not to do my will, but the will of him who sent me" (John 6:38). Simply stated, it is imperative that we set aside our will and seek in all things God's will.

I have acknowledged that God is my Father, the one who created me through the agency of an earthly father and mother and who has infused in me a soul that gives life to my body, making me thereby a living being. My heart lies at the core or ground of this soul. It is through this heart that I connect with my heavenly father and you, my brothers and sisters. Through this heart I listen and learn of God's will. Through a life balanced by prayer, work, and study together with what the rule calls conversion of life, commitment, community, and solitude, I position myself to accept and commit myself to God's will without illusion. Through this life I develop the strength of character to respond willingly to his will "to turn away from my desires." I know that in reality my desires will lead me astray and lead me to do what is wrong in the eyes of God and often in the eyes of my fellow beings. I am mindful of Benedict's admonition, "We must then be on guard against any base desire, because death is stationed at the gateway of pleasure."[9]

The third, fourth, and fifth rungs though of particular significant to the a monk, have relevance to most superior-subordinate relationships when Benedict speaks of patient submission to one's superior for the love of God even under difficult, unfavorable, and unjust conditions. The fifth rung has resonance with AA's admonition to humbly confess all sinful thoughts and deeds committed in secret.

Obedience, the point of the third rung, does not come easy to a child of the twenty-first century. This is a hard one. Notwithstanding, here is where I learn of God's will. I must now be obedient to that will no matter where it leads me. As a layperson or a member of the clergy or religious order, I would do well to place myself in the school of St. Benedict. God's will is to be found in the here and now. God is present to me in each dimension of my life. This is my reality. He has given me the talents and resources to carry out the responsibilities as parent, wife or husband, member of a faith community, and tradesperson or professional. All he needs from me is a response. Oh, that I really listened to him.

Neither is perseverance and patience easy. The only way I can possess either attribute is to be ever-present to God's will. By keeping my eye always on God I am enabled to fight the good fight and keep on trucking. Perseverance is particularly difficult today given life's many distractions. Temptations are everywhere. God help me to persevere, to hold on, to have courage and to be patient despite life's many trials and difficulties.

The fifth rung is a challenge. Here God is asking me to become vulnerable to others. If I am to grow, I must confess my sins not only to God but also to you, my brothers and sisters. Benedict calls for me not only to condemn my own sins but to forgive those of my brothers and sisters.

The message of the sixth rung of the ladder to humility is that the monk ought not to think too highly of himself and be content "with the lowest and most menial treatment" and to regard "himself as a poor and worthless workman in whatever task he is given." The seventh rung advises the monk to welcome humiliation and low status as a blessing "so that I can learn your commandments" (Psalm 118:71).

Humility demands that we aspire to the last place. This is not an attractive doctrine. It is extremely hard. It is also very powerful (if followed). If not understood properly, its practice leads to failure and discouragement. Always to take the last place, to prefer others to one's self—this is not easy; it demands a higher measure of maturity. With this step I am encouraged to strip myself of all pretensions. It is important that I learn to be content to be in the last place. In Benedict's school there is no room for ambition and competitiveness. Esther de Waal[10] says, "Lack of contentment means that I am reliant on externals, of whatever sort, for satisfaction … lets me become trapped in the coils of the competitive society, competing for material goods, social status, the sort of car I drive, the place in which I live. I must not forget that these steps are steps into freedom, and their purpose is to help me to disentangle myself from all that would prevent inner freedom."

Welcoming humiliation is also a hard one to stomach. This step has nothing to do with self-worth. It is all about accepting my wounded-ness and weakness. I have insecurities, doubts, and at times emptiness. I am vulnerable, so I put on a facade to hide my true self. "But," de Waal goes on to add, "if I accept myself as ordinary, weak, frail, in other words, totally human and totally dependent upon God, than I am stripped of any sense of being in some way set apart, different, superior. It is than that my true self may begin to emerge." I become open to learn, to hear God speak to me, to receive his Word, and to act upon it.

The eighth rung of the ladder cautions the monk to do only "what is endorsed by the common rule of the monastery and the example set by his superiors." The ninth, tenth, and eleventh rungs warn the monk to control his tongue, remain silent, not to speak unless asked a question. When responding to this question the monk is advised to speak with modesty, brevity, and seriously without excessive laughter. Finally the twelfth step of humility teaches the monk that he is to "always manifest humility in his bearing no less than in his heart so that it is evident at the Work of God, in the oratory, the monastery or the garden, on a journey, or in the field, or anywhere else." de Waal tells us that Benedict is telling us to "stay in line, keep a low profile, [don't] draw attention to myself." Be willing to be guided by others. Do not become a law unto yourself.

With respect to controlling my tongue, James 3:5–10 says it best,

> So the tongue is only a tiny part of the body, but its boasts are great. Think how small a flame can set fire to a huge forest; the tongue is a flame too. Among all the parts of the body, the tongue is a whole wicked world; it infects the

whole body; catching fire itself from hell, it sets fire to the whole wheel of creation. Wild animals and birds, reptiles and fish of every kind can all be tamed and have been tamed, by humans; but nobody can tame the tongue – it is a pest that will not keep still, full of deadly poison. We use it to bless the Lord and Father, but we also use it to curse people who are made in God's image: the blessings and curse come out of the same mouth. My brothers, this must be wrong.

Not being mirthful, speaking gently, modestly, briefly, and reasonably, and being humble in your bearing no less than in your heart—all three of these last steps are about silence, stillness, and gentleness. Silence is perhaps the most difficult in today's world. If I talk too much, I cannot hear. If I laugh too much, I may miss what is really important or fail to take what I hear seriously. Speech can lead to openness, to learning, and to growth, or it can become a trap into which I plunge. Endless talk can become an excuse for putting off action and achieving nothing. We must learn to be gentle and to respect others. We must be willing to listen rather than dominate and receive rather than control.

Benedict concludes by promising,

After ascending all these rungs of ladder to humility, the monk will quickly arrive at that perfect love of God which casts out fear. Through this love, all that he once performed with dread, he will now begin to observe without effort, as though naturally, from habit, no longer out of fear of hell, but out of love for Christ, good habit and delight in virtue. All this the Lord will by the Holy Spirit graciously manifest in his workman now cleansed of vices and sins.[11]

Hopefully this portion of Benedict's *Rule* has resonance with you. It has stood the test of time, having been written in the early sixth century. It continues to be observed, and it is the primary resource for the governance and spiritual growth in monasteries throughout Christendom. Of course it goes without saying that the *Rule* is meaningless if its adherents do not believe that there is a power greater than them. If we who labor in God's vineyard are able to ascend each of these rungs, we will have begun to acquire the humility that aims for the perfect love of God, which in turn casts out all fear of hell. Our Lenten journey will have reaped for us a certain reward.

Here is a prayer that has resonance with this chapter. It is the Prayer of Abandonment written by the French hermit Charles de Foucauld.[12]

> Father, I abandon myself into your hands;
> do with me what you will.
> Whatever you may do, I thank you;
> I am ready for all I accept all.
>
> Let only your will be done in me,
> and in all your creatures.
> I wish no more than this, O Lord.
>
> Into your hands I commend my soul;
> I offer it to you with all the love of my heart,
> for I love you, Lord,
> and so need to give myself,
> to surrender myself into your hands,
> without reserve,
> and with boundless confidence,
> for you are my Father. Amen.

Endnotes

1   Cary, Sylvia, *The Alcoholic Man* (Los Angeles: RGA Publishing Group, 1990), 4.

2   Wilson, William Griffith, and Robert Holbrook Smith, *Alcoholic Anonymous*, revised as *The Story of How Many Thousands of Men and Women Have Recovered from Alcoholism*, fourth edition (New York: Alcoholic Anonymous World Services, Inc., 2014).

3   Tanquerey, The Spiritual Life, 305.

4   Welch, John, *Spiritual Pilgrims: Carl Jung and Teresa of Avila* (New York: Paulist Press, 1982), 121.

5   Jung, C. G., Civilization in Transition, (*Collected Works of C. G. Jung*) Translators: Gerhard Adler and R. F.C. Hull. (Princeton, NJ: Princeton University Press; 2nd edition 1970), 130

6   Kinsella, Nivard, *Unprofitable Servants: Conferences on Humility* (Chicago: Franciscan Herald Press, 1960).

7   St. Benedict, *The Rule of Benedict in English* (Collegeville, MN: The Liturgical Press, 1981), 32.

8   Ibid

9   Ibid, 34

10 de Waal, Esther, *A Life-Giving Way: A Commentary on the Rule of St. Benedict* (Collegeville, MI: The Liturgical Press, 1995), 64–66.

11 St. Benedict, The Rule of Benedict, 38

12 Foucauld, Charles, Cry the Gospel With Your Life, (10190 Mesnil Saint-Loup, France: Edition Le Livre Ouvert, 1944) 69.

CHAPTER 11

THE SECOND WEEK: "THIS IS MY SON, THE CHOSEN ONE. LISTEN TO HIM."

The Lord, therefore,
displays his glory before chosen witnesses
and so splendidly invest that bodily shape
which he shares with others
that his face becomes as radiant as the sun
and his garments as bright as snow.
By transfiguring himself in this way
his foremost object was undoubtedly
to remove the scandal of the cross
from the hearts of his disciples and
to prevent their faith from being disturbed
over the humiliation of his voluntary passion
by revealing the excellence of his hidden dignity.
—Leo the Great (circa AD 400–461)

On the second Sunday of Lent we celebrate the feast of the transfiguration of Jesus. *The American Heritage Dictionary* defines the word *transfiguration* as a "radical transformation of figure or appearance; a metamorphosis; the sudden emanation of radiance." The Greek word is *metamorpho*, which means to transform literally or figuratively to metamorphose or to change. It is a verb that means to change into another form, to change the outside to match the inside. The prefix *meta-* means to change, and the *morphe* means form. Applied to today's readings, transfiguration means that the interior reality of Jesus is manifested with his exterior reality. Hitherto his divinity had been "veiled" (Hebrews 10:20) by his human form. The transfiguration that occurred on Mount Sinai was a glimpse of his glory. Hence, the overarching theme of today's reading is transformation. Before we discuss the gospel, let us turn to today's other readings, which begin with Genesis 15:1, "… the word of the Lord came to Abram in a vision. He said, 'Fear not Abram, I am a shield to you; your reward shall be very great.'"

At the center of this first reading is a mystery whereby God promises that Abram's successors would be as numerous as the stars in the sky. As proof he offers a covenant, saying to Abram, "Look toward heaven and count the stars, if you are able to count them." And he adds, "So shall your offspring be" (Genesis 15:5). We are not told Abram's complete response, but rather his skepticism as to whether or not this was really going to happen. "… how shall I know I am to possess it?" (Genesis 15:8) he asks. Earlier he had been complaining to the Lord God about having no heir. But after setting an offering according to the Lord God's instructions and falling into a deep sleep, God spoke to Abram in a dream of things that would come to past unto "the fourth generation," (Genesis 15:16) at which time Abram's descendants would inherit a vast land. This is the second covenant between Abram and the Lord God. Abram immediately ends his complaints and places his trust in the Lord God. Surely he must have experienced a tremendous sense of awe, a new dimension of mutuality and reality in his relationship with God. He must also have felt some measure of curiosity, even skepticism. Still he profoundly *trusts* God and his promise. Like the Jew of today, Abram focused more on action than on belief.

In the second reading, Paul, writing from prison, offers the hope that Christ will change the "lowly bodies" of the Philippians "to conform with his glorified body." He prays that they will imitate him and keep the faith, conforming in all things to Jesus Christ and his teachings. Paul certainly recognized that this would meet with considerable difficulty and sacrifice. Of course his prayer is as relevant today for each of us as it was for the early Christian. Just as then, Christians are continually confronted with difficult choices, some of which cannot be evaded. Our journey of transformation, which began with our baptisms, is an ongoing journey. However, we are still living in the "form of a servant" (Philippians 2:7) just as Jesus assumed when he lived among us. Notwithstanding, we look forward to the time when we can confess with Paul, "It is no longer I, but Christ living in me" (Galatians 2:20).

The gospel reading recounts the transfiguration. Jesus and three of his disciples went up on Mount Sinai to pray. While he was in prayer, "the aspect of his face was changed and his clothing became sparkling white. And suddenly there were Moses and Elijah appearing in glory, and they were speaking of his passing which he was to accomplish in Jerusalem" (Luke 9:29–31). Jesus is conversing with Moses, the lawgiver, and Elijah, the prophet, about his exodus, a reference to the Israelite's exodus from Egypt. Through Moses, Jesus is connected to the very origins of Judaism, establishing thereby continuity between the ancient laws and his teachings. Through Elijah, Jesus is connected to the role of the prophet in calling society and its leaders back to the spiritual teaching of ancient Israel.

The exodus of which the three were discussing refers to Jesus' passion and resurrection. Here on the mountain Jesus learns the full extent of the suffering he is about to undergo. From the clouds a voice is heard acclaiming, "This is my Son, the Chosen One. Listen to him" (Luke 9:35). This is the second time God is said to have spoken of Jesus as his Son. The first time was to Jesus himself at the onset of his public ministry. At that time the onlookers only heard thunder. This time God spoke to the disciples. When the cloud disperses, only Jesus remains.

While all of this was going on, Luke tells us that the three disciples were at first overcome by sleep, but upon awakening, they saw Jesus in his glory, Moses, and Elijah. It is safe to say that neither Peter, James, nor John understood what was happening at that time. Many years later Peter reminisces,

> When we told you about the power and the coming of our Lord Jesus Christ, we were not slavishly repeating cleverly invented myths; no, we had seen his majesty with our own eyes. He was honored and glorified by God the Father, when a voice came to him from the transcendent Glory, this is my son, the Beloved; he enjoys my favor. We ourselves heard this voice from heaven, when we were with him on the holy mountain. (2 Peter 1:16–18)

What was the meaning of the transfiguration? In that it was not preceded by any announcement or fanfare, one possible conjecture is that Jesus intended to reveal to his inner circle of disciples his glory as the second person of the Trinity. Another was to underscore the reality that the Law and prophecies of the Old Testament had been fulfilled. The law and the prophets had converged in the person of Jesus. Henceforth, men must listen to Jesus as he speaks of his suffering and death, the way to glory and salvation.

It probably took Peter and his colleagues a long time to fathom its meaning, namely that Jesus, the Son of Man, is God and the Redeemer.

CHAPTER 12

THE PURGATIVE WAY CONTINUED: LANCING THE BOIL

There will be more rejoicing in heaven
over one sinner repenting
than over ninety-nine upright people
who have no need of repentance.

—Luke 15:7

"Deep within his conscience man discovers a law which he has not laid upon himself but which he must obey. Its voice, ever calling him to love and to do what is good and to avoid evil, sounds in his heart at the right moment ... For man has in his heart a law inscribed by God ... His conscience is man's most secret core and his sanctuary. There he is alone with God whose voice echoes in his depths."

—Catechism of the Catholic Church[1]

Conscience

Unfortunately we don't hear much about the conscience today. There are many who don't really understand what it is, or they appeal to the conscience when they are trying to justify some kind of immoral act. They usually say something like, "I'm just acting in accord with my conscience. My minister may teach this and that; however, my conscience tells me something else, and I must be faithful to my conscience." This is simply perverse. They are twisting a truth to serve their particular purpose.

Note that in writing about conscience, I am not writing about an emotional sensation that emanates from a particular ethical or moral situation. In the words of the moralist, conscience does not create its values, but rather it apprehends the truth of the moral order and applies these

163

moral norms to concrete situations. The catechism of the Catholic Church[2] describes conscience as a judgment of reason wherein the human person recognizes the moral quality of a concrete act that he is contemplating, in the process of performing, or has already completed. This is a good definition insofar as it is succinct. The catechism draws out several other dimensions to conscience:

- all are bound to seek, embrace, and live the truth faithfully;
- conscience is experienced as an inner sanctuary or tribunal rather than something external, yet it mediates a universal and objective moral law that is given rather than invented;
- conscience summons us to seek good and avoid evil by loving God and neighbor as well as keeping the commandments and all universal norms of morality;
- conscience is common to all human beings, not just Christians, and it is the very dignity of man, a dignity the gospel protects;
- we will be judged according to how we formed and followed our consciences;
- the moral law and the particular judgments of conscience bind the human person;
- agents may experience anxiety, contradictions, and imbalances in conscience;
- conscience may err out of "invincible ignorance" or by being blamefully corrupted;
- claims of personal freedom or of obedience to civil laws or superiors do not excuse a failure to abide by the universal principles of good conscience;
- conscience must be properly formed and educated by ensuring it is "dutifully conformed to the divine law and submissive toward the Church's teaching office, which authentically interprets that law in the light of the Gospel"; and
- freedom of conscience, especially in religious matters, must be respected by civil authorities and people, not coerced into any religious practice.

Finally, there is implanted in our very nature an intellectual predilection or rule of ethical truth or standard of right and wrong conduct. This law stems from the practical experience of living. This comports with Thomas

Aquinas's observation that conscience is the act of applying our knowledge of good and evil to what we do (or might do). It is reason's awareness of a choice or action's harmony or disharmony with the kind of behavior that leads to genuine well-being and flourishing. It governs our actions, thoughts, desires, words, acts, and conduct. Therefore, it follows that one has a duty or an obligation to take steps to properly inform one's conscience by study and reflection.

An informed conscience leads to good judgment with respect to doing and being good and avoiding evil. It is fostered or rightly formed through a growth in maturity and knowledge of moral principles, prudent judgments regarding truth, and the capacity to apply these principles and judgments in specific circumstances. It is also informed by knowledge of the Word of God as revealed in Scripture, the teachings of one's faith tradition, continued study, prayerful reflection, prudence, and a deep spirituality, all of which enhances one's ability to discern reality as it is and to be open to what is true within the moral order. At times, particularly in highly complex situations, it may be wise to seek advice from a trusted source such as a spiritual advisor.

John Henry Cardinal Newman[3] wrote of conscience as the main guide of the soul, a guide to non-Christian and Christian alike, illiterate and learned philosopher, child and adult.

> Each has within his [or her] breast a certain commanding dictate, not a mere sentiment, not a mere opinion, or impression or view of things, but a law, an authoritative voice, bidding him do certain things and avoid others. I do not say that particular injunctions are always clear or that they are always consistent with each other, but what I am insisting on here is this, that it commands, that it praises, it blames, it promises, it threatens, it implies a future and it witnesses to the unseen. It is more than a man's own self. The man himself has not power over it, or only with extreme difficulty; he did not make it, he cannot destroy it. He may silence it in particular cases or directions, he may distort its enunciation, but he cannot, or it is quite the exception if he can, emancipate himself from it. He can disobey it, he can refuse to use it, but it remains.

Having considered the important topic of conscience, let us now consider the next four steps to spiritual wholeness. To repeat they are as follows:

Step 4: I will make a searching and fearless moral inventory of myself.

Step 5: I admit to God, to myself, and to my confessor the exact nature of my wrongs.

Step 6: I am entirely ready to have God remove all my defects of character.

Step 7: I humbly ask him to remove my shortcomings.

For the benefit of my readers who may be unfamiliar with the particular principles of the Catholic faith as they relate to this section, I will discuss each of these steps within the context of an examination of conscience and the reception of the sacrament of penance, which consists of three parts, specifically contrition, confession, and satisfaction. Step 4 relates to the examination of conscience, while steps 5 through 7 relate to contrition (sorrow for our sins), confession (where a person acknowledges his or her imperfections and sins and with a contrite spirit asks God for forgiveness and the grace to amend his or her life), and satisfaction (where one seeks to actually make amends to either God or those whom he or she has sinned against).

Examination of Conscience

It presupposes that we know when we have sinned and the magnitude of our sins. Are they venial (indiscretions) or mortal (grave)? Are they sins of commission or of omission? Were they committed intentionally or inadvertently? How do we begin an examination of our consciences to determine if we have sinned and the extent of our sins' gravity?

For starters, if we look at the Ten Commandments, we note that the first three are about our relationship with God. Have we in any way sinned against this relationship? The other seven are about our relationships with our neighbors and with ourselves. Have we in any way sinned against these relationships? Have we sinned against our brothers and sisters, the community, or ourselves?

The Hebrew Bible and the New Testament summarize these commandments.

> Hear, O Israel! The Lord is our God, the Lord alone! You shall love the Lord, your God, with all your heart, and with all your soul, and with all your might. Take to heart these

words with which I charge you this day. Impress them upon
your children. Recite them when you stay at home and when
you are away, whether you lie down and when you get up.
Bind them as a sign on your hand and let them serve as a
symbol on your forehead. Inscribe them on the doorposts of
your houses and on your gates. (Deuteronomy 6:4–9)

In the New Testament we also read, "You must love the Lord your God
with all your heart, with all your soul, and with all your mind. This is the
greatest and the first commandment. The second resembles it: You must love
your neighbor as yourself. On these two commandments hang the whole Law,
and the Prophets too" (Matthew 22:37–40).

Penance begins with a searching—at times painful and discomforting—
look at ourselves to see where we have sinned or missed the mark and to
determine the direction of our lives with respect to our relationship with
these commandments, with our God, and with our brothers and sisters.
This calls for recognizing our own baseness (i.e., making a searching and
fearless moral inventory). This does not mean simply listing a number of
individual wrongs but rather analyzing our moral defects, how we manifest
them in our day-to-day lives, and how they affect our behavior. It also means
acknowledging before God not only the fact that our characters are tainted
by these defects but that we are determined to expose them and to eliminate
them, root and branch. The defects include those mentioned in earlier
chapters and others such as: egotism, dishonesty, phoniness, insincerity, and
intolerance.

What is called for here is not a litany of individual wrongs but an analysis
of our defects and how they are manifested in our day-to-day lives. This
calls for considerable humility and self-honesty. We begin by examining our
relationship or connection with God and our neighbor. How conscious are
we of our sins and their verbal expressions, our inner fragmentation, and our
unwillingness to accept who and what we are? What about our moral values—
honesty, truthfulness, integrity, gratefulness, humility, trust, forgiveness, and
love of God, ourselves, and our neighbors? How has our behavior comported
with these values? Where have we fallen short? To what extent have our
choices led us away from God? In which of our values have we ceased to
believe? Why? How aware are we of the distance between us and God? Are
we awake, or are we asleep? Most of us are somewhere in between, not totally
asleep but not really awake. People avoid waking up. I am convinced this is so

because they are afraid to experience the pain they carry within. Little pain is felt during sleep, while living with our eyes open is often painful.

This reminds me of a passage from De Mello's book *Awakening* in which he speaks of spirituality as waking up.[4]

> Spirituality means waking up. Most people, even though they don't know it, are asleep. They're born asleep, they live asleep, they marry in their sleep, they breed children in their sleep, they die in their sleep without ever waking up. They never understand the loveliness and the beauty of this thing that we call human existence. You know, all mystics— Catholic, Christian, non-Christian, no matter what their theology, no matter what their religion—are unanimous on one thing: that all is well, all is well. Though everything is a mess, all is well. Strange paradox, to be sure. But, tragically, most people never get to see that all is well because they are asleep. They are having a nightmare.

De Mello goes on to tell a story about this gentleman who knocks on his son's door. He calls for him to wake up. The son demurs, "I don't want to get up, Papa." He gives three reasons. He says that school is dull, the kids tease him, and he hates school. The father rejoins with three reasons why he needs to go to school. "First, because it is your duty. Second because you are forty-five years old, and third because you are the headmaster."

Most people use staying in bed as a cure-all for irresponsibility. Waking up is so unpleasant. It is easier to stay in a place that you perceive to be safe and comfortable than to extend yourself to take responsibility for being who God wants you to be. And so it is with the realities surrounding the examination of conscience. Wake up! I don't promise you it will be easy or without pain. But I assure you the pain will lead to the healing of your brokenness. With the knowledge learned through this initial step, you are ready for the next step, confessing your sins.

Confession

In my parish community early in Lent we generally have a penitential service. I remember a time when I told my wife that this was to take place in a few days. She indicated that she had already gone to confession a few weeks ago. Moreover, she felt she had no need to go. My response was, "Remember the days when we went to confession every week?"

"I needed to go back then," she replied.

"What's different now?" I asked.

"Dealing with you and the children and the house. I'm okay," she said.

"So now you're perfect?"

"That's right!"

After a few moments of silence she asked, "What time did you say the penitential service was?"

Acknowledging those times when our love for God took a backseat to our desires, when we were less than compassionate toward our brothers and sisters, and when we were not true to our real selves is essential to the Lenten journey. What better place to acknowledge our faults and indiscretions along with our distress, anxiety, and even loneliness than in the privacy of the confessional? The net result of this act is spiritual regeneration and the certitude that God has not only forgiven us but also has embraced us with his compassion and great love for us. It is unfortunate that confession has fallen into disuse, and with it, there has been a decrease in a sense of sin. Indeed, many of us have little understanding of the sacrament of penance apart from confession.

Although the format differs, in the Roman Catholic, Anglican/ Episcopalian, Lutheran, and orthodox communions, confession generally takes place before an ordained priest who represents Christ and who may offer some spiritual advice, administer absolution or forgiveness in the name the Father, Son, and Holy Spirit, and impose a particular penance (satisfaction) that consists of prayers, scriptural readings, reconciliation with anyone against whom the penitent has sinned, charitable acts, etc. The goal of the sacrament is reconciliation with God.

Though the format of the confessional differs in other churches, these basic principles and goals are similar. One significant difference is that in Eastern Catholic churches and the Eastern orthodox church the role of the priest is witness, friend, encourager or facilitator, and advisor, underscoring the fact that the penitent is confessing to Christ, not a mere man. Confession here is almost therapeutic in that the penance imposed is the direct opposite of the sin confessed. For instance, if the sin confessed is stealing, the penance prescribed is to return the item stolen and give alms to the poor on a regular basis. The intention is to heal and purify, never to punish. Sin is viewed as a spiritual illness that only Christ can heal.

This idea of confession and penance has its roots in Scripture. When they came out of Egypt, the Israelites became weary of traveling throughout Edom and tired of the manna God had been providing them as food. They complained, and God was provoked, sending among them venomous snakes. Many people were bitten and died. Once they acknowledged that they had sinned by "speaking against the Lord," they begged Moses to intercede on their behalf with God. God instructs Moses to fashion and place on a standard or pole a bronze serpent figure to symbolize the sins of the Hebrews so that they will acknowledge God as the instrument of their salvation. God instructs Moses that if those who were bitten by a snake would look at the bronze serpent, they would live.

In other words, penance takes root only when we individually and collectively as a community admit to our false selves what wrongs we have done to ourselves and to our neighbors and how we hope to be in relation to God and our neighbor. We confess our sins honestly and openly before God and one another and manifest sincere sorrow and promise to abide by God's commandment of love. Although much is made of being holy and pure, I am of the belief that a deep reading of God's commandments really bids us to be loving and to look at our sins as affronts to the love of God and compassion to our neighbors.

With this step you admit to God, to yourself, and (dependent upon your faith tradition) your confessor, priest, minister, or spiritual director the results of your examination and how your behaviors have been hurtful to yourselves and others. During this confession and with the help of your confessor, you should become aware of the power of sin and to what extent it has become rooted in us and how it separates us from God, from other people, and from our own deepest, truest nature. What is most important here is where we give a name to each of our sins, and if possible, we can identify its roots (what caused this behavior). We recognize that we need to be healed, and we pray that like in the parable of the prodigal son, our father will accept us unconditionally as we are, even in our messiness, selfishness, imperfection, and brokenness. Hopefully the confessor before whom we have bared our souls will listen, accept, and be nonjudgmental. But the important thing is that we have not been talking to him or her but to God. The person before us or with us is simply a vessel through which the Holy Spirit enters our souls and stirs therein a new sense of freedom. The important thing to remember here is that confession manifests our desire to respond to the reality that there is a decided relationship between God and us. But we are not the ones who take the initiative. It is God.

I once heard our Pastor, in one of his Lenten homilies say, "Lent is the season for coming out of the shadows, putting an end to projecting our darkness, and coming clean." Jesus' statement is more direct when he says, "Unless you repent, you will all perish" (Luke 13:3). In a word, a good confession leads to freedom, to putting down the burden of sin and guilt, to opening ourselves once more to the free flowing of God's grace and love. But there is more.

Satisfaction/Making Amends

This is a step that is generally subsumed in the three Our Fathers and Hail Marys, which a priest confessor all-too-frequently tells you to do as penance. But this does not really satisfy the spirit of what one has just gone through in terms of guilt and shame. Something more is called for. To be truly free, amends or reconciliation with those you have harmed must be made if at all possible. You ought to seek their forgiveness, even if you are only able to journal about the harm you perpetrated, how you now feel about your behavior, how the other felt and suffered because of it, and how it affected your relationship. At the appropriate time, if it presents itself, do what you will with this information. Take responsibility for the wrong you have done. Be honest and acknowledge the wrong that might have also been done to you and how you have suffered. Make a promise to yourself to make amends and move toward reconciliation.

And so it is. What better way to enter the Easter season than as one who "has clean hands and a pure heart, [and] who has not taken a false oath by My life or sword deceitfully" (Psalm 24:6).

Our Social Housekeeping

In the final analysis, confession of our sins and bad behaviors is good for the soul. It might even be good for the psyche in that its benefit is positively correlated with the attitude and honesty we bring to it.

Confession might also be good for the collective where the presence of sin is either denied or celebrated in the popular media as the way to go. I have in mind here acknowledging our role in supporting or participating in corporate or political lies, environmental pollution, tax evasion, bribery, failure to pay living wages, and also our tendency to put short-term goals that benefit the few ahead of long-term goals that could benefit the many. Finally confession is good for the collective when we acknowledge our role in promoting or furthering such societal projections as scapegoating, prejudice, racism, bigotry, intolerance, xenophobia, fear, and hatred of the *other*.

Steps 8 and 9 relate to the institutional, systemic, or structural dimensions of our collective sinful life. One says, "I will make a list of all persons I have harmed, and I am willing to make amends to them all." The other says, "I will make direct amends to such people wherever possible except when to do so would injure them or others."

Here I am speaking of the actual sins of the collective, those social, economic, or political sins to which we subconsciously subscribe, in which we participate, and perhaps from which we benefit. To bring these sins home to us we have but to open the local newspaper, listen to the national news media, or drive through certain neighborhoods to see the wide disparity of incomes, where the poor live, go to school, or attend church or where the well-off shop, where there are gated communities in which they live, country clubs and other exclusive places where they socialize away from the riffraff, and the elite well-staffed and equipped schools that their children attend. How do I contribute to or benefit from this state of affairs?

One sees these sins in the ethos of power and so-called right-wing conservative Republican or leftist-leaning liberal Democrat positions when it comes to social, economic, military, or national policies and laws that benefit or favor one group at the expense of another. We see them in the obscene disparities in income that favor 1 percent of Americans over the other 99 percent with the result of a hallowing out of a previously vibrant middle class. The primary sin in these instances is blindness followed by attitudes that promote material acquisition, moral relativism, and feel-good religion. Its principle characteristics are denial, a failure to take responsibility for this state of affairs, a house of cards built on lies and illusions, guilt, obsessions with material acquisitions, nicotine, food, liquor, sex, gambling, guns, etc. The list goes on, and few of us are not guilty. Again how do we contribute to or benefit from this state of affairs?

We are all "people of the lie," addictive and dysfunctional. This we must name our addictions, personal and collective. We must own them. We must put an end to our denial of our sinful reality, our lies, illusions, guilt, and failure to take responsibility. And once again ask ourselves how do we contribute to or benefit from this state of affairs?

Endnotes

1   Catechism of the Catholic Church, Part Three - Life in Christ, Section One - Man's Vocation Life in the Spirit, Chapter One - the Dignity of the Human Person, Article 6 - Moral Conscience, Paragraph 1776; (Libreria Editrice Vaticana, Vatican City, 1994) 438

2   Ibid, Article 6, Paragraphs 1776-1802; pg. 438-442

3   Newman, John Henry, *Sermons Preached on Various Occasions*, eight sermons preached before the Catholic University of Ireland in 1856, 1857, the first year of the opening of its church (New York: Longmans, Green and Co., 1908), 64.

4   Ibid, deMello, Awareness, 5.

CHAPTER 13

THE THIRD WEEK: A SINNER AND THE WATER THAT LEADS TO ETERNAL LIFE

When Jesus heard that the Pharisees had found out
that he was making and baptizing more disciples than John,
though it was his disciples who baptized, not Jesus himself,
he left Judea and went back to Galilee.
He had to pass through Samaria.

—John 4:1–3

Children of Darkness, Children of Light

On this, the third week of Lent, the church holds up for our consideration the story of a Samaritan woman's encounter with a Jewish rabbi. But before we discuss this encounter, it should be noted that this is one of several stories in which Jesus begins to reveal who he actually is.

These stories begin with the Pharisee Nicodemus' visit at night to Jesus in John 3:1–21, where we read of his acknowledgment of Jesus as a very special and unique person, indeed a rabbi who has "come from God as a teacher; for no one could perform the signs you do unless God were with him." Actually we know that Jesus is more than a teacher. He is the Son of God. Nicodemus is a spokesperson for those of us of little and inadequate faith. Jesus' reply is bewildering and perplexing. "In all truth I tell you, no one can see the kingdom of God without being born from above" (John 3:3).

Nicodemus is incredulous "How can anyone who is already old be born? Is it possible to go back into the womb again and be born?" Jesus replies,

> In all truth I tell you, no one can enter the kingdom of God
> without being born through water and the spirit; what is

born of human nature is human; what is born of the Spirit is spirit. Do not be surprised when I say: You must be born from above. The wind blows where it pleases; you can hear its sound, but you cannot tell where it comes from or where it is going. So it is with everyone who is born of the Spirit. (John 3:5–8)

Nicodemus is thinking of a natural birth from a Jewish mother that makes one a member of the chosen people. Jesus rejects this. With the statement that the only thing that flesh can beget or give birth to is flesh, Jesus radically replaces the meaning of chosen people to refer to the children of God as opposed to the children of natural parenthood. He is surprised that Nicodemus, a teacher of the people in his own right, cannot understand him. He bemoans the fact that there are those of the Jews who, despite Jesus's testimony of what he knows and has seen, still do not understand or believe. Nicodemus simply cannot understand or accept the fact that Jesus really knows of whence he speaks. However, we know that the need for begetting from above stems from his coming from above. It is with this night visit with Nicodemus that John begins to lay out the case for Jesus' divinity and his pending death. Jesus is here speaking of his mission and our charge to live by the truth, coming therefore into the light.

Jesus Talks with a Samaritan Woman

It might well have been true that Nicodemus probably knew of the pending plot to capture Jesus and ultimately to kill him. He also undoubtedly knew that the rationale behind such a plot was built on preserving the status quo at all costs because it benefited the Pharisees and the Sanhedrin and their privileged positions. But he could not understand that Jesus was more than a teacher. He was the Son of God.

It was because of these concerns that Jesus left Judea for Galilee. He and his disciples decided to go through Samaria. In actuality he could have gone another longer way by going east across the Jordan River, enter the region of Perea, go north, and once again cross the Jordan River into Galilee, thereby avoiding Samaria, which was the route preferred by pious Jews. Eventually they came to a town in Samaria called Sychar, a tiny village located between Mount Ebal and Mount Gerizim at the intersection of two trade routes

– one from Jerusalem and the other from the Jericho region close to the Mediterranean. It was here that the patriarch Jacob had dug a well bearing his name two thousand years before Jesus was born. The well was about one half of a mile from the village. It was fed by a spring flowing some 150 feet below the surface.

It was believed that this well was on a site bequeathed by Jacob to his son Joseph through his tribes Ephraim and Manassah. The Samaritans, like the Jews, considered Jacob their ancestor.

We don't know the actual season of the year, but we can surmise that it was a long journey. Jesus and his band of disciples were trying to get through Samaria as quickly as possible on their way to Capernaum in Galilee. They stopped at the well, and Jesus, tired from the journey, sat on the ground nearby while his disciples went into the town to buy provisions. It was about midday or the sixth hour. In that part of the world the temperature was probably quite high—perhaps more than a 100 degrees—and the sun was directly overhead.

She had come from the nearby town of Sychar about midday (the sixth hour) to draw water from the well. She was a Samaritan woman put forth by John as a spokesperson for a particular type of faith encounter with Jesus. This was a strange time to come out for water. Was there not a well in Sychar?

Jesus asks her, "Will you give me a drink?" The Samaritan woman, an angry woman perhaps smarting from her treatment at the hands of her fellow Samaritans, is taken aback. She says to him, "You are a Jew, and I am a Samaritan woman. How can you ask me for a drink?" Jews did not associate with Samaritans. Although she did not recognize him as a rabbi, she certainly did recognize him as a Jew. Such a request coming from a Jew was highly irregular. Jews and Samaritans rarely spoke with one another. Furthermore, it was unheard of that a Jewish man, especially a Jewish rabbi, should request water or speak familiarly with a Samaritan woman. She sees only a Jew.

Between her and this Jew stood several barriers—racial, religious, gender, and moral. The Jews spurned the Samaritans as religious and half-breed heretics. They also considered them immoral. Their attitudes toward women—Samaritan and Jew—was at best condescending. Indeed throughout the ancient world the behavior of women was extremely limited. For example, they were not allowed to leave the home of their father or husband without permission, to talk with strangers, or to appear in public venues. When they did leave their homes, they had to be doubly veiled. Religious leaders were forbidden to either directly look at or engage a woman in conversation in public. Moreover, the rabbis taught that it was a sin to touch, drink, or eat from a utensil that a Samaritan had touched. Among other things they taught that Samaritans and their eating and drinking utensils were unclean.

In point of fact, there was much more to the story. After the death of Solomon circa 930 BC, Israel was divided into a northern kingdom of Samaria and a southern kingdom of Judea. Enmity and constant warfare prevailed until 720 BC, when Assyria invaded the northern kingdom, transported most of its citizenry to Medea, the Assyrian capital, and transplanted into Samaria captives from Babylon and other conquered countries. The result of this transfer was widespread intermarriage between Samaritan Jews and non-Jews. Racial purity was lost.

In 587 BCE, Jews from Judea were also taken captive only this time by the Babylonians. They were transplanted to Babylon where they were in exile for almost fifty years. Notwithstanding, they managed to hold on to their traditions and maintain their racial purity. Consequently, to orthodox Jews Samaritans lost the right to call themselves Jews, because unlike them the Samaritans had succumbed to assimilation with non-Jewish peoples.

There is one other factor in this drama. When the Jews returned in 539 BCE to Jerusalem, one of the first things they did was set about rebuilding the temple. The Samaritan Jews offered to help, but they were spurned as impure. They had lost their Jewish heritage and had no right to share in rebuilding or worshipping in the temple. For more than four hundred years this slight simmered and festered into a hot anger well into the days of Jesus. In the meantime the Samaritans developed their own religion based partly on Judaism and partly on pagan ideas, built their own temple on Mt. Gerizim, and developed their own language and version of the Scripture based primarily on the Pentateuch (the first five books of the Hebrew Bible). To traveling Jews from Galilee who were passing through their country, Samaritan Jews would often *invite* them to worship with them on Mt. Gerizim.

Add to this perceived affront was her anger. Maybe the real reason she came all the way out to this particular well was to escape the scorn of the other women who looked upon her with loathing as if she was something less than a prostitute. Whatever her reason, it was unusual and rather dangerous for women to come out to the well at this time of day. Most other women generally came to the well in the morning or in the evening. For them it was a social event.

The woman was taken aback to put it mildly. She responds, "What? You are a Jew and you ask me a Samaritan for a drink?" But obviously this man before her did not feel constrained by the customary protocol between Jews and Samaritans.

All this was as naught to Jesus, who saw only a hurting soul and was determined to breach these barriers and assure her that she was loved by God. He speaks to a Samaritan and a woman at that. He speaks in a public place. And he indicates a willingness to drink from a Samaritan's cup. Step by step he reveals himself as the Messiah who Scripture—Samaritan and Jewish—has promised. And in the end she embraced and drew strength from the realization that she had found God in the person of his Son and was loved mightily in spite of her checkered past.

Instead he replies, "If you only knew what God is offering and who it is that is saying to you: Give me something to drink, you would have been the one to ask, and he would have given you living water" (John 4:10).

The woman, finding this statement at best perplexing, notes that Jesus had no bucket and that the well was deep. In fact, it was a hundred feet deep. She asks how he was going to get this water. She even asks him if he was greater than their ancestor Jacob. Jesus answers, "Whoever drinks this water will be thirsty again; but no one who drinks the water that I shall give will ever be thirsty again; the water that I shall give will become a spring of water within, welling up for eternal life" (John 4:13–14).

And she responds, "Sir, give me some of that water, so that I may never be thirsty or come here again to draw water" (John 4:15).

But she really did not grasp what Jesus was talking about. She thought he was referring to the actual water in the well. This well was a simple well within which ground water percolated and gathered unlike a spring-fed well into which water flowed from aquifers deep within the earth. Water from a spring-fed well was usually sweeter and more satisfying. She still does not understand, but she wants the water if it will enable her to stop coming to the well in the heat of the day. But she does see that Jesus is someone special, someone who possesses superhuman knowledge, perhaps a prophet.

Others hearing this could conceivably think that he was talking about the water of Judaism. Indeed he was, and he is life-giving water that replaces the waters of Judea, Samaria, and any other geographical location. These waters simply quenched for a time one's thirst, forestalling dehydration, providing sustenance to plant and animal life, cleansing one's body, clothing, and physical premises, and/or preparing food or other nonfood substances. These waters were also different from the Torah or other rabbinical or wisdom writings that could not satisfy the drinkers of wisdom who will thirst again and whose desire for wisdom will continue unabated to become even more insatiable. Indeed they will find that their desire can never be satisfied. The more they get, the more they will want

Only the water from Jesus will satisfy thirst forever. Jesus was referring to something else, specifically his teachings and his spirit. He was telling her that he is the living water. He is the water of life. And this water will forever satisfy thirst. He not only promises but delivers divine vitality, revelation, wisdom, and salvation, and whoever drinks it will have a fountain of eternal life spring up within him or her—the gift of eternal life.

Instead of following up on the woman's request, he tells her to go get her husband. She blurts out that she has no husband. Jesus responds that she has told the truth. She also suddenly catches a glimpse of herself, her sordidness, and her immorality. The encounter with this remarkable man spells out for her the inadequacies of her life. It is only in the presence of Jesus that we really see ourselves and are not appalled at the sight and depressing sense of sin. At this point we come to the realization that life as we are living it will not do. We must wake up to ourselves and to the God who loves us.

Jesus lets her know that he knows she has had five husbands and is now living with one who is not her husband. Her response indicates that she was hiding the truth. She is stunned that Jesus knows that she has had five husbands and is living in a sinful relationship with another man who is not her husband. Jesus is calling her to turn her life around. But she must first acknowledge that she is a sinner. He realizes that she is probably searching for happiness. But she must realize she will not find it by living an immoral life. Only God can fulfill her desire.

While this pericope speaks of a certain woman, in reality it speaks *of* and *to* us. In fact, she is but a stand-in for us. Just like her we have many of the same imperfections, hopes, fears, dreams, and burdens. Just like her we struggle "with uncontrollable anger, bitterness, foolish choices, misplaced priorities, hatred, profanity, hypocrisy, lust, greed, envy, pride, nagging doubt, compulsive busyness, broken dreams, and personal failures." Just like her we have our prejudices, racial and religious, social and intellectual. Just like her we fail to address our moral indiscretions. In this pericope Jesus is also speaking to us, you and me.

The woman sees that he is something greater than a teacher, that he is a prophet. Jesus acknowledges her observation and asserts that he is greater than Jacob, their ancestor, and that his teachings will replace the Law or wisdom that both Jew and Samaritan alike regard as God's gift. He adds that salvation, however, will come from the Jews and that he stands firmly within the authentic traditions of all Israel. In short order she recognizes that before her is someone greater than a prophet.

To that end she raises a burning issue with the Samaritans, "Our ancestors worshiped on this mountain, but you Jews claim that the place where we must worship is in Jerusalem." This refers to a controversy between the Jews and the Samaritans over Mt. Gerizian as the proper place of sacrificial worship—the time when Jacob had sacrificed and (according to the Samaritan version of Deuteronomy 27:4) the Israelites had set up the first altar in Palestine. The Samaritans accepted only the Pentateuch as inspired Scripture, and from this came their belief in the coming of the Messiah.

> Believe me, woman, the hour is coming when you will worship the Father neither on this mountain nor in Jerusalem. You worship what you do not know; we worship what we do know; for salvation comes from the Jews. But the hour is coming – indeed is already here—when true worshippers will worship the Father in spirit and truth; that is the kind of worshipper the Father seeks. God is spirit, and those who worship must worship in spirit and truth. (John 3:5–8)

Jesus refuses to be sidetracked. He will have none of this conversation. He thought the conversation and the idea of the temple or mountain was irrelevant in light of who he is, even though it is in Judaism that God's revelation has been safeguarded and through the messiah comes "salvation comes from the Jews." Jesus stands firmly in the authentic tradition of the Jews and Israel. It is not a question of where or how you worship but of who you are and who God is to you. It is a question of being true to who you are. In that truth you can enter into a personal commitment to God.

Finally the woman exclaims, "I know that Messiah is coming. When he comes, he will explain everything to us." She tries again to avoid her personal issue. Jesus presses on and responds simply, "That is who I am, I who speak to you."

In these words Jesus accepts her definition of the Messiah. The woman now sees him as the source of living water. She leaves her jar and goes to call the townsfolk so that they might see the Messiah and come to believe. Jesus plainly claims to be the Messiah with the words *I Am*, the name by which God revealed himself to Moses. "She came in the middle of the day, to draw some water from a well, and she ends up meeting the Water of Life face to face," as one commentator puts it.

At this point the disciples return. The woman runs off toward town, leaving her jar. Could it be that she is now converted and no longer needs this water from Jacob's well. She has had her fill of a new water, the God Jesus who knows her and loves her, filling the void in her life and giving her new reasons to live. She, the outcast, hurries to bring the Word to her fellow villagers. She, whose life had been irrevocably changed by this stranger, speaks across the centuries to you, "If you knew the gift of God and who it is that asks you for a drink, you would have asked him and he would have given you living water." We are at the beginning of the third week of Lent. Each of us would do well to ponder on this phrase in light of the foregoing.

CHAPTER 14

THE ILLUMINATIVE WAY:
BEGINNING TO SEE

Once the soul is purified from past faults by a long and arduous penance, in keeping with the number and gravity of those faults, once it has been grounded in virtue through the practice of meditation, of mortification, and resistance to the disordered inclinations and to temptations, then it enters the illuminative way. This stage of the spiritual life is thus named because the great aim of the soul is now the imitation, the following of Christ, by the positive exercise of the Christian virtues; Jesus is the Light of the World, and whosoever follows Him walks not in darkness.

—Tanquerey[1]

As we have seen, Lent is a time for metanoia, a time of conversion, turning from a life of sin to a Christ-filled life. The operative question in this chapter is this: What are the characteristics of those of the illuminative way?

The illuminative phase is a transition phase between the purgative phase and the unitive phase where we seek a more perfect union or relationship with God by avoiding sin and any attachment to the "ways of the world, the flesh, and the devil." The assumption is that we are serious about not only achieving our salvation but also finding out who we really are. St. John of the cross, according to Garrigou-Lagrange[2], writes that "the entrance into the illuminative way is marked by a passive purgation of the senses … and that the entrance into the unitive way is preceded by a passive purgation of the spirit, a further and a deeper conversion affecting the soul in its most intimate depths." This suggests that the purgative way is devoted to purging one's self of defects or imperfections, confession, repentance, making satisfaction, and finding one's authentic self. At some point during the purgative way we begin to feel the pangs of a desire for holiness. During the illuminative way we find ourselves surrendering our inner being to becoming holy and pleasing to God as a preliminary step to the unitive way, where we abandon ourselves totally to God. We begin to recognize our poverty, and we see the emptiness of honors and dignities and the things of this world. We detach ourselves from these entanglements. We now begin new lives and begin to make progress in our spiritual lives. We become more attuned to the practice of virtue and a desire to become one with Christ. We start to see in ourselves an increase in a desire to serve our brothers and sisters.

Having passed through the purgative phase, we now spend time with holy writ and learn from Jesus' teachings, marvel at his miracles, and experience an increased sensitivity and desire for prayer. We embark on a period of solitary reflection, doing battle with our egoism, self-love, and a multitude of imperfections or habitual faults. We also find ourselves praying for an increase in grace and a perfection or right ordering of love for ourselves, our neighbors, and God. Even if we are overcome by adversity or become disconsolate, we know that as long as we desire to become holy, in time God will provide us with a measure of solace, and we can always find refuge in him as long as we are truly humble.

In this phase we enter more fully in the essence of the Great Commandment or Shema: "Thou shalt love the Lord thy God with thy whole heart and with thy whole soul and with all thy mind and with all thy strength. Thou shalt love thy neighbor as thyself." We learn to love God for his own sake, and not from self-interest, in good times and in trying times, no matter our life's circumstance or the sensibilities of others. We realize that if we are "to put on Christ," this commandment is absolute and without limits, no matter our states in life.

In both instances we must be motivated by a spirit of detachment from worldly goods and become firmly rooted in the knowledge that we are adopted sons and daughters of a God who loves each of us with an abiding love.

In the previous chapter we essentially began a transformation process designed to open our souls to God, discern the obstacles hindering our relationship with him, and purge ourselves of these stumbling blocks. It was presumed that this purgation would lead to the illuminative phase of the spiritual life where we will extend and build upon this transformation. We will learn new ways of hearing God and being with him in prayer. We will discuss the various tools of prayer (i.e., meditation, contemplation, *lectio divina*, which refers to holy reading, and journaling). This discussion will serve to address the final three steps in AA, which speak to the maintenance, sustenance, and growth of what we have accomplished thus far. Specifically these steps include the following:

1. I will continue to take personal inventory, and when I am wrong, I will promptly admit it.
2. I seek through prayer and lectio to improve my conscious contact with God, praying only for knowledge of his will for me and the power to carry it out.
3. I will try to practice these principles in all my affairs.

Prayer: Conversations with God

On one of his many journeys Ignatius Loyola, one of the founders of the Jesuits, had hired a porter to carry his bags and those of his associates. From time to time the small band of men would stop and pray together. As the porter watched them, he wondered what they were doing, and as the days went by, he began to want to do what they were doing. Ignatius, when the porter's desire became known to him, realized that this humble man was, through his desire to pray, praying the finest prayer of all.

For many of us prayer has become an enigma. It is difficult even to talk about it since nothing is more personal than one's prayer life. Each person is his prayer. When one thinks about prayer, he thinks of his own experience of it rather than of what prayer is. When you talk to someone else, you are talking to someone whose experience is also an individual experience. So I ask you, the reader to bear with me as we discuss this enigma.

And so peace! *Shalom!* Peace be with you!

This was the first greeting of the risen Lord. And it is the heartfelt need and desire of every human person. It is the great concern of our times. But there can be no peace in this world of ours and no peace among nations unless there is first peace in our hearts. How do we find peace? How do we come to possess it so that we can say and bring to our brothers and sisters peace?

The answer is prayer. But what is prayer? "Prayer," says one of the early fathers of the church[3], "is conversation with God, contemplation of the invisible, the angelic mode of life, a stimulus towards the divine, the assurance of things hoped for." To pray implies a conversation between two entities (i.e., a speaker and one who hears what is spoken). The presumption is that the latter also listens and understands what is spoken. There is also the further presumption that the conversation is two-way. Both parties are in turn speaker and listener. Unfortunately some of us forget to listen. But God always hears us.

According to Merton,[4] prayer is a "yearning for the simple presence of God, for a personal understanding of his word, for knowledge of his will, and for capacity to hear and obey him." Its aim is purity of the heart, "an unconditional and totally humble surrender to God, a total acceptance of ourselves and of our situation as willed by him." It means ridding ourselves of our delusions of self, worth, merits, and estimates of our personal capacities.

Kataphatic or Apophatic Prayer

There are many types and styles of prayers. However, in both Western and Eastern Christianity there are essentially two types—kataphatic and apophatic prayer. The first type of prayer is characterized by content (i.e., words, images, symbols, or ideas), whereas the second has no content. It simply calls for emptying the mind of words and ideas and resting in the presence of God. It is usually referred to as the prayer of negation. Centering prayer is an example of apophatic prayer. Kataphatic prayer, on the other hand, generally encourages the use of images and imagination. It is oriented to feelings and sensual stimuli. It is generally referred to as the way of affirmation.

Kataphatic Prayer

Kataphatic prayer forms are varied and are probably the type with which we have the greatest familiarity. It refers to those prayers that call for some sort of external action, usually verbal expressions we recite from memory or reading. Generally they are characterized as vocal and as private or public worship that is spontaneous or formal. It does not matter how many words are actually used, but it does matter how fervent we are in "talking with God." Our interior disposition should match our external demeanor, be it praising or petitioning God. It is appropriate to call upon our entire being—body, soul, and heart. They may invoke multiple images as in poetry, scripture recitation, icon meditation, the rosary, litanies, or music, such as in hymns, chants, or performances featuring sacred themes. They may be formal as in the Mass or other religious ceremonies, the Liturgy of the Hours, the stations of the cross, or adoration of the blessed sacrament. Retreats such as the Ignatian Exercises are also examples of kataphatic prayer.

The prayer that Jesus taught us, specifically the Lord's Prayer, is the definitive example of this prayer form. In Sunday school or catechism classes you were taught that it embodied the following four characteristics of the perfect prayer:

- praise and adoration of our heavenly Father,
- contrition or sorrow for our sins and the expression of our intent to repent and amend our ways,
- thanksgiving for God's many blessings, and
- petition for our particular needs or the needs of those for whom we pray.

Vocal prayer often leads to meditation.

Meditation is a form of mental prayer and requires a period of quiet reflection and focus. When we meditate, we are applying our thinking, reasoning, imagining, sensing, visioning, or other faculties to the consideration of some truth, mystery, or spiritual principle. We are reflecting on or calling to memory what we have read, seen, experienced, or heard in vocal prayer, be it liturgical or otherwise. Often meditation excites in us some emotion, realization, or discernment as to what God is calling us to be or do. Other times meditation helps us to confront ourselves, to come to grips with our particular illusions, and to face reality.

Merton[5] has a somewhat different perspective. He finds that meditation is not so much about the reasoning of the mysteries of faith as it is about prayer of the heart that seeks "a direct existential grasp, a personal experience of the deepest truths of life and faith, finding ourselves in God's truth." It is listening for God's will and seeking to understand his will for me. It is coming to grip with my relationship to God as my Creator and as his creation, God as my redeemer and me as a sinner. Given Merton's perspective, there comes a point in our meditation when we become still. We are beyond images, words, and thoughts. The mind ceases to process, and we enter a realm of quiet rest. We are on the threshold of the apophatic prayer form. It is possible that we are aware of being embraced by God, even though it might be hard to describe how one knows this. This is a taste of contemplation.

Aphophatic Prayer

In its simplest terms apophatic prayer or the "way of negation" is typified by its simplicity, the absence of images or words, darkness, and the emergence of intuition wherein. At times the Holy Spirit speaks in a still, small voice. Examples of this prayer form are contemplation and centering prayer.

Contemplative prayer is spending time with God. It requires nothing more than listening in silence for God's soft whisper. It is prayer without words. It is being with God … and knowing it. It is unlike meditation, where the mind is actively working. It is the proper aim of both *lectio divina* and centering prayer.

The great mystic Teresa of Avila[6] defines contemplative prayer as nothing else than a close sharing between friends; it means taking time frequently to be alone with God, whom we know loves us. Contemplative prayer seeks him "whom my soul loves." According to Merton,[7] contemplative prayer is "the highest expression of man's intellectual and spiritual life." He adds elsewhere[8] that it is being in the presence of God. It is the perfection of love and knowledge. It goes beyond concepts and apprehends God not as a separate object but as the reality within our reality, the being within our being, the life of our lives. It is a mystery in which God reveals himself as the very center of our own innermost selves. And "it is the highest and most paradoxical form of self-realization, attained by apparent self-annihilation."

In a word, contemplative prayer is a deeply personal encounter with God. This encounter is beyond the grasp of reason. It is realized within the depths of one's very being. Here contemplative prayer is realized as a gift, a grace whereby God establishes a covenant relationship within us and makes us like unto himself in his divine image and likeness.

Some who engage in contemplative prayer are given the grace of what the mystics call a prayer of ecstatic union. They enter a stage in which they become unconscious for a period of time. This is not sleep in the usual sense, for the attentiveness of prayerful posture is generally maintained during prayer. Ecstatic experiences may last for seconds to minutes. Upon returning to consciousness, there is a sense of having missed a period of time, but you may have no knowledge of how long. Not everyone experiences this. It might simply be a phase through which one passes. The fruit is generally deep serenity and inner healing.

The mystics also tell us that there is another stage where there is no longer any obstacle in the soul to receiving contemplative graces. It is the stage of transformation. All of our faculties are receptive to the energies of the Holy

Spirit. God's will becomes our will. We are one with God. We may appear quite ordinary, but in reality we have become liberated and have begun to enjoy something of the joy of heaven even while we are on earth. Life is now prayer, and prayer is now life. Contemplation has helped us to discover and live out our lives on a level of truth—truth to ourselves and truth to God and to others. The question remaining is how to experience contemplation. Here I would like to suggest two mutually supportive ways, *lectio divina* and *centering prayer*.

Lectio Divina: Sacred Reading

The Scriptures are the primary source of lectio. Generally they are the richest resources for discovering the Word of God. But it is not the only resource. You can turn to other both ancient and modern spiritual writings, spiritual masters of earlier ages and traditions, and others such as Thomas Merton, who speaks to late-twentieth-century men and women.

This is a time-honored method of prayerful reading of Scriptures or other spiritual texts. We listen to God's voice, and we respond to it. This requires a special adjustment for those of us who approach most readings, including the Holy Scripture, as an intellectual exercise of the mind to understand. Lectio is more than this. It is an intellectual exercise of the heart where we absorb God's Word. This requires us to read slowly and deliberatively, letting God's Word sink into the very fabric of our being or, as Merton puts it, "into the ground of our being."

This poses some special challenges to those of us living amid the clamor and speed of the high-tech information age. The notion of reading slowly seems a bit foreign to most of us who have grown accustomed to doing things as quickly and efficiently as possible. In addition, some of the values of our highly materialistic culture with its emphasis on achieving and acquiring have spilled over into the reasons many of us have for reading in the first place. We often see it as a way of acquiring information, gaining insight, and possessing knowledge about one thing or another. Most of us can relate to the popular adage "So many books, so little time" because of our own tendency to want to accumulate more and more books regardless of those we have on our shelves and those we have scarcely any time even to skim through. Sacred reading, on the other hand, is something entirely different. In order to incorporate this particular practice into our lives, some of us may need to change some of our attitudes and approaches to reading.

Sacred reading is the exact opposite of speed reading or information gathering. To begin with it requires taking the time to slowly and deliberately read through a selected text with the purpose of listening and responding to what is written. It helps if you can set aside a certain period of the day as well as a specific place where it will be possible to devote your full attention and energies to the kind of reflection required by this kind of prayer. In addition, since sacred reading involves an inner receptivity on the part of the reader, it isn't the sort of thing that can be undertaken when one is feeling distracted, tense, or preoccupied with other things that need to be done later.

Assuming we choose the Scriptures, the slow, reflective reading of a selected passage or text can be richly rewarding to our spiritual lives, provided we are open to what we are encountering. Responding to the Word of God involves more than the purely cognitive act of reading and thinking about written words. We also use our emotional and intuitive faculties to respond to the rich array of images, symbols, and metaphors we find in scriptural passages and to ponder their implications in our own lives[9]

People who have grown to love the special graces they encounter through lectio are usually hesitant to prescribe a structure or procedure for others who would like to learn what's involved. It's more a matter of finding one's own rhythm and pace in order to arrive at a balance between reading, listening, reflecting, and responding to the specific text being encountered.[10]

Notwithstanding those of us just beginning to explore lectio, let me offer an outline or method. To begin, there are seven principles of lectio.

- Lectio is not aimed at confirming and reinforcing our individual approach to life but at breaking into life to enrich and deliver us from our limitations.
- Lectio is a long-term activity needing fidelity and constancy.
- Lectio is connected with our personal sense of vocation; its aim is to hear God's call.
- Lectio applies the Word of God to our own life situations.
- Lectio should be done in a peaceful manner so that it may be punctuated by prayer.
- Reading is not only an inner experience but an experience of the whole body.
- When something speaks to us in lectio, try to retain it in memory and savor it.

Often the most ordinary cause of dryness in prayer is a defect in genuine spiritual reading. Lectio rectifies this defect. It is fundamentally different from other types of intellectual reading and feeds the soul directly. Just as there are seven principles of lectio, the actual doing of Lectio consists of five phases.

At the outset lectio involves trying to become as present as possible to God's Word. Our intention should be not so much to get something out of it as to become totally receptive to God, to offer him the adoration of our stillness and receptivity, to receive with meekness God himself, to become in our hearts one with God. Hence, stillness of the body is a real help in becoming attentive. It also provides an atmosphere of prayer for others when lectio is done in a group.

- The first step of lectio is preparatory. Any preparation you can do on the text will aid you in moving toward prayer. For example, look up references and footnotes, go over the liturgy of the day, familiarize yourself with the customs of New Testament times, learn Greek and Hebrew (Aramaic), and read your text in the original.

- The second step is lectio per se. Read the text through once to remind yourself of its content. Then go back to the beginning and slowly reread the text sentence by sentence. This reading serves to focus and center us.

- The third step is what is called *meditatio.* Take the words of the sentence you have just read and repeat them to Jesus. Change pronouns if necessary. Just repeat the sentence to him. It does not have to make sense. Also repeat to Jesus whatever freely enters your mind. Do not try to think up something to say. Allow the process of free association to work. (According to Jung, the process of free association can stir long-forgotten memories or reveal things hidden in the unconscious.) Simply by repeating to Jesus the sentence from Scripture and whatever freely and easily comes to mind, I am exposing myself to a response from him, whatever it might be. Go on to the next sentence in the same way. Read and repeat. This is basically a right-brain activity like reading a love letter over and over again, savoring each word, making every thought your own, pondering and perceiving hidden lessons in the Word of God, acquiring the mind of Jesus.

- The fourth step of lectio is called *oratio* or prayer. One sentence or phrase may strike you in a particular way. You may see a new meaning in it. It may take fire in your soul. It may act upon your heart (e.g., pierce it, purify it, burn it, delight it, feed it, heal it, or make it whole). At this point it has become your word, your prayer. It is an experience and a recognition. The Word of God moves from your lips to your mind, and now you are led into your heart. Oratio is the response of your heart to God's Word and his grace. Remain here as long as you wish or go on to the next sentence.

- The final step of lectio is *contemplatio*. This is the outcome of lectio; it is an immersion, a deepening of our relationship with the Trinity. It is real contact with the Jesus behind the gospel. It is a receptivity to the love that the Holy Spirit pours into our hearts. It is our humble surrender to the loving will of the Father. It is a communion in which he forms us into his image and likeness. Here the Spirit prays in the human spirit. One experiences a state of inner harmony. Carnal motions are quieted. The flesh is not at odds with the spirit. The person is in a state of spiritual integration. As love, God is no longer an abstraction but a concrete reality. This moment can be fleeting or prolonged, subtle or pronounced. They can come and go again. If you experience this moment, enjoy it. Listen to Merton[11] in *New Seeds of Contemplation* when he says,

Contemplation is ... life itself, fully awake, fully active, fully aware that it is alive. It is spiritual wonder. It is spontaneous awe at the sacredness of life, of being. It is gratitude for life, for awareness, and for being. It is a vivid realization of the fact that life and being in us proceed from an invisible, transcendent and infinitely abundant source. Contemplation is, above all, awareness of the reality of that source.

Ten years later[12] in *Contemplative Prayer* he writes,

Contemplation is the summit of the Christian life of prayer, for the Lord desires nothing of us so much as to become, himself, our "way," our "truth and life." This is the whole purpose of his coming on earth to seek us, that he may take us, with himself, to the Father. Only in and with him can we reach the invisible Father, whom no man shall see and live. By dying to ourselves, and to all "ways," "logic" and "methods" of our own we can be a numbered among those whom the mercy of the Father has called to himself in Christ ... No logic of our own can accomplish this transformation of our interior life.

Merton adds in subsequent writings that prayer, reading, meditation, and contemplation fill the apparent void of one's (monastic) solitude and silence with the reality of God's presence, and thus, we learn the true value of silence and come to experience the emptiness and futility of those forms of distraction and useless communication that contribute nothing to the seriousness of a life of prayer. Lectio ... is essentially a "prayer of silence, simplicity, contemplative and meditative unity, a deep personal integration in an attentive, watchful listening of the heart." The response such prayer calls forth is not usually one of jubilation or audible witness. It is a wordless and total surrender of the heart in silence.

Centering Prayer

Basil Pennington, one of the principal teachers of centering prayer, tells a story[13] of his last meeting with Mother Teresa in Calcutta. As they were finishing breakfast, he asked her for a word of life to take home to his brothers at the Trappist Monastery in Spenser, Massachusetts. He writes, "And she looked at me with those deep, deep eyes. She had deep brown eyes that sort of invite you to enter into them, and she said, 'Father, tell them to pray that I don't get in God's way.' So I have been praying ever since that I don't get in God's way ... That's the secret: to let God be in us and through us all he or she wants to be." That is the secret of centering prayer—to open ourselves to God's entry into the inner recesses of our being.

Remember when one of John the Baptist's disciples asked Jesus, "Where do you dwell?" The answer is that he dwells in intimate love in you and me. And he is always there. He is always at home. The problem is that most of the time we are out to lunch. Centering prayer could be called in a way the prayer of coming home to dwell in intimacy and quiet love with the Lord. More traditionally it is the ancient prayer of the heart, the prayer in the heart, the prayer of presence, the prayer of simple regard, and the prayer of quiet. It is the natural culmination of vocal prayer, lectio, meditation, and contemplatio.

The name *centering prayer* was inspired by Thomas Merton. He used it often in his writings. We must go back to our true selves so we may find our own centers, our true being, where we also find God, who is constantly bringing us forth in his love.

One thing Merton constantly insisted upon was that this kind of prayer or contemplation wasn't something esoteric and it wasn't something just for a special few. Certainly contemplation is very special. There is nothing more special than union and communion with God, but it was meant for every one of us who have been baptized in Christ. We have been baptized and made one with the very Son of God, a oneness beyond anything we can discern. Contemplation is the work of the Holy Spirit working within us through his gifts of wisdom and understanding.

There is the apocryphal story of a young man named John Cassian, who early in the fourth century realized that what he was looking for was not in the books he was studying in Rome. He traveled throughout Asia Minor and Mesopotamia, joined an order of monks, and continued his travels throughout Arabia until he and a traveling companion came upon a hermit named Abba Isaac, reputed to be the holiest and wisest of the desert fathers. John Cassian asked Abba Isaac to speak to them about prayer. Abba Isaac gave them a beautiful conference on prayer. They were enthralled. When they awoke the next morning, they realized that they had indeed been exposed to a beautiful and edifying explanation of prayer; however, they were puzzled by the question, "How do we pray?" And so they went running back to Abba Isaac to ask him how to pray.

And old Abba Isaac said to them, "Aha. I see you are a true seeker, so I will teach you what I learned from the holiest and oldest and wisest of the desert fathers when I was a young man. We should be content with the poverty of a single, simple word, but a word that expresses all that we are. It is not the words that matter. It is the intention of the heart, the fullness of our being." He taught them the Jesus Prayer, the prayer of the heart, which is the deepest place within us, the source of life and love and being, the center.

A century or so later Benedict de Nursia wrote a rule for monasteries, and in the last chapter of his rule he said, "Do you really want to learn how to pray? Go to John Cassian."

How Do You Do Centering Prayer?

Centering prayer begins by choosing a sacred word as the symbol of your intention to consent to God's presence and action within. A single syllable word is best. But choose a word that is meaningful to you. It may be *Jesus*. It may be *Lord*. It may be *love, father, mind*, or whatever. The word is not important. The purpose of the word is just to help us to remain quietly with the Lord, to be all there for him.

There was a wise and kind father who wrote for his spiritual son, a young man who was twenty-four years old, "Just sit quietly." For the most of us that's the best posture for prayer. Find a decent chair with good back support and just sit quietly. Close your eyes. As soon as you close your eyes, you begin to appreciate Jesus when he says, "Come to me all who labor and are heavily burdened, and I will refresh you."

Prayer is supposed to be a refreshing experience. Jesus was a good Jew, and so when he said, "You, I will refresh you," he meant all of you, body, mind, and spirit, the whole of who you are. So prayer should refresh you physically, mentally, and spiritually. So take a moment just to get settled comfortably and close your eyes. In a way the chair kind of takes the body a second to kind of rest the body, it takes the spirit a moment to rest in God.

Listen to Basil Pennington's comments at a 2001 retreat conference that I attended. The following are taken from my notes:

- In the center of your being lives God—Father, Son, and Spirit. Experience his presence and be touched and transformed by Him.

- Simply sit, relaxed and quiet, enjoying your own inner calm and silence. For a few minutes, listen to his presence and allow yourself to be touched by it. God lives inside your silence. Listen to whatever he wants to share with you.

- In time perhaps a single word will come, such as *Jesus, Lord, love*, or perhaps a phrase such as "Jesus Christ, Son of God, have mercy on me." This word or phrase is a symbol of your intention to be open to God. Slowly and effortlessly repeat your word. Allow it to lead you more and more deeply into God's presence at the center of your being, where you are in God and God in you. Surrender to his refreshment and recreation.

- Center all your attention and desire on him, leaving your faculties at peace, allowing him to draw you into his perfect prayer of adoration, love, and praise. Let it happen. Whenever you become aware of any thoughts or images, whenever you find your mind wandering (and it will), simply return to the sacred word to gently nudge you back into a state where there are no thoughts intruding on your presence to God. Turn inward toward God as if you are gazing upon him. See him with the eyes of your heart. Turn off any mental interruptions. Do this for about twenty minutes. As you end this prayer, remain in silence for a few more minutes before you open your eyes. Move into a slow recitation of a favorite prayer, such as the Lord's Prayer. Savor the words. Listen to them and absorb them into your being. Rest in the Lord. Open your eyes.

Dom Basil promised, "If you are faithful to this method, you will soon discern in your life the maturing of the fruits of the Spirit: love, joy, peace, patience, gentleness, and kindness, and yes, shalom, peace."[14]

We have thus far discussed the principle forms of kataphatic and apathetic prayer. There are other forms of prayers that combine elements of both forms. They include the Liturgy of the Hours and the Jesus Prayer that comes to us from Eastern orthodoxy. We will conclude this chapter with a meditation on the Lord's Prayer, which also provides us with an illustration of both forms.

The Liturgy of the Hours: The Prayer of the Universal Church

> O Lord, open my lips
> And my mouth shall proclaim your praise;
>
> > -Psalm 51:15

> O God. come to my assistance.
> O Lord, make haste to help me.
>
> > -Psalm 70:1
> > -Customary Antiphons recited prior to each hour

We have already seen that prayer and praying are essential for our life of faith. Like breath to the human body, prayer makes the spirit live. Without it, faith dies. Yet a person who prays grows in spirit and life. Up to this point I have been speaking of prayer as conversations with God. For the most part this prayer is done in private. The Liturgy of the Hours, which is the church's formal daily prayer, is generally done in choir or as the divine office or breviary of clergy and/or laity. In this prayer the church as a collective acknowledges that prayer is God's gift and asks him to give and strengthen that gift in each of us.

The Liturgy of the Hours is the richest single prayer resource of the Christian church. It provides prayers, psalms, and meditation for every hour of every day. It has existed from the earliest times to fulfill the Lord's command to pray without ceasing. Never monotonous, always new, it provides the means for the whole world to unite, to pray together, and to sanctify every hour every day of every year. All over the world hundreds of thousands of clergy, nuns, monks, religious, and laypeople pray the liturgy daily in public and in private, in tin shacks and cathedrals, in palaces and prison camps. Every minute of every day this prayer rises to the heavens. Someone someplace is praying.

The Liturgy of the Hours has a long history. Its roots are found in Jewish practices that precede Jesus. We learn in the Hebrew Bible that God commanded Aaron and his successors (Exodus 29:38–40) to offer a morning and evening sacrifice. While in exile in Babylon, the Jews read aloud and sang the psalms and hymns from the Torah. Scholars opine that this may have been in fulfillment of David's words, "Seven times a day I praise you" (Psalm 119:164), as well as, "The just man meditates on the law day and night" (Psalm 1:2). These practices continued after the people returned to Judea and the temple was rebuilt and lasted to the time of Jesus and his disciples, who continued to frequent the temple for daily prayer. After Jesus' death and resurrection we have evidence (Acts 2:15; 10:9; 10:3; 13) that in addition to morning and evening prayer, which generally accompanied the sacrifices, there was prayer at the third, sixth, and ninth hours of the day. Early Christians continued to pray at these hours. In place of the bloody sacrifices of the temple, they celebrated the breaking of the bread (the Eucharist).

In the first century of the early church, Christians gathered with other believers, their bishops, and their clergy to pray in the morning and the evening and to rise during the night and keep vigil. They were even encouraged to pray during the *watches* of the day (the third, sixth, and ninth hours) while they were performing necessary works. This practice of praying at specific hours continued throughout the early church into the second and third centuries. However, it was not until the desert fathers and mothers in their efforts to live out St. Paul's command to "pray without ceasing" (1 Thessalonians 5:17) that a measure of formality entered into the praying of the hours. With the development of monastic communities in both the east and west, a practice of unbroken, fixed-hour prayer grew and a cycle of prayer composed for the most part of the psalms became the norm. By the fourth century the idea of canonical hours began to take their present shape. With Benedict of Nursia this idea became known as the divine office or *Opus Dei* (the work of God).

The composition of this divine office relies heavily on the psalms and canticles as well as readings from the Old and New Testaments. Each day's prayers are linked with the feasts and seasons of the liturgical year as well as the natural rhythms of the day, especially the alternation of light and darkness. The actual office consists of the following:

- the Ordinary, where prayers or hymns that are daily recited or sung are found;
- the Psalter, which consists of 150 psalms divided into each canonical hour during a four-week period and forming the basis of the liturgy as the foundation of Christian prayer[15];
- the Proper of Saints, where is found special readings and prayers in memory of those who have entered into glory;
- the commons, a compilation of special prayers for and readings of the apostles, the evangelists, martyrs, confessors, abbots, virgins, holy men and women, the dedication of the churches, and the Blessed Virgin Mary;
- special offices (readings and prayers) and the office of the dead; and
- the actual hours of prayer, consisting of the following:
  o Invitatory—An introduction to the divine office of the day
  o The Office of Readings[16]— which were originally offered in the middle of the night (4:00 a.m.).
  o Morning Prayer, (Sunrise or in the early morning).
  o Midmorning Prayer (9:00 A.M.)
  o Midday Prayer (noon).
  o Midafternoon Prayer (3:00 P.M.).
  o Evening Prayer (Sunset).
  o Night Prayer (At Dusk no later than 8:00 P.M.)
- Each hour's structure is similar in that its composition consists of:
  o A hymn.
  o Antiphons—this serves to introduce the psalm or canticle.
  o Psalms and/or canticles

- o A reflections on the psalm or the canticle
- o Readings or lessons—These are extracts from Scripture or the fathers and mothers of the church.
- o Prayers and intercessions

In both the Jewish and Christian traditions all the people—priests and laypeople alike—prayed the divine office. Somehow it became the province of the clergy and religious for many centuries. Happily the Liturgy of the Hours has been encouraged as appropriate for all Christians. It is a principal means for achieving unceasing prayer, mindfulness of God, and transformation in Christ. In monastic communities the Liturgy of the Hours join with lectio divina and/or Centering Prayer as the monk's principal efforts at unceasing prayer.

The Jesus Prayer: The Prayer of the Heart

I first came across the Jesus Prayer several years ago. I was struck with its brevity and simplicity and direct appeal to Jesus. But it was not until I read a small book written by an anonymous author called *The Way of the Pilgrim* that I came to appreciate its power. It is the story of a man whose one desire was to learn how to pray constantly. He was advised to say this prayer eight hundred times a day the first day until he had reached several thousand times per day and he was no longer saying it. It seemed like it was saying itself within his heart. Hence, its alternate name is the prayer of the heart.

The Jesus Prayer centers on the name of Jesus. Its power lies in his name. It is a prayer that comes to us primarily from the orthodox tradition as a method of contemplation. Attributed to St. Simeon, who is called the new theologian (949–1022), the prayer has come down to the present through the practice and teachings of countless monks and laypersons. The monks on Mt. Athos are particular devotees of the prayer. It is offered as a way in which to focus one's inner life.

The Jesus Prayer is rooted in the gospel. Indeed it sums up the whole of the gospel. In the first part—Lord Jesus Christ, Son of God—the name of Jesus invokes the incarnation when "by the power of the Holy Spirit he was born of the Virgin Mary and became man" (Nicene Creed). We affirm Jesus as the Word of God, one with the Father, become man of flesh and blood and dwelling among us. In the Old Testament whenever a Jew deliberately and attentively spoke the name of God, he in effect placed himself in the presence of God. By invoking the name, Jesus, whose name in Hebrew means *God saves*, we place ourselves in the presence of the living word of God. Jesus is the name of God's Son, "the Name which is above all names" and of whom it is written "all beings should bend the knee at the Name of Jesus" (Philippians 2:9–10). It is in the name of Jesus that the disciples were empowered to cast out devils, heal the sick, and preach to the masses.

The post-Easter appellation, Christ, speaks to the risen Jesus as foretold in the prophecies of the Old Testament. Jesus has become the Christ—in Greek Christos or the Anointed One, in Hebrew Messiah. He has resumed his divinity as the Son of God. He is Lord, and "no one can say Jesus is Lord except by the Holy Spirit" (1 Corinthians 12.3)

The second part, "have mercy on me, a sinner" speaks to the right relationship with God. Recognizing our sinfulness as well as our estrangement from God and our brothers and sisters is the first step in our spiritual journey. Through this prayer we admit our need for a Savior and for God's mercy. Yet the very word *mercy* in English does not have the same richness as its Greek source, *eleison*, which comes from the same root as *elaion*, which means olive tree and the oil thereof. The image of the olive tree in Genesis is manifest in the story of Noah and the returning dove, which brings back a small branch from an olive tree, now the traditional symbol of peace. The metaphorical message here is that God's wrath has come to an end. Man has an opportunity to get it right. In the parable of the Good Samaritan we learn that he put olive oil on the wounds to the man who had fallen among brigands. This oil had the properties of healing and soothing. Another use for olive oil we learn in the Old Testament is the anointing of kings and priests—an image of God's grace coming down and flowing over them, giving them a new power to carry out their duties, even though they might appear to beyond their human capabilities. In a word, God's mercy goes beyond forgiveness. He offers us peace, healing, and the grace of his power. This mercy or *elaion* expresses the complex and rich relationship of love between God and us.

I conclude this section with a few observations of Theophan the Recluse, a nineteenth-century Russian spiritual writer.[17] He offers the following guidelines for those interested in the Jesus Prayer as a way to deepen their spiritual lives. He indicates that there are three levels to saying the prayer.

He says that the prayer begins as an oral prayer, a simple recitation. As you enter more deeply into the prayer, you cease to be bothered by distractions. At this point our minds are focused on the words of the prayer, and we begin to speak them as if they were our own. In the third level the prayer becomes part of who we are. It enters the heart and like the prodigal son returns to the Father. It is at that point when the Holy Spirit cries out within us, "Abba, Father" (Galatians 4:6).

This is the goal of all spirituality—to return to the Father as his adopted sons and daughters through Christ in the Holy Spirit. It is in our hearts where we find his kingdom. Here we cry out with the Holy Spirit, "Abba, Father." Lord Jesus Christ, Son of God, have mercy on me, a sinner.

Let Us Pray as Jesus Taught Us

Jesus himself taught us to pray. How many times have we rushed through the Lord's Prayer without really listening to what we are saying? We should not only recite it but pray it. We should realize to whom we are speaking.

> And when you pray, do not imitate the hypocrites: they love to say their prayers standing up in the synagogues and at the street corners for people to see them. In truth I tell you, they have had their reward. But when you pray, go to your private room, shut yourself in, and so pray to your Father who is in that secret place, and your Father who sees all that is done in secret will reward you. In your prayers do not babble as the gentiles do, for they think that by using many words they will make themselves heard. Do not be like them; your Father knows what you need before you ask him.
>
> —Matthew 6: 5–8

I am reminded of a story about an African Trappist monk who was asked what the topic of his meditation was. His response was, "The Lord's Prayer." When further asked how long he had been meditating on this prayer, he responded, "Oh, about twenty years, and I am still on 'Our Father.'" You may not want to take this long, but you should take enough time to allow this prayer to enter into your heart, where you will find our Father.

Take time to listen to each part of the prayer. I offer the following meditation. I suggest you copy this essay into your journal and add your thoughts as they come to mind to each segment. Take your time.

The Lord's Prayer

So you should pray like this:

> Our Father in Heaven, may your name be held holy,
> your kingdom come, your will be done,
> on earth as in heaven. Give us today our daily bread,
> And forgive us our debts, as we have forgiven those
> who are in debt to us. And do not put us to the test,
> but save us from the Evil One.
>
> Yes, if you forgive others their failings, your heavenly Father
> will forgive you yours; but if you do not forgive others, your
> Father will not forgive your failings either.
>
> -Mathew 6:9-14

Our Father in heaven - We are praying to our Father—that is to say that you and I and all others in the community of mankind are praying a corporate prayer, not a personal prayer. I am not calling on my Father. I am joining with you to call on the Father, the God of us all, for you and I are brothers and sisters, no matter our country or skin color or religious beliefs. Our God is the same Creator of Adam and Eve. He is the God of Abraham, Isaac, and Jacob, the *I Am* who brought Israel out of bondage in Egypt, who through Moses laid down the law upon Mount Sinai, who spoke through the prophets and now through his beloved Son, Jesus, the seed that crushes the head of the Serpent as he promised. This is our Father, the Creator of the universe, the solar system, this planet Earth with its atmosphere, seas, land, and all creatures large and small, all vegetation, you, and me.

The relative pronoun *who* underscores the *person* of God the Father, but could it also be speaking of the other persons of the Trinity? The verb to be *"art"* (rather than "is") conceivably reveals the fact that in speaking to God the Father, we are also speaking to God the Son and God the Holy Spirit - three persons, one God.

In heaven— Where is heaven? We have been taught that it is "out there," but could it be "in here" in our hearts?

And so <u>we</u> call on the Father not as an individual but as a body of men and women, a community of brothers and sisters, children of God. The tenor of this call as to underscore that this father knows us as his children.

May your name be held holy - In the Lord's Prayer the word hallowed is generally recognized as meaning "holy." It also means sacred or praiseworthy. God's very name is holy now and forever. It is so sacred that the ancient Jews dared not pronounce it. At the burning bush Moses was told that his name was *I Am*. Subsequent writers of Scripture referred to him as Yahweh, Adonai, Elohim, or simply the letters YHVH[18]. Today orthodox Jews refer to him as G-D. His name is sacred and holy.

Your kingdom come—Where is God's kingdom? Is it in and of this world? Is it in an incorporeal place, a clime of spirits? Is the church reflective of this kingdom? What is the nature of this kingdom? Is it out there? From whence will it come? Will I know it when it comes? Could it be that in Jesus, as the Christ, we have seen this kingdom? Have we seen those who rise up against this kingdom (i.e., Satan and his minions) yesterday and today? When will he establish this kingdom on earth as it is in heaven? Who among us will be among the elect, the damned?

Your will be done, on earth as in heaven—I am reminded of Jesus' prayer in Gethsemane, "Father, not my will but yours be done." As a human my will is informed by faulty information and at times misleading impulses, not to mention limited powers of reason and my propensity for sin. God is not so limited. His wisdom is unsurpassed. His will is omnipotent, good, holy, and just. But he calls you and me to surrender our wills completely, to pray that others will do the same no matter where they are in the world. Of course we know that Satan still roams the world like a hungry lion, seeking to devour us and to entice us and to cut us off from him and fellowship with one another. May God's will prevail. May those among us who defy that will know the error of their ways. May we all be subject to him.

Give us today our daily bread—Today I ask for food for my bodily and mental sustenance. I also ask for food for my spiritual sustenance. I ask only for that which is appropriate and sufficient for this present day. I ask not only for myself but also for my brothers and sisters wherever they may be, nearby or far away. These include my neighbors, relatives, friends, here and abroad, those in harm's way, imprisoned, sick or hospitalized, grief-stricken, or depressed.

And forgive us our debts, as we have forgiven those who are in debt to us— Forgive what we have done and failed to do. Also forgive those who have sinned against us, against those of us who pray this prayer. Each day help us to keep our sins before us and to know sorrow and remorse. Help us live together without sins of laziness, lack of bodily discipline, self-indulgence, envy, hatred, and corrupting ambition. Give us the strength to bring our transgressions before you as we pray for forgiveness.

And do not put us to the test—We know that the Tempter is on the prowl. We know that he attacks us in diverse ways so that we might fall into his clutches. Sometimes these attacks are subtle, sometime direct onslaughts. For example, we might be beset with doubts and uninformed consciences. Other times when we least expect it, we are overwhelmed by pride, prurient desires of the flesh and envy, anger, or a desire to have that which does not belong to us. Still other times we give in personal aggrandizement, cruel lies that harm our brother or sister, impatience, despair, and theft. The list is endless. Help us to be aware of our weaknesses and not to expose ourselves unnecessarily to temptation. As St. Benedict advises us, when tempted, dash the temptation against the feet of Jesus.

But save us from the Evil One—Here we pray that we do not give into the previously mentioned sins. We seek to not only avoid doing evil but also the near occasions of evil. We also seek our inheritance as adopted children of God. We seek to not only live a holy life but to die a holy death, our sins having been forgiven by right living and humility.

Over the years we have added the following to what Jesus taught us:

For yours is the kingdom, the power and the glory forever and ever—We are part of that kingdom by virtue of our relationship to Jesus. In Jesus our prayer is made holy. God's name remains sacred. His kingdom is realized, and his will is completed. As Jesus' disciples our sins are forgiven. We are protected against temptation, and we are bought to eternal life to see the Father face-to-face as did Moses. *Amen, or So be it.*

Conclusion

No one said this stage would be easy. In fact, it is not uncommon for it to last many years following the purgative stage. Ignatius Loyola[19] writes that one generally goes through periods of great desolations (dryness, boredom, trials, suffering, or darkness)) and consolations (joy, solace, or relief). Yet John of the Cross[20] (Dubay, 1989) observes that when one is in this stage, one's prayer life and occupation with God is much easier and of greater joy than in the purgative stage.

Even Jesus makes it clear that it would be difficult. He nonetheless calls each one of us to be holy. Will you answer that call? Will you make that little extra effort to be sanctified and allow the Holy Spirit to flow through you by the grace of the heavenly Father so you can shine before the world as Christ does? Your survival—as does mine—depends on it! It is a matter of life or death! It is a matter of eternal joy or eternal suffering! Once we pass on to the other side and the spiritual world, there will be no second chance! If we reject God's grace and present calling, all we will be able to say for eternity is this: "I wish I would have done things differently!"

Now is our chance to do things different! Now is our chance to walk the path of light that Christ gave us. Now is our chance to become saints. Let us walk together, saints on earth, in purgatory, and in heaven, encouraging one another to answer our callings so that we can all rejoice eternally as saints and children of God. That is what Christian life is all about. This is what the following chapter is all about.

Endnotes

[1] Tanqueray, The Spiritual Life, *454.*

[2] Garrigou-Lagrange, Reginald, *Three Ways of the Spiritual Life* (Publisher unknown, 1938) Kindle Electronic Edition Location 473 of 1863

[3] Theodorus the Great Ascetic, circa 200 CE, *A Century of Spiritual Texts*, Paragraph 60 in The Philokalia, Volume Two, Compiled by St. Nikodimos of the Holy Mountain and St. Makarios of Corinth; translated from the Greek and edited by G.E.H, Palmer, Philip Sherrod, and Kallistos Ware, (London: Faber and Faber, 1990) pages 25-26

[4] Merton, Thomas, *Contemplative Prayer* (Garden City, NY: Image Books Doubleday, 1971), 67.

[5] Ibid

[6] Dubay, Thomas, *Fire Within: St. Teresa of Avila, St. John of the Cross, and the Gospel on Prayer* (San Francisco: Ignatius Press, 1989), 57–58.

[7] Merton, Thomas, *New Seeds of Contemplation* (New York: New Directions Publishing Corporation, 1961a), 1.

[8] Merton, Thomas, *The New Man* (New York: Bantam Books, Inc., 1961b), 10–11.

[9] Casey, Michael, *The Undivided Heart* (Petersham, MA: St. Bede's Publications, 1994).

[10] Louf, Andre, *The Cistercian Way* (Kalamazoo, MI: Cistercian Publications, 1983).

[11] Ibid, New Seeds of Contemplation, 1.

[12] Ibid, Contemplative Prayer, 93

13 Lopes, Milton, *Notes from a Private Conversation with the Lay Cistercians of Our Lady of the Holy Spirit Monastery* and Basil Pennington, Abbot (Conyers, GA 2001).

14 Lopes, Milton, Notes (2001) from retreat conference at Our Lady of the Holy Spirit Monastery, Conyers, GA with Basil Pennington. Abbott

15 It should be noted that the Psalter was the basis of Israel's prayer centuries before Christ and the foundation of the Church's prayer from the time of the apostles

16 The Office of Readings contains substantial material for meditation in the form of biblical readings and a selection from one of the church fathers or mothers who lived from the earliest centuries of the church or from old homilies whose authors have been forgotten or from the writings or biographies of the saints.

17 St. Theophan the Recluse, "On Prayer, letters 42 and 51." *Orthodox Life*, vol. 32, no. 4 (July-August, 1982): 21-30. Translated from the Russian by Fr. Stefan Pavlenko.

18 Or the Greek tetragrammaton, meaning four letters

19 Ignatius Loyola, *The Spiritual Exercises of St. Ignatius* (New York: Image Book Doubleday, 1533).

20 Dubay, Fire Within, 51.

CHAPTER 15

THE FOURTH WEEK:
BLIND FROM BIRTH

As long as day lasts
we must carry out the work of the one
who sent me;
the night will soon be here
when no one can work.
As long as I am in the world
I am the light of the world.

—John 9:4–5

In this pericope we are brought face-to-face with the suffering of one human being—a man blind from birth who unexpectedly comes by chance into contact with Jesus. His disability is palpable as is the pain of his parents. One can only imagine the financial, emotional, and relational toll blindness must have taken on this man and his family. However, this chance encounter provides the evangelist with another powerful opportunity to speak to how Jesus reveals himself to us. You and I must also be cured of our blindness so that we may see God. This account is not so much about physical blindness as it is about spiritual blindness.

Jesus is still in Jerusalem. It is the Sabbath day. He sees a man blind from birth. He is moved with compassion and seizes upon the moment as an opportunity to once again do the will of his Father and thereby display the glory of God.

But first imagine what physical blindness is like. Imagine never being able to see the beauty of God's creation, the light of the sun or the moon or the stars, a tree or a bird on one of its branches or a flower, a mountain or a river or the ocean, a sunrise or a sunset. Imagine never actually seeing an animal or another person, not even your mother or father or yourself in a mirror. Imagine never seeing the smile of another person or the handiwork of an artisan, artist, or architect. Imagine never seeing a landscape from the deck of a boat sailing down a fabled waterway in Europe or Asia or Africa. Imagine never seeing what is playing on television or in the theater or on the stage. Your whole life would be impacted by your blindness, and you couldn't do anything about it.

Now imagine what it is like to be spiritually blind, having no appreciation for God's manifestation of himself in creation, in his holiness, and in his mercy, love and grace toward each of us unworthy sinners that we are. Imagine being unaware of our own sins or immoral behaviors. Imagine—or better yet realize—how we struggle in our lives for God's guidance, how we are unable to grasp the meaning or purpose of our lives or envision the kind of person God wants us to be. Imagine how we fail to recognize God's presence and grace in our lives or the extent to which we are blind to our faults and failings.

And then we encounter Jesus and begin to understand that the blind man's story is our story too.

Let's get on with our story. Those with him also see this blind man, and they ask, "Rabbi, who sinned, this man or his parents, that he should have been born blind? Neither he nor his parents sinned." Jesus answered, "he was born blind so that the works of God might be revealed in him."

Not only is sight to be restored, but the light is given to one who never had it—a free gift of God through Jesus. It should be noted that the Jews believed that every affliction was the punishment for sin and that the sins of the parents would be punished in their children. Jesus does not concern himself with this. He is more concerned with doing God's work and offering this man a sign of divine light—saying, "We must work while there is daylight," rather than saying we should toil in darkness and sin (meaning spiritual darkness). Jesus' time on earth is drawing to a close. While there is still time, he is compelled to do the work for which God has sent him. The blind man must be cured.

After saying this, he spat on the ground, made some mud with the saliva, and put it on the man's eyes. "Go," he told him, "wash in the Pool of Siloam." (This word means *sent.*) So the man went and washed and came home with sight. Spittle is a sign of baptism. It was customarily believed to have medicinal properties, particularly if it came from a great personage. Smearing the man's eyes is equivalent to anointing. The blind man does as he is told, and he is given the ability to see for the first time. Having washed in the waters of Siloam, he sees for the first time. His chance encounter with Jesus and his act of obedience to Jesus' instructions—not his faith—resulted in his sight. No longer must he live in darkness. Yet he did not know who it was who had cured him, only that he was called Jesus. Trying to get to the bottom of a supposed violation of Jewish Sabbath law, the Pharisees set about questioning the blind man and then his parents, who attested to the fact that he had been blind from birth but pleaded ignorance as to how he was cured so as to avoid taking a stand against Jesus. It was common knowledge that anyone who attested to Jesus' legitimacy as the Messiah would be expelled from the synagogue. For a second time they called before them the cured blind man. This time they put to him a series of questions that increased in hostility.

This time in response to the Pharisees he surmises that Jesus is a prophet and even disputes their assertion that this Jesus is a sinner, saying, "That is just what is so amazing! You don't know where he comes from and he has opened my eyes! We know that God doesn't listen to sinners, but God does listen to people who are devout and do his will. Ever since the world began it is unheard of for anyone to open the eyes of someone born blind; if this man were not from God, he wouldn't have been able to do anything." Here we have a man cured of blindness standing toe-to-toe with the Pharisees, giving as good as he got.

For such *arrogance* the Pharisees throw him out of the synagogue. Their justification is that Jesus performed this miracle on the Sabbath day. Healings on this day violated their understanding of the law of God, which stated that a person could perform no work on the Sabbath day. To the Pharisees healing a person was considered work. Therefore, Jesus was a sinner, a lawbreaker, one who did not obey God's law or proper religious rules. He was not from God because he did not obey the laws that they thought were important or fit their understanding, perceptions, or expectations of what a genuine man of God should be. Unfortunately this is not unlike many of us who consider ourselves religious or spiritual because we keep the rules and regulations of our chosen religion and rituals, the letter of the law if not its spirit.

As the blind man gains physical sight, they lose spiritual sight. The Pharisees represent that part of ourselves that rejects spiritual growth. It is our wiser, arrogant, intellectual, rational, self-centered self that insists that spirituality must fit our rules and conditions, our perceptions, and our time frames. The Pharisee represents that part of ourselves that goes along with spiritual transformation only so far as there is a payoff that redounds to our benefit, whether it be social acceptance, good feelings, or a nonthreatening stance to our sense of well-being. Moreover, the Pharisee in us is too busy to be worried about anything other than getting ahead, making more money, looking attractive, fearing death, and currying favor because these are reinforced every day thousands of times by society or our zeitgeist.

The Pharisees suffered from spiritual blindness. They were blind to the Holy Spirit. They had religion, but they did not have the Holy Spirit. They loved their religious traditions but did not love their neighbors in need. They were blind to the human misery, suffering, enormous pain, and trauma of their brothers and sisters who came across their path every day. They had no compassion in their hearts.

Who among us is not aware of those who go to church on a regular basis yet are blind? They attend religious services, give money, pray, and know the Bible chapter and verse, yet they are spiritually blind to the power of the Holy Spirit and to the misery around them. There is much spiritual blindness inside and outside of the church. Perhaps the most hidden and grievous sin of our time is spiritual blindness that corrupts our religious beliefs and practices, our marriages, our parenting, our work habits, and our personalities.

Being aware of our spiritual blindness is to take the first step towards what we earlier called metanoia. We turn away from our blindness and begin to turn toward Jesus and his healing grace of spiritual sight. We repent and ask him to heal us. We turn away from the voices of the Pharisees within us that are counseling evil and self-centeredness. It has been observed that it takes a lot of work to find Jesus and to stand with him, but it also takes a lot of work to ignore him. Are you the blind man looking for spiritual sight or the Pharisee thinking that what you know to be spiritually true? The reality is we are a mix of both. Let us see Jesus. He is standing in front of us. "For judgment I came into this world, that those who do not see may see, and that those who see may become blind."

Hearing that the Pharisees had thrown the blind man out of the synagogue and having undergone a sort of trial, Jesus seeks him out. When he finds him, he asks "Do you believe in the Son of Man?" Of course the man was perplexed, not knowing what Jesus was asking. He says, "Tell me so that I may believe in him." And Jesus responds, "You have now seen him. In fact, he is the one speaking with you." Jesus identifies himself as this "Son of Man." Now it was probably known by most Jews of the time that one of the titles of the Messiah was Son of Man. Another was the Anointed One. Still another was the Son of God. At this point the man begins to understand the true identity of Jesus and says, "Lord, I believe," and he worships him. Jesus then says, "For judgment I came into this world, that those who do not see may see, and that those who see may become blind."

Barclay[1] writes,

> Jesus came into this world for judgment. Whenever a man is
> confronted with Jesus, that man at once passes a judgment
> on himself. If he sees in Jesus nothing to desire, nothing to
> admire, nothing to love, then he has condemned himself.
> If he sees in Jesus something to wonder at, something to
> respond to, something to reach out to, then he is on the way
> to God. The man who is conscious of his own blindness, and
> who longs to see better and to know more, is the man whose
> eyes can be opened and who can be led more and more
> deeply into the truth. The man who thinks he knows it all,
> the man who does not realize that he cannot see, is the man
> who is truly blind and beyond hope and help. Only the man
> who realizes his own weakness can become strong. Only the
> man who realizes his own blindness can learn to see. Only
> the man who realizes his own sin can be forgiven. The more
> knowledge a man has the more he is to be condemned if he
> does not recognize the good when he sees it.

Those who see are blind; those who are blind see. As John Chrysostom put
it, "The Jews cast him out of the Temple; the Lord of the Temple found him."
If the Pharisees had less knowledge of eternal matters and were ignorant of
the good when they encountered it, they could have been forgiven. But in that
they purported to possess such knowledge, they are worthy of condemnation.

Note that the blind man began by calling Jesus a *man*. "A man called
Jesus opened my eyes." He was amazed. Never had he met or heard of a man
with such powers.

He moved on to call him a *prophet*. "He is a prophet." A prophet is one
who conveys to man the Word of God, one who lives close to God and is
privy to his inner councils.

Finally he confesses that Jesus is the *Son of God* when he hears Jesus' *I
Am*. Really there is no other way to describe him.

Upon reflection the woman at the well underwent a similar conversion.

At first she only saw a man, a Jewish man at that.

His behavior toward her led her to believe that he was a special person for
whom the social restrictions between a man and a woman, Jew and Samaritan
had not salience.

After much conversation she was moved to call him a prophet.

In short order after they heard Jesus utter the "I Am" proper only to God himself, she and the blind man recognize that they are in the presence of the divine.

Endnotes

1   Barclay, William, *The Gospel of John*, vol. 2 (Philadelphia, PA: The Westminster Press, 1975), 50.

CHAPTER 16

THE UNITIVE WAY:
LESSONS FROM THE SERMON
ON THE MOUNT

Seeing the crowds, he went up the hill.
There he sat down and was joined by his disciples.
Then he began to speak. This is what he taught them.
                                        —Matthew 5:1–2

He then came down with them and stopped at a piece of
level ground
where there was a large gathering of his disciples
with a great crowd of people from all parts of Judea and
from Jerusalem
and from the coastal region of Tyre and Sidon who had come
to hear him.
                                        —Luke 6:17–18

This is the last of what some theologians call the three stages of spiritual perfection. We have seen that in the purgative stage we begin our journey with a decision to turn our lives around—metanoia. We acknowledge our individual sins and the roles we play in the commission of the sins of the collective we call society (i.e., sexism, racism, failing to address the needs of our brothers and sisters, etc.). We realize that to become the disciples of Jesus we need help, and so we seek the aid of God's Holy Spirit to purge ourselves of our shortcomings and evil inclinations, to overcome our temptations, and to take steps to avoid the occasions of sin. But there is more. This phase of the spiritual life also enables us to come into contact with our true selves, to be who we really are. This means that we begin to shed the false selves we present to the world.

In the illuminative stage we continue our journey. At this stage, ever-mindful of our dependency on God, we devote our energies to advance in virtue, particularly in the love of God, our neighbor, and ourselves. If we have done our work in the purgative phase of our journey we should be stronger and better able to withstand temptation, particularly mortal sin. But we still need to be on the lookout for the occasions of sin, particularly venial sin or allowing our minds and hearts to be distracted by any number of desires or imaginations. Hence, in this phase we need to strengthen our resolve to become more of whom we really are and to grow in our relationships with one another and with God. In this phase we seek to progress in the spiritual life and in all the theological and moral virtues.

This third phase goes well beyond the focus of the twelve-step program. We are now in the realm of spirit. It embodies an inner life of contemplation. Here Christ is literally the life of our souls. We know a great peace. Our hearts, souls, and minds are fixed on God. We are united with him by a great love, which permeates and directs everything we think, do, or say. We see God in our brothers and sisters and in all of his creation. Love energizes us in the performance of both the corporal and spiritual works of mercy of which we spoke in an earlier chapter. Love also is the driving force in our prayer life, which is now less dependent on verbiage and more motivated and enlightened by the inspirations of the Holy Spirit.

The very word *unitive* bespeaks "union with." In this context, union is the hoped-for result of the gift of contemplation, which opens us up to extraordinary graces and virtues. For some this leads to mysticism. For others it leads to exceptional deeds on behalf of their fellow men and women. This is not to say that the soul in this state of being is without a sense of anguish or desolation. Many feel keenly the heaviness or pain of their peculiar cross. We recall the anguish of Mother Teresa, for whom the feeling or the absence of God in her life was a pressing burden. Nonetheless, she persevered in the knowledge that God was present in her life in a most edifying way. She knew that life on this plane was a time for purification of the interior life and a strengthening of her relationship with God despite her personal millstone. She knew what she had to do—love God and carry out his work—and she knew in the end she would meet him and enjoy his embrace.

Here the Beatitudes are of immeasurable help. Together with the preceding phase this is what Lent is all about. We have identified our tools. During Lent we try to "put it all together." We realize that the path on which we trod is not one that we necessarily chose, but we actually abandon ourselves to divine providence. We understand that it is God, through his Holy Spirit, who is really in charge. At this stage our goal is habitual and permanent union with God, which is the real purpose of the unitive phase.

I think it appropriate to spend some time listening to and commenting upon Jesus' Sermon on the Mount, where he describes the characteristics of the saints and what must be done for one to qualify to be called a child of God. He gives specific details.

Wherever it took place, mountain or valley, Jesus presented to his followers his essential teaching or revelation of God's will. Whether intended for his disciples or for whomever else was drawn to his message, what follows molds and shapes the Christian identity.

The sermon begins with blessings and sayings (Matthew 5:3–16) similar to those in the book of Psalms and in the Hebrew Bible's wisdom literature. In the middle there are six scripture interpretations (Matthew 5:17–48), instructions on how to practice the art of discipleship (Matthew 6:1–18), and comments about social and economic behaviors (Matthew 6:19–7:12). The sermon ends with a preview of the last days (Matthew 7:13–27). Here Jesus describes a community characterized by justice, piety, and shared resources. This community was markedly unlike the Palestine of his day, which was characterized by wide disparities in wealth and considerable injustice. While a few prized and enjoyed power, possessions, and status, most Palestinians suffered under Roman rule and the greed and venality of the Jewish court.

Luke's rendition of the beatitudes parallel Matthew's first, second, fourth, and eighth. He adds several antithetical *woes*. In comparison to Matthew, Luke emphasizes the quality of virtue and its activity. He speaks of actual poverty, hunger, and mourning. Matthew, on the other hand, emphasizes the spiritual dimension but nonetheless is cognizant of the impoverished and destitute condition of the poor class who constituted the vast majority of the then Greco-Roman world. Hence, both sets of Beatitudes speak to Jesus' preference for the powerless and the poor. Each one identifies those who are without resources or options and who yearn for God's intervention and blessings. Each one identifies the consequences of Roman rule and promises God's victory over it. Let us look more closely at these Beatitudes. We will use Matthew's account, augmented by those of other writers, particularly Pope Leo the Great whole Pontificate ran from 440–461 CE,[1] and whose sermons on the Beatitudes have informed generations of clergy and others who are accustomed to daily readings of the divine office.

How Happy Are the Poor in Spirit? Theirs
Is the Kingdom of Heaven.

First the saints are those who are poor in spirit. Embracing a spiritual attitude in all things, they are detached from the world, living *in* the world but not *of* the world. The poor in spirit have little valuable worldly possessions if any. While these Christians are poor in worldly wealth, they are rich in spiritual wealth. While they are poor in this world, they find their joy and peace in their daily personal relationship with the Lord Jesus. Spiritually they are rich. They are unlike the avaricious who measure their worth by how much money they make, how resplendent their possessions, or how much power they possess over others. Like Dives they will one day die, and their money, possessions, and power will be for naught (Luke 16:19–31).

The kingdom of heaven is to be given to those who are humble and not tied to their possession or lack of worldly goods. Matthew's emphasis is less on the literal lack of possessions by the poor than their lowly condition. He knows that their poverty does not allow them the arrogance and assertiveness of the wealthy but imposes habitual and servile deference. This is just as true in our times as it was in his time. Matthew acknowledges that though the poor are more likely to be disposed to the blessings of humility than those who are rich, there are many wealthy people who are disposed to using their abundance to help others. They consider their greatest gain to alleviate the distress of others. Humility is available to rich and poor alike. Leo adds, "Blessed, therefore, is that poverty which is not trapped by the love of temporal things and does not seek to be enriched by worldly wealth, but desires rather to grown rich in heavenly goods."

He brings our attention to the apostles who left their belongings and families to follow Jesus and to become "fishers of men [and women]." "Abandoning all their worldly property and possessions they were enriched with eternal goods." They rejoiced to have nothing of this world and to possess all things with Christ. We are told that there was a time when Peter was en route to the temple and a lame beggar asked him for alms. Peter responded, "Silver and gold I have not; but what I have I give to you. In the name of Jesus Christ of Nazareth, arise and walk." The man got up and walked, praising God. Peter, though poor in silver and gold, was rich beyond belief. He was rich in divine grace.

Luke also mentions this beatitude when he says to his disciples and those others who had come to hear him, "How happy are you who are poor; yours is the kingdom of God … But alas for you who are rich; you are having your consolation now." The first comment is addressed to those of his immediate disciples who are present—the poor, the destitute, and the hungry. The second comment is addressed to those who are not present and who do not acknowledge Jesus or his teachings and who are generally rich, full, and self-satisfied.

Happy Are Those Who Are Meek.
They Shall Inherit the Earth.

The saints are the meek, those who humble themselves before others, those who are willing to serve rather than be served. Their meekness is rooted in their relationship with God to whom they surrender everything. With Job the meek person cries out, "Naked I came into this world, naked I shall leave. The Lord gives and the Lord takes. Blessed be the name of the Lord."

In present times the word *meek* is not part of our vocabulary. It is not what most of us would use in describing ourselves. Our culture finds it offensive. It has the connotation of a *milquetoast*, a *pushover* or a *sucker*. To survive in this world we are taught to be self-assertive. The media and contemporary education and training systems reinforce this position by presenting the successful person as aggressive and determined to secure his or her rights, to take care of *numero uno*, and to get out of life as much as he or she can, whether or not the person deserves it or has a right to the spoils. We are daily fed the bromide of actualizing your potential, entering into your magnificence, making yourself as indispensable as possible, promoting yourself at the expense of others. There are even churches that promote this doctrine of prosperity and self- aggrandizement.

It is acceptable to look with contempt at the meek, the gentle, and the humble. The mantra is this: "It is a dog-eat-dog world out there. We need to be tough and not gentle, or else we will be either eaten alive or steamrolled."

Jesus' declaration flies in the face of current perceptions of reality. Later in Mathew 11:29, we hear him saying, "Shoulder my yoke and learn from me, for I am gentle and humble in heart." It seems to follow that the word *meek* is to be defined within the context of the first two beatitudes—the first being poverty of spirit, a sense of our insufficiency and nothingness, a realization of our unworthiness and unprofitability, the other being a mourning and sorrow for our deficiencies and sins. Accordingly this leads me to define meekness as self-emptying, what the saints call self-abnegation, the antithesis of not only pride but self-will, stubbornness, and the like. Such meekness can only be realized through the good graces of God. Only through these graces are we enabled to control our tempers, cease being resentful, avoid getting even, and turn the other cheek.

Pope Leo[2] has a different point of view. He zeroes in on the word *earth*, recalling the words of Ash Wednesday, the first day of the solemn season of Lent. *"Meménto, homo, quia pulvis es, et in púlverem revertéris,"* which translates to, "Remember man that thou art dust, and unto dust thou shalt return." Ashes, though a symbol of penance, are a reminder that our bodies were made from the dirt or mud of the earth (in Latin *humus*, the root of the word humility) by our Creator, who breathed into them a living soul. We are creatures made in his likeness and image. When we die, we shall in time assume a new body, a body "transformed by a joyous resurrection and clothed in the glory of immortality." No longer will we be at war with sin, but we will realize the original integrity of body and soul that we possessed upon our creation as man and woman. Leo adds, "Then, truly will the meek inherit the earth in perpetual peace, and nothing will be taken from their rights, for this perishable nature shall put on the perishable and this mortal nature shall put on immortality. Their meekness and gentleness will be the key to their reward; what was a burden will have become an honor."

Hence, the meek person is quiet, patient, forbearing, gentle, submissive, and humble. But do not confuse this with weakness. Though Jesus possessed all of these characteristics, he was a strong man in every sense of the word. He had the strength of character to carry through the judgment of his Father. "The cup which my Father has given me, shall I not drink of it?" (John 18:11). Led, not dragged "as a lamb to the slaughter," reviled, he did not seek revenge. Buffeted, he did not strike back. He was meek and humble, gentle and strong. He was resigned to the will of his Father and thus bore patiently the insults and injuries he received. Yet when the time presented itself for him to stand up to evil, he was more than ready. Note how he rebuked the evil spirits he found in his brothers and sisters. See how with a knotted whip he drove out the merchants out of concern for his Father's house. Marvel at his replies to Pilate, who claimed to have the power of life or death over him. "You would have no power over me ... if it had not been given you from above," was Jesus' response as he stood before the procurator, regal in his bearing, wearing a crown of thorns and a purple robe that covered his beaten, whip-lashed body. This was not a weak man.

With all this said, Jesus knew full well what he was saying when he declared this beatitude, which is reminiscent of Psalm 37:11, "But the meek shall inherit the earth; and shall delight themselves in the abundance of peace." I don't know about you, but this seems to be a pretty good deal, or to put it another way, the risk-reward ratio is decidedly in our favor.

Happy Are Those Who Mourn. They Shall Be Comforted.

The saints are those who mourn. They long for the day when they will receive their blessed hope, the day when they will be eternally united with Christ and their loved ones, the saints of the church. Many suffer because of social injustices, their cries reaching up to the heavenly throne for justice. While they may not inherit justice in this world, surely they will inherit eternal and divine justice in the kingdom of God. And those who did not heed the suffering and cries of the oppressed will pay a heavy penalty in due time.

Leo tells us that this mourning has nothing to do with ordinary worldly distress but rather with sin, one's own sin or the sins of another. It also relates to the extent of human evil. He writes, "Indeed, he who suffers it, for his wickedness plunges the sinner into punishment, whereas endurance can raise the just man to glory."[3] Other commentators contend that this beatitude echoes Isaiah 61:1, "He has sent me to bring good news to the poor, to bind up hearts that are broken," and Isaiah 61:3, "To comfort all those who mourn and to give them for ashes a garland; for mourning robe the oil of gladness, for despondency praise." They also suggest that this beatitude refers to those who have no joy in this world and who mourn the evils of Israel's many sins. Another somewhat unorthodox rendering of this beatitude by Aramaic scholar Douglas-Klotz[4] translates the Aramaic verb "to mourn" as "confusion or turmoil, to wander, literally or figuratively." "To be comforted" in Aramaic can also mean "to be untied inside, to return from wandering, or to see the face of what one hopes for." Accordingly he translates this second beatitude as follows:

> Ripe are those who feel at loose ends,
> coming apart at the seams;
> they shall be knit back together within.
> Blessed are those in turmoil and confusion.
> They shall be united inside.

Finally Luke's rendition says, "Happy you who weep now; you shall laugh … Alas for you who laugh now; you shall mourn and weep."

Christ himself provides us a model regarding mourning when we see him weeping at Lazarus's grave and another time mourning over Jerusalem. We ourselves have many causes for which to mourn within our families and among our friends and associates—the hardships and travails of our brothers and sisters who are starving, being killed, denied access to education or employment, experiencing unbelievable forms of discrimination and physical torture, such as rape, child abuse or molestation, the misdeeds of those in high places. The list goes on. How often do we notice or hear of these injustices, crimes, and other horrid events yet barely raise our eyebrows? How often do we mourn over our sins?

Happy Are Those Who Hunger and Thirst for What Is Right. They Shall Be Satisfied.

The saints are those who hunger and thirst for righteousness. They see the many wrongs in the world. They see the victims of these wrongdoings. They pray for peace and for their enemies. Here we can associate with personal and worldly righteousness. On a personal basis, how often have we been taken advantage of by someone who abused our goodness or our forgiveness? How often have we wished that the truth would come out and righteousness would flourish? On a worldly basis we see many things that offend us. Children suffer because of divorce. Crimes are on the rise. Abortions flourish in many cities. Some countries are torn by war. Some families are starving to death because rich nations will not share their food unless it is being paid for. The recent midterm election is a case in point. It is this writer's opinion that it was a travesty in terms of naked hatred, lies, innuendos, rabid racism, ugly accusations, incredible ignorance, ugly manifestations of fear-mongering, the corroding influence of money furthering narrow interests at the expense of the common good, pandering to the basest passions of the electorate, a 24-7 news cycle, an electorate that wants it all but is unwilling to pay for any of the services it demands, an education system that has been decimated and serves only the well-healed, a wealthy plutocracy that possess an oversized amount of the riches of this country at the expense of a middle class that is rapidly falling into poverty. Yes, the list goes on—all for which we should hang our collective heads in shame. All these things disturb our spirits and give rise to a hunger and thirst for righteousness.

Note that this is not hunger or thirst in the usual sense. This beatitude speaks to having a good relation with God (i.e., submitting to his will). Unlike the Pharisees, who taught that such good relations were realized simply by observing the Law according to strict Pharisaic standards, Jesus insisted that his disciples were called to a higher standard. He teaches that those who hunger and thirst are hungry and thirsty for what is right and just, virtuous and moral. Those who would be his disciples are on fire with love for God and neighbor. Luke adds the idea that one who would follow Jesus must be willing to share in his rejection. They must be willing to take up their crosses and follow him. To those who are not willing, they already have their comfort.

This beatitude calls upon each of us to take steps to comport our will to that of God's. Just as Jesus in the garden acknowledged and accepted the will of his Father, so must we if we would be his disciples. This means that our love for God and our neighbor must extend to the ill and infirm, the hungry and thirsty, the naked and homeless, the destitute and desolate, and the institutionalized, including those in prisons or asylums.

With the exception of the institutionalized, these people are in our neighborhoods, towns, and cities. We see them every day, but more often than not we pass them by with not so much as a word or glance that acknowledges them as our brothers and/or sisters, much less as a human being. As long as we ignore them and take no steps to provide them the basic rights to which every human should be entitled, such as healthy food, clean water, decent housing, affordable and adequate medical care, safe environments, access to quality education, basic justice, and opportunity without regard to race, ethnicity, gender, sexual orientation, or physical handicap, we really cannot call ourselves followers of Jesus. As long as we take no personal responsibility for such injustices, we cannot call ourselves Christians.

We can lay no claim to being on fire with love of God. We give the lie to being hungry and thirsty for what is right and just. We cannot say that we want what God wants or that we are in sync with his will. Our very prayer life or attendance to our religious obligations is really a farce. Jesus promises satisfaction only to those who seek to do his Father's will, and that goes beyond mouthing mere words on Sunday and going about business as usual on Monday. Can you honestly say that you are seeking to do his will?

Happy Are the Merciful. They Shall Have Mercy Shown Them.

The saints are the merciful, those who are willing to forgive the trespasses of others as God the Father forgives their trespasses. As humans, they also understand the weaknesses of human nature. They seek to uplift and encourage their brothers and sisters in Christ so all may share in the eternal glory that awaits the saints. Do we not all pray that we will be forgiven our mistakes that offend others? But how quick are we to forgive others who have done wrong against us? Did Jesus not say that we will be judged by the measure that we judge others? If we cannot forgive others, can we expect divine justice to forgive us?

Mercy is the ability or capacity to feel and express compassion for another, particularly in circumstances where the other is in a particularly difficult or crisis-ridden situation, such as a grave illness, debilitating disability, old age, or serious personal or emotional difficulties. It also presumes that the person with this gift of mercy either has the wherewithal to provide the necessary help and support and the desire to stick with the person or persons until the situation is rectified. Such persons desire also to help others without being judgmental.

Mercy is a frequent theme in Scripture. Matthew illustrates it with the parable of the merciless servant (Matthew 18:23–35) and his description of the last judgment (Matthew 25:31–46). In response to those who would rebuke him for eating with "tax collectors and sinners," Jesus replies, "it is not the healthy who need the doctor, but the sick. Go and learn the meaning of the words: 'what I want is mercy not sacrifice' (Hosea 6:6) And indeed I did not come to call the virtuous, but sinners" (Matthew 9:13). In Matthew 15:32, Jesus gives voice to his feelings when he sees the crowds that had been following him for three days. "I feel sorry for all these people; they have been with me for three days now and have nothing to eat. I do not want to send them off hungry, they might collapse on the way." He then goes on to multiply seven loaves of bread and a few small fish to feed the crowd of four thousand men plus many women and children. Jesus again speaks of mercy in Matthew 23:23, where he calls the scribes and Pharisees hypocrites because they are more concerned with minor issues in the Law rather than more weighty ones like "justice, mercy, and good faith." In Luke 7:13, Jesus has mercy on the mother of a son who had died. "When the Lord saw her he felt sorry for her," and he restored the young man to life. He is described as so filled with mercy that he sometimes wept (John 11:35). His mercy extended to children for whom he had much love and concern (Matthew 19:14). Perhaps the best-known accounts of mercy is Jesus' parable of the Good Samaritan (Luke 10:30–37). But it is in Matthew's description of the last judgment that we hear Jesus portraying himself as the Son of Man, separating the sheep on one side and the goats on another.

To the sheep, who represent those who have been faithful to the Son of Man, he says,

> Come you whom my Father has blessed, take for your heritage the kingdom prepared for you since the foundation of the world, For I was hungry and you gave me food. I was thirsty and you gave me drink. I was a stranger and you made me welcome … naked and you clothed me … sick and you and you visited me … in prison and you came to see me.

To the question "Lord when did we do these things?" the Son of man replies, "In so far as you did this to one of these, to one of the least of my brothers, you did it to me." To the goats he states before he consigns them to the eternal fires of hell, "In so far as you neglected to do this to one of the least of these, you neglected to do it to me" (Matthew 25:31–46).

From this pericope the Christian churches have constructed and commends to the faithful what are known today as the corporal works of mercy. They include

1. to feed the hungry,
2. to give drink to the thirsty,
3. to shelter the homeless and to welcome the stranger,
4. to clothe the naked,
5. to visit the sick, and
6. to visit the imprisoned.

The churches add a seventh corporal work of mercy—to bury the dead.

While mercy is the responsibility of all people from the perspective of social justice, it is also a call to holiness. Many of us think that we are on the right track if we simply adhere to the letter of the Ten Commandments. But we are called to do and be more. We are called to adhere to the spirit of the commandments. We are called to that aspect of holiness, which is called love, and mercy is at its core.

Spiritual Works of Mercy

Often we forget that mercy goes beyond relieving our brother and sister who is in physical distress. The church also finds in Scripture that mercy extends to those in spiritual distress as well. Here are what the churches recommend to us as the spiritual works of mercy and those scriptural passages that support this commendation.

- To admonish the sinner, they says, "There will be more rejoicing in Heaven over one repentant one sinner than over ninety-nine upright people who have no need of repentance" (Luke 15:7).
- To instruct the ignorant, they say, "Go out to the whole world. Proclaim the gospel to all creation" (Mark 16:15).
- To counsel the doubtful, they say, "Peace I bequeath you, my own peace I give you, a peace the world cannot give, this is my gift to you. Do not let not your hearts be troubled or afraid" (John 14:27).
- To comfort the sorrowful, they say, "Come to me, all you who labor and are overburdened, and I will give you rest" (Matthew 11:28).
- To forgive all injuries, they say, "And forgive us our debts, as we have forgiven those who are in debt to us" (Matthew 6:12).
- To bear wrongs patiently, they say, "Love your enemies, do good to those who hate you, bless those who curse you, pray for those who treat you badly" (Luke 6:27–28).
- To pray for the living and the dead, they say, "Father, I want those you have given me to be with me where I am" (John 17:24).

To perform these works of mercy—corporal and spiritual—is the responsibility of all who call themselves Christians, not just the clergy and religious people, such as nuns and brothers, or those laypeople who are part of organizations dedicated to a particular charism. It extends to each of us in the interactions within our families and those among our acquaintances and friends who are lonely, sick, or troubled. They need our compassion and attention. We don't have to go afar to find people who have been victimized by the vagaries of a weak economy and have lost their jobs and their sense of self-worth because they can no longer find meaningful work or are the recipients of prejudice and discrimination because of their race, ethnicity, or religion. Sometimes to be merciful in a given situation is inconvenient. Visiting the imprisoned or the sick comes to mind. Going out of your way to help the battered woman or the confused teenager who finds herself pregnant also comes to mind. Think of the Good Samaritan, who went out of his way at no small expense to take care of the Jew who was victimized by robbers.

Mercy is charity in the true sense of the word. As such it springs from a good heart, a heart that is aligned with the love of God. It is not social work in its disparaged sense. It involves giving of ourselves out of love. It is a spiritual encounter. It is serving Jesus himself. It is never condescending. It restores dignity to the person who is the recipient of our mercy. It honors him over and above relieving him of physical or spiritual suffering. In the final analysis our salvation is in direct correlation with the quality of the mercy with which we treat the least of our and Jesus' brothers and sisters.

Happy Are the Pure of Heart. They Shall See God.

Jesus introduces a new approach to purity. In the Hebrew Bible purity is achieved by ritual ablution as described in Leviticus, in which elaborate prescriptions are laid out with respect to the cleanliness of beasts, priests, and other men and women. The idea of purity of heart was a frequent point of contention between Jesus and the Pharisees. In Matthew 15:10–20, Jesus explains what he means by this beatitude.

> What goes into the mouth does not make a man unclean; it is what comes out of the mouth that makes him unclean … Can you not see that whatever goes into the mouth and passes through the stomach, is discharged into the sewer? But the things that come out of the mouth come from the heart, and it is these that make a man unclean. For from the heart come evil intentions: murder, adultery, fornication, theft, perjury, slander. These are the things that make a man unclean. But to eat with unwashed hands does not make a man unclean.

Mark 7:14–23 adds to this list of evil intentions malice, deceit, indecency, envy, slander, pride, and folly. In the final analysis purity of heart is revealed primarily in speech, which reveals one's thoughts and desires.

Purity has its genesis in the Word of God (John 15:3) and comes from holiness of life as espoused by Jesus. Paul reminds us that it issues forth as the perfection of charity or "from a good conscience and sincere faith" (1 Timothy 1:5) and from hearts that are free from sinful attachments to other people, creatures, or material things. It speaks to chastity, which is to be morally clean in thought, word, or deed. It goes well beyond sins of the flesh, referring rather to abstaining from anything that is contrary to revealed truth. It means the alignment of our will with that of God. It is not simply the ritual purity of the Hebrew Bible. As Jesus clearly points out, it is interior.

Its reward is being admitted to the presence of God, where we shall see "no longer in a mirror or obscurely, but face to face." St. Leo the Great[5] writes,

> The blessedness of seeing God is justly promised to the pure
> of heart. For the eye that is unclean would not be able to see
> the brightness of the true light, and what would be happiness
> to clear minds would be a torment to those who are defiled.
> Therefore, let the mists of worldly vanities be dispelled, and
> the inner eye be cleansed of all the filth of wickedness, so
> that the soul's gaze may feast serenely upon the great vision
> of God.

The saints are the pure of heart. They see the goodness of God in all things. They are those who have a sincere heart in all their actions. When the fruits of the Holy Spirit flourish through them, they do not seek worldly rewards in return for their charitable acts of goodness. In love, they reach out to others, seeing Christ in all without discrimination.

Happy Are the Peacemakers. They Shall Be Called Sons and Daughters of God.

The saints are those who are peacemakers. They are the called children of God in that they bring worldly comfort to those who suffer. They unite the divided and reunite the alienated. They make life a little easier for all. If there were no peacemakers, all would be suffering greatly in this world.

When the average person thinks of peace, particularly in the aftermath of September 11, 2001, not far from his or her thoughts are concerns about security, arms production, international terrorism, rogue states, jihadist movements, and armed conflict in the Mideast, Africa, and parts of Asia. In truth, from 1900 - 2014 there have been more than 322 documented wars.[6] If we think of peace as the absence of war and violence, we have seldom if ever experienced it. Throughout the 20th century there has not been single day of global peace on earth.

In this context whatever brief moment passes for peace is simply "when everyone stops to reload." It is within this context that the United Nations was founded. Its goal was and is to foster peace throughout the globe. It has proven to be an elusive goal; some have even called it a pipe dream. This is true as long as we define peace in terms of armed conflict instead of the laying down of arms. At this point, let's examine other definitions of peace.

The very word *peace* gives rise to many emotions. *Merriam-Webster* defines it as a "circumstance or physical condition: freedom from war, harmony, agreement" or "a state of mind: calm, tranquility, quietness, contentment, the absence of anxiety." Its antonyms include war, anxiety, disorder, disturbance, disruption, conflict, or commotion.

In Scripture, the word *peace* takes on a different dimension or perspective. It is an idea that permeates the Bible. It is a story of creation and redemption, peace lost and peace restored. In Genesis and throughout the Hebrew Bible we read of man's creation in a state of grace, sanctifying, preternatural, and actual. In the garden there was peace. We read further of his loss of this peace and all but actual grace through his disobedience. Man broke his relationship with God. In the New Testament we read of his redemption, the restoration of sanctifying grace, and the gift or covenant of peace promised in Ezekiel 37:26, which says, "I will make a covenant of friendship with them—it shall be and everlasting covenant with them." We know the Hebrews repeatedly broke and abandoned this covenant. Yet God forgives them by sending his only begotten Son to redeem us. Jesus personifies a new covenant of peace through the shedding of his blood on our behalf.

The Hebrew word for peace is translated as *shalom*, a word usually meaning rest, favor, health, and prosperity. It was a familiar biblical greeting. It denotes well-being, totality, completeness, fulfillment, maturity, soundness, and wholeness. The Greek equivalent of shalom denotes a joining together of what had previously been separated or disturbed. It is frequently used to signify quietness or rest, satisfaction or contentment, living a full life, or freedom from trouble. It could be used to denote everything that makes for a man's highest good. It is the peace that only God provides, the peace of his Spirit.

In this context peace naturally flows from the purity spoken of in the preceding beatitude. James 3:17 writes, "The wisdom that comes down from above is essentially something pure; it is also peaceable, kindly and considerate; it is full of mercy and shows itself by doing good; nor is there any trace of partiality or hypocrisy in it." Peace follows purity and humility. To lay aside one's quarrel with another and accept peace, it is first necessary to come to the realization that bitterness and hatred is counterproductive. In Hebrews 12:14, we read that there is also a connection between peace and holiness. They are inextricably linked with each other. This calls to mind Psalm 85:11, which says, "Justice and well-being kiss peace." Hence, true peace is connected with purity and righteousness.

Before we discuss the idea of a peacemaker, it might be helpful to touch upon the obstacles he or she faces. They include separation, alienation or estrangement, isolation or exclusion, hostility and wrath, and enmity between two or more parties. The peacemaker seeks to bring about some form of reconciliation that brings them to an end and restores peace, access, and fellowship with God, a restoration of the indwelling of the Holy Spirit, joy, peace of mind and soul, and love.

And now what is a peacemaker? The prime example of the peacemaker is Jesus. What he preached is rightfully called the gospel of peace. It is a message about peace between men and between men and God. It is also a gospel of reconciliation. As used by Jesus, the peacemaker is one who reconciles quarrels. The peacemaker engages in the Christian charism of reconciliation. In Matthew 5:23, Jesus admonishes the person who has a quarrel with his brother to "leave your offering there ... before the altar, go and be reconciled with your brother first, and then come back and present your offering."

Another dimension of the role of the peacemaker rests in the difficulty he or she has in bringing it about. "Do not suppose that I am come to bring peace to the earth; it is not peace I have come to bring, but a sword" (Matthew 10:34). This looks to be contrary to Matthew 5:9, but it is not. Jesus is telling us that peace comes at a price. There is going to be strife before there is peace. A conflict has to be resolved. This is where the peacemaker comes in. It requires bringing truth to power and falsehood. And this causes strife. People do not accept or embrace the truth when it goes against their perceived interests. They often are upset at the person who confronts their sinfulness. They must be convinced by the central truth of the gospel and be reconciled to each other and to God. The peacemaker is one who sees clearly that truth and sin cannot coexist. Acknowledgment of one's sins by each party to the conflict and the love of God and he who has been wronged are the conditions under which peace is realized.

I conclude with two powerful examples of peacemaking. The first story[7] recounts a process once practiced by the Native American tribe of Dakota (Sioux) Indians. One of the young men of the tribe had been murdered. His family was enraged and came together to determine how to deal with the killer. As they debated among themselves, one of the tribal elders sat quietly in their midst and listened intently. In time he reflected back to them what he had heard and felt. He realized that they felt insulted and desired revenge. But he spoke to them of a better way.

> That the fire of hate may not burn on in his heart or in ours, we shall take that better way. Go now to your homes. Look over your possessions and bring here the thing you most prize—a horse, say, or weapons, or wearing apparel, or a blanket. Easy ways and empty words may do for others … Let us take the harder way, the better way.
>
> The gifts you bring shall go to the murderer, for a token of our sincerity and our purpose. Though he has hurt us, we shall make him … a relative, in place of the one who is not here. Was the dead your brother? Then, this man shall be your brother. Or your uncle? Or your cousin? As for me, the dead was my nephew. Therefore, his slayer shall be my nephew. And from now on he shall be one of us. We shall regard him as though he were our dead kinsman returned to us.

In time the slayer was brought into the tipi. He was offered the pipe of peace and presented with the gifts. He was ritually accepted as a kinsman. Deeply moved, he began to weep. "You see," explained the narrator of this story, "he had been neatly trapped by loving kinship. And you may be sure that he proved himself an even better kinsman than many who had the right of birth, because the price of his redemption had come so high."

The second story is of a scene from a film of the Truth and Reconciliation Commission in South Africa during the year 2000.[8]

> An elderly black woman faced several white security police officers. One of them was a Mr. Van de Broek. He had just confessed to the brutal murders of the woman's son and her husband several years before. He and his cohorts had made

her witness their murder. Her husband's last words had been, "Father, forgive them."

A member of the Commission turned to the elderly woman and asked her, "What do you want? How should justice be done to this man who has so brutally destroyed your family?"

She replied, "I want three things. I want first to be taken to the place where my husband's body was burned so that I can gather up the dust and give his remains a decent burial."

She paused and continued, "My husband and son were my only family. I want, secondly, therefore, for Mr. Van de Broek to become my son. I would like for him to come twice a month to the ghetto and spend a day with me so that I can pour out to him whatever love I still have remaining with me. And finally, I want a third thing. I would like Mr. Van de Broek to know that I offer him my forgiveness because Jesus Christ died to forgive. This was also the wish of my husband. And so, I would kindly ask someone to come to my side and lead me across the courtroom so that I can take Mr. Van de Broek in my arms, embrace him, and let him know that he is truly forgiven."

As the court assistants came to lead the elderly woman across the room, Mr. Van de Broek, overwhelmed by what he had just heard, fainted. And as he did, those in the courtroom—friends, family, neighbors—all victims of decades of oppression, brutality, and injustice began to sing, softly, but assuredly, "Amazing grace, how sweet the sound that saved a wretch like me."

In both of these stories relationships and forgiveness have been reclaimed. In both stories the work of the peacemaker is evident. Harmony between man and man as well as God and man has been restored. Indeed, happy are the peacemakers. They shall be called sons (and daughters) of God.

Happy Are Those Who Are Persecuted in the Cause of Right. Theirs Is the Kingdom of Heaven.

The saints are those who are persecuted for sake of righteousness. Obligated to speak up against injustice, they are oppressed so that they may be silenced. In some nations some are beaten, and some are imprisoned. Others are even murdered. How often has it been heard that when someone tried to break up an argument between two people for the love of Jesus, the two arguing parties turned against the peacemaker? Or how often has someone been persecuted for speaking up against corporate greed or chicanery or abuse? Did Jesus not warn that those who would do his work would be persecuted because of his name? It is obvious that goodness does not blend in with evil. If one seeks righteousness, he must expect persecution. In the end he will gain the kingdom of God. The saints are those who are slandered and falsely accused of all kinds of evils because they promote the sacred words of Jesus and the eternal kingdom that awaits the righteous.

Persecution is the lot of those who would follow Jesus Christ. The very word persecution or its cognates are found in Scripture more than seventy-five times. *Webster's* defines it as "being pursued, followed after, suffer, to run or chase after with hostile intent, to hurt or to hunt down." It speaks to overt and covert rejection, insult, physical injury, torture, beatings, assault, and even death or martyrdom for the sake of righteousness.

Righteousness simply means living life according to the teachings and example of Jesus (i.e., good deeds, piety, truthfulness, love of neighbor, living a virtuous life, and steadfastness in keeping God's commandments and avoiding immorality and sin in all their manifestations).

St. Leo opines that what is striking about this last beatitude is the promise that persecution's reward in this context is "to be filled with the Lord himself." He adds that this beatitude goes to the heart of the true meaning of the first and great commandment, "You shall love the Lord your God with your whole heart, your whole soul, your whole mind, and your whole strength, for to love God is nothing else than to love righteousness." Be righteous, "so that the Creator may shine forth in his creature, and the image of God be reflected in the mirror of the human heart as it imitates his qualities." [9]

In a homily on this beatitude, St. Gregory of Nyssa[10] writes that "persecution steadfastly borne, whether it be torture, threat of death, deprivation of livelihood, separation from loved ones, or whatever, purifies our souls, turning them to God. Hence the promise that those persecuted for the sake of righteousness will possess the Kingdom of Heaven." Gregory adds,

> But when the living Word … penetrates into a man who has truly received the faith, it cuts through the things that have badly grown together, and disrupts the fetters of habit. Then he will throw off the worldly pleasures bound to his soul, like a runner casts a burden from his shoulders, and will run light and nimble through the fighting ring, since he is guided in his course by the President of the contest Himself. For he looks not to the things he has left behind, but to those that come hereafter, and so he does not turn back his eyes to the pleasures that are past, but he goes forward to the Good that lies before him.

Conclusion

The saint is the salt of the earth, the light of the world, and the one who keeps the commandments yet whose virtue goes beyond them. Not content with the command you must not kill, the saint harbors no anger toward his brother and does not call him a fool or renegade. but seeks his forgiveness. The saint does not commit adultery but refrains from looking at a woman or man with lust. He does not give into revenge but offers his enemy his other cheek and indeed loves him and prays for those who persecute him. He gives alms and prays in secret. He trusts that the Lord will provide for his needs and refrains from judging others, treating others as he would like them to treat him.

While it is a spiritual blessing to be called to be a saint and a child of God, emotionally and psychologically it is a heavy burden to carry in this world. It means to carry the cross that Jesus carried. It means to persevere without looking back. It means to forgive seven times seventy times. It means to keep loving as the heavenly Father loves even when our love is being rejected by those we love. It means not being of this world while living in this world. It means to live as a shining star. It means to reject the evils of this world. It means to place God first in our lives. It means to love everyone without exception as God loves us and we love him.

It means to feed the hungry, dress the naked, and give a home to the homeless. It means to visit the sick and the prisoners. It means to turn away from the abuses of foods, alcohol, drugs and prostitution. It means to turn away from gambling, pornography, adultery, and other immoralities. These are guidelines that teach us how to achieve our own sanctification so we may be pleasing to God.

In this chapter we have seen how the beatitudes provide the means by which we can complete the twelve-step program. When taken together, they provide the steps to maintain, sustain, and grow a spiritual life that is conducive to the right attitude toward the holy season of Lent. Moreover, they provide the means whereby we can truly become who we were meant to be, our true selves. They enable us to get beyond our self-deception and the fake identities we have constructed over a lifetime (i.e., those false or phony ideas we harbor about ourselves and we telegraph to our respective worlds). The Beatitudes help us to come to grip with the true nature of our circumstances and interior lives and to overcome the lies we have internalized and the energy we put forth to promote and maintain them.

We have looked at developing a spiritual life through the lens of the three stages of spiritual growth. Several times we have implied that these stages are not necessarily linear in progression. We will slide back into the preceding stage more than once. Some parts of our lives may be in the illuminative stage, while other parts are still in the purgative stage. We may be blissfully in the unitive stage at the beginning of the day and still find ourselves ensconced in the quagmire of life's vicissitudes in the afternoon, sliding back even to the purgative stage.

Endnotes

1. St. Leo the Great, "Sermon on the Beatitudes, Matthew 5:1–9" sermon 95. In *Nicene and Post-Nicene Fathers—Second Series*, vol. 12, edited by Philip Schaff and Henry Wace; translated by Charles Lett Feltoe (Buffalo, NY: Christian Literature Publishing Co., 1895), revised and edited for New Advent (2009) by Kevin Knight at http://www.newadvent.org/fathers/360395.htm

2. Ibid, "On the Beatitudes, Part V: The Blessedness of the Meek."

3. Ibid,

4. Douglas-Klotz, Neil, *The Hidden Gospel: Decoding the Spiritual Message of the Aramaic Jesus* (Wheaton, IL: Quest Books Theosophical Publishing House, 1999), 49.

5. St. Leo the Great, On the Beatitudes part VIII.

6. En.wikapedia.org/ListofWars#Wars

7 Prevalett, Elaine, *Toward a Spirituality for Global Justice: A Call to Kinship* (Louisville, KY: Sowers Books & Videos, 2005).

8 Francis Reid and Deborah Hoffmann, Filmmakers, Long Night's Journey into Day, South Africa's Search for Truth and Reconciliation (Berkeley. CA: Iris Films, 2000)

9 Leo the Great, Sermon on the Beatitudes

10 St. Gregory of Nyssa, "The Lord's Prayer/The Beatitudes," trans. Hilda C. Graej. In *Ancient Christian Writers: The Works of the Fathers in Translation*, ed. Johannes Quasten, S.T.D., and Joseph C Plumpe, No. 18: (New York, NY: Paulist Press, 1954), p. 171.

CHAPTER 17

THE FIFTH WEEK: LAZARUS

The Death of Lazarus

We have seen how Jesus begins to reveal his divinity in his nighttime encounter with Nicodemus, a member of the Sanhedrin. Here he teaches that "unless a man be baptized [born again of water and the Spirit], he shall not enter the kingdom of heaven." His dialogue with the woman at the well continues his revelation of his divinity. Again the image of water is front and center. Even though he initiated the conversation by asking for a drink of water, Jesus replies in response to the woman's surprise that a Jew would be asking a Samaritan for water, "If you only knew what God is offering and who it is that is saying to you: Give me something to drink, you would have been the one to ask, and he would have given you living water" (John 4:10).

You will recall that she became confused, and noting that Jesus had no bucket and that the well was deep, she asked him how he was going to get this water. Jesus answered, "Whoever drinks this water will be thirsty again; but no one who drinks the water that I shall give will ever be thirsty again; the water that I shall give will become a spring of water within, welling up for eternal life" (John 4:13–14).

And next we are told that Jesus mixed his spittle with mud and made a sort of plaster that he smeared on the blind man's eyes, and then he told the man to go wash his eyes out in the pool of Siloam. And he saw for the first time after that.

In each of the previous situations Jesus uses water as an image with which to manifest his compassion by helping Nicodemus begin to come out of the darkness of the night, the Samaritan woman to see the real reason behind her unhappiness, and the blind man to experience the gift of sight. Through his compassion each person came to see Jesus as divine with life-giving powers. The death of Lazarus provides yet another opportunity to continue these themes. John takes the death of Lazarus to another level by attributing to

Jesus life itself. Here he identifies himself with the resurrection and exclaims that by raising Lazarus from the dead, he, the Son of God, will be glorified.

Lazarus was the brother of Mary and Martha. They lived a few miles outside Jerusalem in a village called Bethany. The sisters had sent word to Jesus that their brother was gravely ill. When Jesus heard of his friend's illness, instead of hurrying to Bethany, Jesus tarried a while—two days to be precise. He told his disciples of Lazarus's sickness, saying, "This sickness will not end in death, but it for God's glory so that through it the Son of God's may be glorified" (John 11:4).

After two days Jesus said to his disciples, "Let us go back to Judea." The disciples were surprised that he would consider going into such hostile territory where the Sanhedrin had made it known that he was a marked man. "But rabbi," they said, "a short while ago the Jews there tried to stone you; are you going back there again?" Jesus knew that his hour had not yet come. He still had time for his appointed work before the darkness arrived. Alluding to his nighttime visit by Nicodemus, he answered, "Are there not twelve hours of daylight? No one who walks in the daytime stumbles, having the light of this world to see by; anyone who walks around at night stumbles, having no light as a guide ... Our friend Lazarus is at rest; I am going to wake him. fallen asleep; but I am going there to wake him up" (John 11:5–11).

Although his disciples thought otherwise, what Jesus really meant was that Lazarus was dead and had been dead for four days. It was now the right time for Jesus to go up to Bethany and be glorified. It was at this point that Thomas said, "Let us also go, to die with him" (John 11:16).

Jesus rejoiced at Lazarus's death. It is an occasion for revealing the presence of God in Jesus. It is also an opportunity to confirm and strengthen the faith of his disciples. Even though he is speaking of impending danger and death, Thomas in effect sums up the common destiny of all Christians, which is to die with Christ and to live with him upon his resurrection. Bonhoeffer says it well when he states that when Christ calls a man, he calls for him to die.

His waiting several days before going to Bethany is similar to other times when Jesus refused to cooperate with family and friends. He is operating on God's time, not man's. His hour and his relationship to God govern his actions, not human timeliness and expectations. In addition by choosing to return voluntarily to Judea in the face of death threats, Jesus showed he chooses death freely. His life would end at the time and place where God wills it. None of his enemies could alter this fact.

By the time Jesus arrived, Lazarus had been in the tomb for four days. The Jews believed that the soul of the dead remains near the body of the deceased for three days but departs on the fourth day, which establishes the finality of a person's death.

Upon his arrival he found many Jews from Jerusalem and other areas in the vicinity of Bethany. They had come to comfort Martha and Mary.

Martha came out to meet Jesus while Mary stays at home.

> "Lord," Martha said to Jesus, "if you had been here, my brother would not have died. But even now I know that God will grant whatever you ask of him." Jesus said to her, "Your brother will rise again." Martha said, "I know he will rise again at the resurrection on the last day." Jesus said, "I am the resurrection. Anyone who believes in me, even though that person dies, will live; and whoever lives and believes in me will never die. Do you believe this?" 'Yes, Lord,' she said, 'I believe that you are the Christ, the Son of God, the one who was to come into this world'" (John 11:21–27).

Martha's words contain both complaint and confidence even in the face of death. She knows that God will listen to Jesus. In effect Jesus is actually saying that physical death is our common lot but that faith in him brings the believer to life again in the resurrection. Physical death can never affect the believer.

In articulating the "I am the resurrection and the life" saying, Jesus announced that the promise of the resurrection is not lodged in some distant event but is available now in him. Jesus shares completely in God's ability to give life. As the resurrection and the life, Jesus defeats the power of death in the future and in the present.

Jesus' words reminded Martha and the readers of the revelatory significance of the miracle that is about to take place. Jesus' prayer directed attention to the real author of the miracle, God. Everything that Jesus says and does has been given to him by God.

Mary, having been called by her sister Martha, came to Jesus, fell at his feet, and said, "Lord, if you had been here, my brother would not have died."

Jesus is "deeply moved in spirit and is troubled." He asks where they have laid Lazarus. "Come and see, Lord," they replied.

Jesus wept.

Then the Jews said, "See how he loved him!"

Johannine scholars have long-debated over what the statement that Jesus wept means. Several have suggested that the Greek should be translated "disturbed in spirit," reflecting thereby the belief that Jesus was angry in addition to feeling sorrow. However, one looks at this passage, it does indicate strong emotion. We can imagine Jesus shuddering, indignation, distress, or hurt. It has been suggested that he was angry because he found himself face-to-face with the manifestations of Satan's realm of evil, the thought of his ultimate betrayal by one of his own, the effects of sin, and the bitter cost and power of death in human lives.

Notwithstanding, Jesus' weeping highlights the biter cost and power of death in human lives and so underscores the significance of Jesus' ultimate victory over death. Martha's protest draws attention to the reality of death that confronts Jesus at the tomb.

The bottom line is we can't really fathom the death of Jesus' emotions. But one thing is certain. He did set out to raise Lazarus from the dead. Martha believes that Jesus is the Messiah and that her brother, Lazarus, will rise on the last day.

> Sighing again, Jesus reached the tomb; it was a cave with a stone to close the opening. Jesus said, "Take the stone away." Martha, the dead man's sister said to him, "Lord, said by now he will smell; this is the fourth day since he died." Jesus replied, "Have I not told you that if you believe, you will see the glory of God?" So they took the stone away. Then Jesus lifted up his eyes and said, "Father, I thank you for hearing my prayer, I myself knew that you her me always, but I speak for the sake of all these who are standing around me, so that they may believe it way you who sent me."
>
> When he had said this, he cried out in a loud voice, "Lazarus, come out!" The dead man came out, his hands and feet bound with strips of material, and a cloth over his face. Jesus said to them, "Unbound him, let him go free" (John 11:38–44).

"I Am the Resurrection and the Life."

Jesus is the resurrection and the life. No one who believes in him will die

It is now time to enter into Lazarus's death, and he does so with voice that a befits his identity as the Word. He called Lazarus in a loud voice. A loud voice symbolizes the presence of God. His voice penetrated into the open cave and reached the ears of the dead. Lazarus comes out of darkness into light.

Death is imaged as an imprisoning reality blocking the hands, nose, eyes, mouth, and ears of people. The feet are also bound so that people cannot walk. Jesus' command is to reverse this condition. God's glory is to free people and let them go. As Moses told Pharaoh centuries earlier, God's command is, "Let my people go!" Now, however, it is spoken to death by the one who calls himself "the resurrection and the life."

The Bible is clear that death is a result of sin. God told the first humans that disobeying his law would result in death (Genesis 2–3). Adam and Eve disobeyed God in the garden of Eden and death entered the world (Romans 5:12). Death and suffering are the result of disobeying God, and we all disobey God.

Every human is born fearing death. We understand intuitively that death means separation. Yes, we try to prevent physical death. But we realize that there is nothing final about death. John 11 is the story of Jesus, the almighty Son of God, encountering death and beating it into submission. We see that the story of Jesus raising Lazarus from death is a sign to us that death itself is vanquished. Jesus has the power to raise dead men and women back to life.

Jesus began by telling Martha that Lazarus will rise again. Martha, being a good Jew, professes faith in the final resurrection from the dead. Jesus stopped her and makes a bold theological claim, "I am the resurrection and the life." Jesus wants us to know that apart from him, not only will Lazarus remain in the grave, but every dead man and woman will stay dead as well. This statement makes more sense when we finish the rest of John's gospel. Jesus, the resurrection, will die. God declared that sin would bring death, and God himself innocently died on behalf of sinners. But he did not remain in the grave. More powerful than death, Jesus bursts into life three days after his burial. Because Jesus paid the death penalty for sin, sinners who trust in him find life. Christians may still fear the threat or mode of death, but the more we encounter Jesus as the resurrection and life, the less we fear death. For the Christian physical death only transitions us into more life.

When Jesus came to the tomb, he did not initially act as someone who has power to reverse death. We see him groaning and weeping. John goes to lengths to show us the depth of Jesus' sorrow over Lazarus. Jesus is not a distant God detached from the suffering of his creatures. Jesus suffers alongside us and even dies with us. As we encounter the suffering Jesus, we become people who enter into the suffering of others. We die alongside them. Within our church membership we have close friends who are dying, and our church walks alongside them. In our neighborhoods we know many who are dying, sick, and suffering. We weep with them, walk alongside of them, serve them, and point them to Jesus.

The raising of Lazarus surely strengthened the faith of those who witnessed the miracle. There were, however, thousands of people who died in Israel while Jesus walked the earth. They begged God for immediate healing that never came. As we read this story, we are tempted to ask, "Why didn't Jesus raise all the dead in the tombs?" The answer to that question is the cross. Remember, the real sickness we suffer from is not physical but spiritual. On the cross Jesus died in our place. We still live in a world affected by sin. We still experience physical sickness and sin, but Jesus has given us life beyond this life, and one day he will deliver us from the very presence of sin. As we pray for miracles, we realize that Jesus' resurrection was the ultimate miracle that bought our life. In the meantime we suffer faithfully for Jesus, pointing people to the cross and begging them to trust what Jesus did for them there. God is most glorified in us when we are most satisfied in him in the midst of suffering and death.

Jesus gives life just as he gave sight. Lazarus's return to life is a sign or gift, for he will die again. (Note that he emerges from the tombs still in his burial clothes.) Jesus, on the other hand, comes to life, leaving his burial clothes behind. Jesus is raised from the dead and will never die again! He has conquered sin and death!

All Jesus' miracles are signs of what he is and what he has come to give man, but in none of them does the sign more closely approach the reality than is the gift of life. The physical life that Jesus gives to Lazarus is still not in the realm of the life from above, but it is so close to that realm that it may be said to conclude the ministry of signs and inaugurate the ministry of glory. Thus, the raising of Lazarus provides an ideal transition to Gethsemane and its aftermath. Moreover, the suggestion that the supreme miracle of giving life to man leads to the death of Jesus offers a dramatic paradox worthy of summing up Jesus' career.

The Plot to Kill Jesus

The die has been cast. By coming back to Bethany, Jesus seals his fate. This miracle not only gives rise to the Sanhedrin's decision that Jesus must die. More significantly Jesus will soon return to the glory of his Father in heaven. It is simply a matter of time. The Sanhedrin and other leading figures among the Jews have decided that the troubling activities of Jesus and his small band must be stopped. They are drawing too much attention to themselves, and this is proving detrimental to the position of the chief priests and Pharisees with respect to their relations with the Roman authorities. They fear that "if [they] let him go on in this way everybody will believe in him, and the Romans will come and suppress the Holy Place and our nation." Caiaphas, the high priest, adds the following prophecy: "You do not seem to have grasped the situation at all; you fail to see that it is to your advantage that one man should die for the nation, rather than that the whole nation should perish" (John 11:48–51).

The high priest is also fearful that that Jesus is putting at risk the privileged status of the chief priests and Pharisees within Judea. The people are beginning to follow him. He is upsetting the status quo. He has to be stopped. And so Jesus becomes a marked man and realizes that his movement among the people is being stymied. From this point on the Jewish authorities set out to put into motion their plans to put Jesus to death. The word is out that he should be arrested upon his coming into Jerusalem for the Jewish Passover.

PART 4

AGONY AND EXULTATION

CHAPTER 18

THE LAST WEEK OF LENT:
A FIVE-ACT PLAY
RENDEZVOUS WITH DEATH

Rejoice Jerusalem, your king is coming to you.
He comes not to invite the self-righteous to a change of heart,
but to rescue those who are immersed in sin.
—Andrew of Crete (AD 660–740)

Hosanna

This chapter commemorates the week of the passion, death, and resurrection of Jesus of Nazareth. Though we are still in the desert this week is the highpoint of the Christian year. It is a week that is observed throughout Christendom with solemn liturgies and services that in Roman Catholicism culminate in what is called the Easter Triduum and in Eastern orthodoxy, the Great Pascha. Other Christian traditions observe this week with daily liturgical services in churches that bring to mind key themes from Jesus' ministry and/or informal gatherings in homes as they celebrate the Christian version of the Passover Seder supper. The overarching theme throughout this week focuses on suffering, humiliation, and death in contrast with resurrection as the promise of newness and life. By enduring the darkness of Good Friday with its shadows and gloom, by coming to grips with the horror and magnitude of evil and sin and its consequences, by experiencing the despair and confusion of the disciples, and by seeing Jesus hanging on the cross, we come to realize the price he paid to restore our relationship with God. It is against this backdrop that we begin to appreciate the significance of Easter Sunday morning. This week provides each of us with the opportunity to examine our own lives and faith journey and experience the transformative power of the liturgy and the gospel.

Palm Sunday/Passion Sunday: What Is Its Significance?

Holy Week begins with Palm Sunday. On this day we remember the triumphal entry of Jesus into Jerusalem astride a donkey. I posit that by entering Jerusalem astride a donkey, Jesus declares his authority. It is a messianic event. In antiquity it was customary for a person of royalty to enter a village or city upon a mule or colt as a sign of peace. Palm Sunday summons us to behold our King, the Word of God made flesh. This event summons us to acknowledge Jesus as the Christ. Yet we cannot understand this event apart from Jesus' passion. Jesus, our King, seated on a dumb beast, strides toward his coming betrayal, trail, conviction, and the horrors of the cross. In a few days he will bear our sorrows and transgressions and make of himself an offering for our sins (Isaiah 53). Our King is on his way to death to accomplish the mission for which he was born. But by this time next Sunday we will see him glorified in his resurrection and shortly thereafter ascend into his kingdom, which is not of this world.

Palm Sunday is about more than Jesus mounted on a donkey. It is also about Jesus, the Christ ever-present among his disciples, in his church, in every Eucharist, prayer, and sacrament, in every act of love, kindness, and mercy. This Jesus comes not only to die for us but also to liberate us from the darkness of sin and the bondage of death. Jesus is he who vanquishes death and gives life, whose mercy is boundless and whose kingdom is a present reality.

Looked at metaphorically, Jesus' kingdom is not one of geography but of spirit. It is internal, inside each one of us. It does not lie in the distant future. We have but to go inside to find it and identify with Jesus Christ. Scripture tells us that the kingdom of God is not only at hand (Matthew 3:2; 4:17) but within us (Luke 17:21). The kingdom is a present reality as well as a future realization (Matthew 6:10). Theophan the Recluse[1] writes,

> The kingdom of God is within us when God reigns in us, when the soul in its depths confesses God as its Master, and is obedient to him in all its powers. Then God acts within it as master "both to will and to do his good pleasure" (Philippians 2:13). This reign begins as soon as we resolve to serve God in our Lord Jesus Christ, by the grace of the Holy Spirit. Then the Christian hands over to God his consciousness and freedom, which comprises the essential

substance of our human life, and God accepts the sacrifice; and in this way the alliance of man with God and God with man is achieved, and the covenant with God, which was severed by the Fall and continues to be severed by our willful sins, is re-established.

This kingdom lodged within the grounds of our very being is the life of the Holy Trinity. It is a kingdom of holiness and goodness. Let us lift up our palm branches, and with the angelic host along with our brothers and sisters, we can cry out with a loud voice, "Blessed be he who orders all things for our good. May he give us peace and joy. Indeed, the glory of the Lord will shine on us."

Shortly before revealing to his followers his decision to go up to Jerusalem, we find Jesus walking somewhere outside Caesarea Philippi, a town in Northern Palestine near Mount Hermon, where it is reputed that he and Satan had long ago met. Satan promised to give him all that could be seen from this mountain "if you will kneel down and adore me ....be my servant." Of course Jesus refused and rebuked Satan.

Jesus asks his followers a rather innocuous question, "Who do men say I am?" Some said that he was John the Baptist back from the dead. Others said that he was Elias or Elijah. Still others said he was Jeremiah. Suddenly the impetuous Simon blurts out, "You are the Christ, the Son of the Living God." In a word Simon is acclaiming Jesus as the Messiah.

One can imagine Jesus stopping and turning to Simon as he says,

> Simon son of Jonah, you are a blessed man! Because it was no human agency that revealed this to you but my Father in heaven. So I now say to you: You are Peter and on this rock I will build my community. And the gates of the underworld can never overpower it. I will give you the keys of the kingdom of heaven: whatever you bind on earth will be bound in heaven; whatever you loose on earth will be loosed in heaven. (Matthew 16:17–19)

Jesus then tells his disciples not to repeat what they had just witnessed. In no way will he be the kind of Messiah the Jews are expecting.

Although the other disciples do not fully comprehend Jesus' words, they know that he is saying something significant. "It was hidden from us," Mark would write years after the event, "and we were afraid to ask him about it all." If this was not confusing enough, imagine their confusion when he tells them that he must go up to Jerusalem and be killed. Simon Peter again blurts out that he should not speak thusly, and Jesus' sternly admonishes him by saying, "Get behind me, Satan! You are an obstacle in my path, because you are thinking not as God thinks but as human beings do" (Matthew 16:22–23). Only moments before this he called Simon a rock and made him the leader of his church. Now he is the recipient of Jesus' ire. This was the same Simon who would later betray Jesus by denying he knew him. This same *rock* would turn into a pebble. Years later he would be martyred and would not flinch in his love or devotion. He would prove himself to be Peter, the rock upon which Jesus' church would be built.

But the story does not end here. The most meaningful drama of history is about to unfold. Jesus is entering his last days on earth as a living human being. With his entry into Jerusalem as the Messiah but not the one the people had been led to believe was coming, Jesus begins his short ministry in the city of David. His moment is upon him. And so the journey to Jerusalem begins. But before recounting his entry into the city, let's pause and ask, "Why Jerusalem?"

Jerusalem was the Holy City. It was where the temple was. It was the center of Jewish life. However, it was a city under the thumb of Rome and controlled in its name by a cabal of priests, scribes, and Pharisees. It was a city that epitomized the dominance of imperial Rome and its vassals who, according to one writer, made Jewish culture, tradition, and Law so oppressive that ordinary people had little room for maneuver.

Jesus challenged this prevailing and oppressive order by denying that it represented God's will. He contended that this order prevented people from seeing the real meaning of life, our relationship to God, and our bond to one another. God never gave the dominant group the prerogative to interpret what is right and what is wrong, what is good and what is evil. Nor did he intend for his people to be beholden to arcane restrictions and laws governing every facet of life. In addition he characterized the scribes and Pharisees as hypocrites and "whitened sepulchers." No wonder the priests and others were out to get him.

So why did Jesus go to Jerusalem? The answer in a word was *to die*. In Luke 13:33, he said, "It would not be right for a prophet to die outside Jerusalem." And so Jesus goes to Jerusalem. His time draws closer. The curtain rises and the greatest of tragedies begins.

ACT 1

THE JOURNEY TO JERUSALEM

Rejoice greatly, fair Zion;
Raise a shout, Fair Jerusalem!
Lo, your kind is coming to you
He is victorious, triumphant,
Yet humble, riding on an ass,
On a donkey foaled by a she-ass.

—Zechariah 9:9

When they were approaching Jerusalem at Bethpage and Bethany, which was close by the Mount of Olives, he sent two of his disciples ahead and said to them,

> Go to the village facing you, and as you enter it you will at once find a tethered colt that no one has yet ridden. Untie it and bring it here. If anyone says to you, "What are you doing?" say, "The Master needs it and will send it back here at once." They went off and found a colt tethered near a door in the open street. As they untied, some men standing there said, "What are you doing, untying that colt?" They gave the answer Jesus had told them and the men let them go. (Mark 11:1–6)

It appears that Jesus had made preparations for his entry into Jerusalem by securing a colt. He leaves nothing to chance. He virtually stages his entry. What is generally not known is that the timing coincided with the entry into Jerusalem on the west side of the city by Pilate and his imperial forces to preserve the peace and to keep down any possible insurrections. Coming from Bethany, Jesus enters from the direction of the Mount of Olives, which is on the east side of the city. The contrast is apparent—Jesus as the man of peace and the suffering servant compared to Pilate, the man of war the conquering general. Jesus is on a simple colt, and Pilate is astride a stallion. Jesus has the people, and Pilate is followed by his legion of soldiers.

This scenario is also not what the religious leaders of the times had expected. They expected the Messiah to come at the head of an army as a majestic conqueror. The people are taken aback. Puzzled, they nonetheless see that this Jesus is of God, though a different Messiah. One reason for their puzzlement was the popular belief that the coming of the Anointed One was traditionally associated with the region around the Mount of Olives. It was the hill of oil and of anointing.[2]

> Then they took the colt to Jesus and threw their cloaks on its back, and he mounted it. Many people spread their cloaks on the road, and others greenery which they had cut in the fields. And those who went in front and those who followed were all shouting, "Hosanna! Blessed is he who is coming in the name of the Lord! Blessed is the coming kingdom of David our father! Hosanna in the highest heavens!" And Jesus entered Jerusalem and went into the temple; and when he had surveyed it all, as it was late by now, he went out to Bethany with the twelve. (Mark 11:7–11)

Recorded in all four of the Gospels, this occasion was marked by crowds of Jews who were in Jerusalem to celebrate the Passover. They had heard of Jesus' teachings and miracles, particularly the raising of Lazarus from the dead. Brandishing palm branches, they proclaimed him as the Messiah and King. These were many of the same people who in five days would cry out for his crucifixion. Within these five days he will be betrayed, tortured, and die on the cross.

What a scene this must have been. Having been less than successful in spreading his teachings in Galilee, here comes Jesus astride a young colt. The crowds are wild with enthusiasm. Using their clothes as saddles and waving palm branches, they cry out, "Hosanna! Blessed is he who comes in the name of the Lord." But do they really understand to whom they are lavishing this praise? Why does Jesus, who usually shunned such public settings, here go out of his way to invite public praise and adulation? Why does he allow the people to identify him as the Messiah? It could not have been for his sake. He doesn't need for anyone to stroke his self-esteem.

Could it be because the people then and we now need to praise him? Could it have been a sign of the imminent coming of the kingdom of God and his judgment of Israel? Or does the words of Peter, "You are the Christ, the Son of the Living God," echo through the people's *hosanna*? We will soon find our answers after his death on the cross and the observation of the Roman centurion that he is truly the Son of God. At that time the meaning of Jesus' messianic mission will begin to become clear. After Easter it will become manifest for all times. But first, on to the temple.

ACT 2

MY FATHER'S HOUSE IS A ROBBERS' DEN

Destroy this Temple and in three days I will raise it up."
—John 2:19–20

Most of us know of Jesus putting together a makeshift whip and driving out traders and oxen and sheep and other animals together with merchants and money changers from the temple while crying out that they were making of his Father's house a marketplace. In Mark 11:15–18, we read,

> So they reached Jerusalem and he went into the Temple and began driving out the men selling and buying there; he upset the tables of the money changers and the seats of the dove sellers. Nor would he allow anyone to carry anything through the Temple. And he taught them and said "Does not scripture say: My house will be called a house of prayer for all peoples? But you have turned into a bandits' den."

Long before this event the psalmist in Psalm 69:10 exclaimed, "My zeal for Your house has been my undoing." That zeal Jesus displays in full measure. He is indignant. The temple was intended to be the center of Jewish worship and praise of God. What Jesus finds is a marketplace where animals were sold and bought ostensibly for sacrificial offerings to line the pockets of money changers and religious leaders.

So what is Jesus talking about when he says, "Destroy this Temple and in three days I will raise it up"? Most commentators tend to believe that he is aware of the vested interests that are one in their desire to do away with him, yet he is also aware of the moral turpitude prevalent in God's house. By the same token he is also talking about his pending crucifixion and resurrection. I think there is more.

I contend that Jesus was not only speaking of his body that would die on the cross and in three days rise from the grave. He was also talking about building a new temple, the temple that would become his church, a union of all Christians into a spiritual body with Jesus as its head and a community of persons, you and me, as its members. He was not talking about a building of stone and mortar, but of people, flesh and blood. He was talking about what the Roman Catholic tradition expresses as "the Mystical Body of Jesus." In this context the word "Body" derives its meaning from the analogy used by St. Paul in 1 Corinthians 12:27, "now Christ's body is yourself, each of you with a part to play in the whole," and in Colossians 1:18 when he speaks of Christ as "the Head of His Body, that is the Church." In this new temple the Holy Spirit of God dwells.

No wonder Jesus was so zealous. No wonder he was so upset about Jerusalem's temple of brick and mortar, the forerunner of his living temple being turned into a marketplace catering to the inordinate passions and lusts of humankind. No wonder he was disappointed that his contemporaries were lacking in respect for the old temple as the dwelling of God on earth and the place where he would come into contact with his chosen people through prayer and sacrifice. No wonder he is disappointed today when we enter his new temple, the church, of which he is the cornerstone, without a sense of reverence or respect for his presence, forgetting why we have come together in community and to whom we are praying. No wonder Jesus is disappointed when you or I, the people of God, abuse the temples that are our bodies with prurient and sinful pleasures and passions.

And so I ask, "Have we turned his church into a marketplace where we go to make a deal with God, promising to change our lives if only he would give us something? Or have we polluted God's houses of prayer and our bodies with sinful and unholy trafficking in the name of God and religion?" With the coming of the paschal feast, to what extent does the cleansing of our temples need to be undertaken so that we can celebrate without "the yeast of malice and evil" but "with sincerity and truth?" (1 Corinthians 5:8; John 4:24).

ACT 3

BETRAYAL

Judas Iscariot, one of the Twelve
approached the chief priests
with an offer to hand Jesus over to them.
They were delighted to hear it,
and promised to give him money;
and he began to look for a way of betraying him
when the opportunity should occur.

—Mark 14: 10–11

In truth I tell you,
one of you is about to betray me,
one of you eating with me. They
were distressed and said to him,
one after another, 'not me, surely?'
he said to them, 'It is one of the Twelve,
one who is dipping into the same dish with me.
Yes the Son of man is going to his fate,
as the scriptures say he will,
but alas for that man by whom the Son of man is betrayed!
Better for that man if he had never been born.

-Mark 14:18-21

His name was Judas, Judas Iscariot. He was one of the Twelve. Unlike most of Jesus' small band of followers, he was not from Galilee but rather from Judea, where the name Judas was very common. His surname, Iscariot, however, is something of a mystery. One theory is that he was from a town in Judea called Iscariot. Another theory is that his surname is a corruption of the Latin *sicarius*, which means murderer or assassin. Accordingly several historians posit that he belonged to the Sicarii (also known as "dagger-wielders), an anti-Roman terrorist Jewish group active throughout Palestine. Others associate him with the zealots, another fanatical group that had included another apostle, Simon. In reality little is known of him, although he is mentioned many times in the New Testament. Seldom is his name mentioned without the appellation *traitor*. All we really know are the basic contours of the

251

betrayal of Jesus by one of his own. The rest is simply conjecture or the stuff of novels and film. There are many questions that have yet to be answered.

Here is what the evangelists have told us, though not without several points of inconsistency from one evangelist to the other. Jesus chose him to one of the twelve apostles. Like his brothers Judas was a practicing Jew. We assume that Jesus was a shrewd judge of character and must have seen some redeeming qualities in Judas. Likewise, Judas must have seen in Jesus someone worthy of following and initially accepted the sacrifices required to be his follower. As keeper of the purse, he handled the accounts of the group, which speaks to the level of trust Jesus placed in him. It also indicates that he possessed a measure of education and was literate. He more than likely shared in their ministry. That's it—aside from the fact that he betrayed Jesus.

We do not know what prompted him to approach the religious authorities and agree to betray Jesus for thirty pieces of silver, roughly the equivalent of four months wages for a day's labor in that period. Apparently this agreement was entered into prior to the Passover meal. It is during this meal that Jesus announces to his disciples that one of them will betray him. After he blesses and breaks the bread, Jesus whispers to Judas to go do what he has to do. The others at table seem to have no idea why Judas is leaving, where he is going, or what he is about to do.

After the meal Jesus and the remaining disciples go out to the garden, where he leaves them behind while he goes a bit farther into the garden to pray. In time Judas arrives with a group of armed men. He kisses Jesus as a sign that this is the man for whom they have come. Jesus is taken from the garden to the chief priests.

After the trial by the priests Jesus is taken to Pontius Pilate, scourged, and crucified. Mortified by what he had set in motion, Judas repents, but he is so upset that he goes out and hangs himself but not before he confesses to the priests that he has betrayed an innocent man and throws the thirty pieces of silver on the ground at their feet. The priests recognize that this is blood money and they cannot simply put it back into their treasury. So they purchase a plot of ground to bury paupers and the like.

This in effect is all we know. Questions abound. Why did Judas set out to betray Jesus? Why did he hang himself? What was his mental condition? Given today's development of medical and psychiatric knowledge of mental disorders, the customary condemnation of Judas's suicide no longer seems appropriate. Answers are in short supply. We do know from the Scriptures that he was remorseful, and we also know that God's love is boundless. These facts alone should produce some measure of doubt as to history's blanket consignment of Judas to hell. There are those who contend that the betrayal had been foretold by the Old Testament prophets Jeremiah and Zachariah. The early first century Egyptian Christian philosopher and theologian Origen of Alexandria (circa 185-254 CE), called Judas's betrayal a great mystery, a mystery of tragic proportions, yet one for which we can only feel the most profound gratitude. He suggested that Judas' betrayal, though an exercise of his free will, is not beyond forgiveness. Despite the gravity of his act, Judas still has some hope of forgiveness. There still remained a remnant of good in him. It is clear that he did repent of his act.[3] For this view of Judas, Origen was posthumously condemned as a heretic, despite the fact that he suffered a martyr's death on behalf of the faith. But I am getting ahead of myself. We have not yet been to supper. Much of what I have spoken of here took place after the Last Supper.

ACT 4

A CALL TO HOLINESS

I am the bread of life.
Your fathers ate manna in the desert and they are dead;
but this is the bread which comes down from heaven
so that a person may eat it and not die.
I am the living bread which has come down from heaven.
Anyone who eats this bread will live for ever;
and the bread that I shall give is my flesh, for the life of the world.

—John 6:48–51

God wills us to be holy, to share in his life. By baptism he gives us the germ of his life. By the Eucharist, the great prayer of the community, he gives us himself.

God is love. He loves each one of us greatly. "Before I formed you in the womb, I knew you," (Jeremiah 1:5) God tells the reluctant prophet. God created the world and all it contains. He intentionally sustains all of creation in existence. You and I exist because God literally loved and willed us into being. The dignity of every human being derives from the fact that life finds its origin in God and that each person is destined to live forever with him. Human life is thus eternal. We are immortal. And our lives are lived well to the degree that they prepare us for eternity. We are made for eternity. Each of us are made in God's image to grow by grace in his likeness. We are made to be holy.

By baptism he gives us the seed of his life, by which we become his adopted sons and daughters, sharing in his divinity. By the Eucharist he gives us his Son, by which this divinity is nourished. By confirmation he gives us his Holy Spirit, who strengthens and increases within us a more perfect adhesion or union with the Trinity.

Such is, as Abbot Marmion[4] tells us, God's plan in its general outline. Marmion urges us to enter more and more deeply by the light of faith into the design of God by conforming our lives to the teachings of Jesus. He tells us that we shall only be pleasing to the eternal Father if he recognizes in us the features of his Son. Only then will he be well pleased with us, as he was when his Son walked in our midst. Marmion writes,

God is a Father. Long before the created light rose upon the cosmos, God begets a Son to whom He communicates

254

His nature, His perfections, His blessedness, His life, His very being … In God then is life, life communicated by the Father and received by the Son. He has, with the Father, one and the same individual divine nature; and both, although distinct from one another in person-hood, are united in a powerful, substantial embrace of love, whence proceeds that third person, the Holy Spirit.

Marmion suggests that this becomes a reality only by cooperating with the Holy Spirit and the graces he showers us with. We also need a faith strengthened by love accompanied by prayer and by the sacraments. Above all we are strengthened by the sacrament of the Eucharist, the very sacrament of union that nourishes and maintains the divine life in us. "Whoever eats my flesh and drinks my blood lives in me and I live in that person" (John 6:56).

This is the secret of the inmost life of God, of whom St. Paul (Ephesians 1:4–7) writes,

Thus he chose us in Christ before the world was made to be holy and faultless before him in love, marking us out for himself beforehand to be adopted sons, through Jesus Christ. Such was his purpose and good pleasure, to the praise of the glory of his grace, his free gift to us in the Beloved, in whom, through his blood, we gain our freedom, the forgiveness of our sins.

Hence, holiness is receiving from Christ as a share in his divinity. It is a mystery in which we are made also fully divine (even though we are fully human). But how is this holiness to be realized by you and me?

It is to be realized in prayer, through which we become like Jesus, pleasing to the Father. Through prayer we take on the features of his Son. We become identified with him. Strengthen by faith and by the sacraments—above all by the sacrament of the Eucharist—we become united with the Father, and his life is nourished and maintained in us.

The Eucharist is more than a community meal of bread and wine. It is the reception of the very body and blood, which is understood within "the context of the redemptive activity whereby he [Jesus] gives himself … to his own."[5] It is a representation of the Hebrew Paschal feast, at which is recounted the meal the ancient Hebrews partook of on the night before they set out on the exodus from the land of Egypt. For those of us gathered around the altar, a reincarnation of the Paschal table, the Eucharist involves a representation of Jesus' redemptive work, the fulfillment of the old covenant, and the inauguration of the new covenant. Through his ministry Jesus invites his people to the table, where he gives himself sacramentally in body and blood in a Paschal sacrifice that is consummated upon his physical death on the cross. He thus gives to us, his church, the special gift of himself, his body and blood, in the form of bread and wine. In uniting ourselves with him we are transformed into his likeness. We become holy. We become divine.

Jesus offered the people true bread, the bread of God, which comes down from heaven and gives life to the world. They responded enthusiastically, "Sir … give us that bread always." Jesus' reply was unexpected and challenging. "I am the bread of life. No one who comes to me will ever hunger; no one who believes in me will ever thirst" (John 6:34–35).

In uttering these words, those who heard him thought he was preaching cannibalism, and finding this a hard and disgusting idea, they walked away. Yet his disciples remained. When Jesus asked why they stayed, they replied, "Where should we go?" He had the words of eternal life. Later as they were celebrating the Passover with Jesus, he returns to these words. We read in Matthew 26:26–28,

> Now as they were eating, Jesus took bread, and when he had said the blessing he broke it, and gave it to the disciples. "Take it and eat," he said, "this is my body." Then he took a cup, and when he had given thanks, he handed it to them saying "Drink from this, all of you, for this is my blood, the blood of the covenant, poured out for many for the forgiveness of sins."

There is a lot here. Notice first that Jesus very plainly says, "Take (eat) this bread; drink this wine." He did not say, "This is a symbol of my body. This is a symbol of my blood." He very plainly said, "This is my body. This is my blood." What it all comes down to is that under the species of bread and wine Jesus extends to us a new covenant, his body and blood, both of which shall be shed for you and me. Jesus becomes the sacrificial victim.

Jesus, as living bread, is the Word sent by the Father.

This is the same Word that was in the beginning and the same that came into the world and became flesh (John 1:1–14) so that man might have eternal life. Just as the bread given by the angel to Elijah was able to sustain him in his journey to Horeb (1 Kings 19:8), so the Word made flesh, when eaten, can sustain each of us on our journey to eternal life. When in Eucharist we eat the Word become flesh and blood under the species of bread and wine, we become one with Jesus. What was once an ordinary piece of bread and an ordinary cup of wine in Eucharist becomes the very body, blood, soul, and divinity of Jesus. Catholics refer to this process as transubstantiation. This bread and wine is changed into Jesus, the Word of God. At the Last Supper and on the cross, Jesus offers himself as both priest and sacrificial victim for the remission of our sins. Today bread and wine is changed into the body and blood of Jesus by an ordained priest at the moment of the consecration, the most sacred point in the Mass.

Jesus goes to considerable lengths in explaining the Eucharist. He recalls that the manna in the desert and the multiplication of loaves only fed the hungry. There was no promise of eternal life. His body and blood, however, was real food and did promise eternal life. "Unless you eat the flesh of the Son of Man and drink his blood you have no life in you ... he who eats my flesh and drinks my blood abides in me and I in him" (John 6:53–56). The Jews who heard this understood what he was saying. They heard it not as a symbolic statement but a literal one. To "eat someone's flesh" and to "drink someone's blood" were hard sayings in those days, as seen in Isaiah 9:20, Jeremiah 46:10, and Deuteronomy 32:42. This seemed to them to be in conflict not only with ordinary human sentiment but also with their laws prohibiting the consumption of the blood even of animals (see Genesis 9:4, Leviticus 17:10–14, Acts 15:19–21).

But there is more. An important phrase in this pericope is the expression "I Am." This is the name of God spoken to Moses in Exodus 3–14. Jesus uses the name of God to say, "I am the bread of life." Later in John 14:6–7, we hear Jesus repeating the same expression. "I am the Way; I am the Truth and life. No one can come to the Father except through me. If you know me, you will know my father too. From this moment you know him and have seen me."

Jesus is God, eternally existent, the Creator, the Alpha and the Omega, unchanging, the same yesterday, today, and tomorrow. The people of Israel hearing the name of God presented them with a defining moment. Even though he had established a covenant with Abraham, Isaac, and Jacob, this was the first time he had made his name known to them. And now Jesus, the incarnate one, goes further. He gives himself to us under the species of bread and wine. He tells us that he is truly the bread of God, which has come down from heaven to give life to the world. When we eat his flesh and drink his blood, the reality is that we are in effect eating God. We are eating divine food. God, the great I Am, is giving himself to us so that we might become who we really are and we might know him on this plain and the time when we enter glory.

The Eucharist becomes the prayer of the community of God's sons and daughters. "He who eats my flesh and drinks my blood lives in me and I in him." (John 6:56) To many these words are hard and confusing, but we must eat and drink if we are to know eternal life and if we are to share in Jesus' divinity.

The Eucharist cannot be explained without reference to the cross and Calvary. The Last Supper looked not to the end. It looked forward into the future. It is complete only in that it culminates in the bloody sacrifice of the cross, by which Christ gained for us, you and me, redemption and grace. This very sacrifice is reproduced on the altar at the sacrifice of the Mass. It is a reenactment of the night before he died when he took bread and wine in his hands, gazed upon he Father, and declared them his flesh and blood as he says, "Take and eat. Take and drink."[6] But there is more. This bread and wine, which is mingled with water, also represents you and me. We, too, are changed into the body and blood of our Lord. We become transformed into Christ as sons and daughters of the Father.

Bread is not just ordinary human food. It is for countless thousands food in a preeminent way. The human destination, the need of our bodies, gives to bread itself a peculiar dimension. We recognize something of ourselves in it. In the book of creation, we read, "With the sweat of your brow, shall you eat your bread." The farmer must till the soil and sow the seed. He must reap and gather his wheat into the barn. The wheat must be threshed and the chaff separated. The grains have to be crushed and pulverized and kneaded and cooked in the fire of the oven. Only then do we have bread to nourish our bodies. Only after we have sweated can we eat.

What is said about bread is equally true of wine. The culture of the vineyard requires special care. Vines must be planted in fertile soil that has been cultivated and cleared of stones. When the grapes are ripe, they must be harvested and placed in a press where they are trodden, and the resultant juices are placed in casks to ferment until they become wine suitable for drinking.

Bread is thus the symbol of Christ, the true bread, insofar as it feeds and sustains human life. What earthly bread achieves only imperfectly, Christ accomplishes in a perfect way when he surrenders himself to death on our behalf. On the altar he dies, according to his own Word, as the grain sown in the earth, in order to rise from death as the life-giving Lord.

The vine is the classical symbol of the people of Israel. It is a symbol of God's care and choice and a symbol of gratitude and fidelity. Christ is the true vine. "I am the vine, you are the branches. Whoever remains in me, with me in him, bears fruit aplenty." (John 15:5) Only in him is life and fruitfulness possible. The wine of the vine, which rejoices the heart of man, becomes the sign of redemption, forgiveness of sins, the community of God and man, and the new and eternal covenant in Jesus' blood.

At the moment the celebrant extends his hands over the offering as the high priest did of old over the victim about to be slain, he recalls all the gestures and words of Jesus at the Last Supper. Raising high the bread, he intones, "This is my body." Doing likewise with the cup of wine, he intones, "This is my blood." At these words Catholic Christians together with other historical Christian churches (e.g., Eastern orthodox and Byzantine Christians, Lutherans, Anglicans, some Episcopalians, and others) believe that the bread becomes the body of Jesus Christ and the wine becomes his blood. By his express will and his formal institution, Jesus renders himself present—really and substantially with his divinity and humanity—under the species of bread and wine. On the altar he mystically separates his flesh and blood, which upon the cross were physically separated, a separation that bought death. The same Jesus who was slain upon the tree is slain upon the altar, although in a different manner, and this slaying, this immolation, which is accompanied by the offering, constitutes a true sacrifice.

Receiving this bread and wine in Communion ends and completes the sacrifice. The mysteries of redemption and sanctification enter into our lives. In uniting ourselves so intimately with the victim, Jesus himself, we are transformed into his likeness. We become holy, and we become divine. We become sharers of Jesus' thoughts and his sentiments. Jesus communicates his virtues to us and enkindles in us the fire that he came to cast upon earth, the fire of love and charity, which unites us in him.

Through Jesus' supreme act of reconciliation we are made members of his body and members of one another. We become holy.

Conclusion

Before concluding this segment, it should be mentioned that both Roman and Orthodox Catholics and many other Christian religions see nothing in Scripture that would contradict these teachings and that the reality beneath the visible signs in the Eucharist is the body and blood of Christ. Despite the assertions of many Protestant traditions that the Bible implies that the bread and wine are not in reality changed into Jesus' body, from the earliest of times both Roman Catholics and Orthodox Christians—and others such as some Anglicans—continue to believe to the contrary.

In the arguments between Roman Catholicism and Protestantism in the sixteenth century, the Council of Trent[7] declared subject to the ecclesiastical penalty of anathema anyone who

> "denieth, that, in the sacrament of the most holy Eucharist, are contained truly, really, and substantially, the body and blood together with the soul and divinity of our Lord Jesus Christ, and consequently the whole Christ; but saith that He is only therein as in a sign, or in figure, or virtue" and anyone who "saith, that, in the sacred and holy sacrament of the Eucharist, the substance of the bread and wine remains conjointly with the body and blood of our Lord Jesus Christ, and denieth that wonderful and singular conversion of the whole substance of the bread into the Body, and of the whole substance of the wine into the Blood—the species only of the bread and wine remaining—which conversion indeed the Catholic Church most aptly calls Transubstantiation." (Canons 1526–1527)

Interestingly many Protestants now celebrate the Eucharist with greater frequency and no longer consider such a practice as *purely Roman*. Some denominations even consider Christ to be present in the Eucharistic elements, though, with very few exceptions, none totally subscribe to the concept of transubstantiation.

Finally in the words of Benedict XVI[8],

> In the Eucharist, we ourselves learn Christ's love. It was thanks to this center and heart, thanks to the Eucharist, that the saints lived, bringing to the world God's love in ever new ways and forms. Thanks to the Eucharist, the Church is reborn ever anew! The Church is none other than the network—the Eucharistic community—within which all of us, receiving the same Lord, become one body and embrace the word.

Through Jesus the Christ's supreme act of reconciliation, we are made members of his body and members of one another. We are purified of our sins. We are strengthened against Satan's onslaughts. And a deep and holy joy permeates our being and strengthens our union with the Godhead.

In recognizing the presence of the body and blood, the soul and divinity of our Lord Jesus Christ in the Eucharist under the species of bread and wine, our eyes and hearts become attuned to see the image and likeness of God in the unborn child, the frail elderly, the chronically and terminally ill, the rich and impoverished and downtrodden, the homeless, the orphaned and the addicts, the distressed and the confused, the bereaved and the disconsolate, Protestant, Catholic, Jew, Muslim, Hindu, and Buddhist, atheist and agnostic, those of different colors and ethnicities, for all are God's children. We are all made in his image and likeness.

ACT 5

THE REDEMPTION, JESUS DIES FOR OUR SINS

They then took charge of Jesus,
and carrying his own cross he went out to the Place of the
skull or,
as it is called in Hebrew, Golgotha,
where they crucified him with two others, one on either side,
Jesus being in the middle.

—John 19:16–18

In the wee hours of the morning in the garden to which he had come to pray, after a common meal celebrating the Passover, they come for him. Kissed by a disciple—Judas—he is singled out to the temple authorities, who arrest him. Alarmed, one of his companions draws a sword, cutting off the ear of the high priest's servant. Jesus heals the man. A youth flees the scene, leaving behind the sheet that covers his nakedness. His other companions scatter we know not where. Only two of them are bold enough to follow where they are taking him. Before long one of them will deny he knows him.

We know the story only too well. But why is Jesus arrested? Of what is he charged? Why is he so feared by the authorities? Why was he crucified? There is some evidence that the initial cause was his sensational entry into Jerusalem during the high holy days of Passover, that occasion wherein the Jews celebrated the liberation of their ancestors from bondage in Egypt. Jerusalem was the political and religious capital of Israel. Passover was the most important annual festival of the Jews. During these days Jewish pilgrims came to the city from all over the world. The crowds were such that the Roman prefect, Pontius Pilate, felt compelled to come into the city with military reinforcements to maintain security. It was a time of heightened tensions, what with the presence of zealots and others intent on casting off the yoke of Rome and the tyranny of Herod Antipas, the puppet king.

But scholars tell us that there were more deep-seated reasons. From the vantage point of the authorities, Jesus was a threat to the existing order, where Israel was a vassal state of Rome and where the bulk of the national wealth was in the hands of a few—the Romans, the king, and the priests. Only a pittance was available to the general populace.

262

Now here comes this itinerant preacher who acts as if he is the long-awaited Messiah and raises questions about such things as marriage, family, nation, relations with authority, and dealing with other individuals and groups. His ideas conflict with what was commonly accepted about the system, social norms and the law, religious customs and practices, attitudes toward the poor and the outcast, tax collectors and prostitutes, the temple and its priests and other clerics. Here comes Jesus with claims of authority that dismay his critics, enrage the religious authorities, and challenge the system. Moreover, he prophecies that Jerusalem and the temple will be destroyed. This man must be unmasked now. He must be shown to be a heretic or a false prophet, an enemy of the Jewish and Roman law and of the temple.

And so the authorities attribute his miracles to demonic power. They claim that his teachings make a mockery of the Sabbath. His teachings are heretical in that he regards the law and the social order as irrelevant. He seduces the people by challenging the whole social system and encouraging rebellion. He has to be taken seriously. He confuses and upsets the people, who are ignorant of religion or politics with his challenges to the ruling class. In his behavior among all sorts of people, particularly the irreligious and morally unstable, he degrades God and his law and encroaches upon God's prerogatives by personally assuring and guaranteeing forgiveness of sins. Furthermore, unless he is silenced, the Romans will take matters into their hands, thinking that a rebellion is eminent. Untold numbers will suffer. He must be done away with before the people rise up.

From Jesus' perspective, if he wanted to announce his message to all of Israel, he had to do it in David's city, the Holy City, the religious center of the nation. Jerusalem is where he had to announce God's kingdom and will. Contrary to his disciple's expectation, Jesus was about to meet his destiny. It seems obvious that he was aware of the consequences of his sensational entry into the city. Surely he realized he might lose his life, perhaps violently. Surely he was aware of all the scriptural references to the fate of those who preceded him (Isaiah, Jeremiah, Amos, Micah, Zechariah, and others).

Another way of looking at this matter from Jesus' perspective is that his death was something greater than an historical necessity. Nothing less than paying the ultimate price of laying down his life was called for. Jesus knew that the cross would exemplify his life and was the penalty he had to pay for challenging the social system of his day, but more importantly it was also the key to understanding his messianic vocation. Jesus knew that it was only through his suffering and death, going through the darkest and longest night, that there would be the dawn of a new day. In his death he would redeem sinners and build a new kingdom, one that accords with God's will. He knew that in the final analysis his death on the cross would trump evil.

Compassion unto the End

> Jesus, remember me when you come into your kingdom …
> In truth I tell you today you will be with me in paradise.
> —Luke 15:42–43

There are two others with him on Golgotha, one on his left, the other on his right. We are told that they were common thieves. One of them began to taunt and vilify Jesus. "If you are who you say you are, come down off your cross and save us also." (Luke 23:39) The other upbraids his fellow miscreant, reminding him that they had indeed committed criminal acts and deserved their punishment, while Jesus had done nothing to deserve crucifixion. He then turns and asks Jesus to "remember me when you come into your kingdom." And Jesus responds, "This day you will be with me in Paradise."

Imagine that you or I are that criminal. Indeed we actually are not unlike him. How often have we forgotten who we are? How often have we made several regrettable turns in our sojourn on this earth? How often have we made the wrong decision by choosing our way rather than God's way? How often has it been all about me? We really don't know the specifics of the good thief's criminal past. Nor is it important that we do. Suffice it to say that he, like us, was probably guilty of more than a few sinful acts. But now that is all behind him. Simply by refusing to berate Jesus or blame anyone else for his misdeed but rather asking that Jesus remember him when he "comes into his kingdom," the Good Thief's future beyond death is assured. "This day you shall be with me in Paradise."

We have no way of knowing if he believed Jesus to really be the Messiah. Perhaps he thought Jesus was a king of some sort or simply a holy man. But I think the thief thought him to be not so much king or holy man but the Messiah that Scripture had promised. Maybe he did not know what he was asking. Perhaps he simply meant, as one writer puts it,[9]

> Remember me—not for who I have been all my life, nor for
> what I have done to bring me here but for who I have been

in this hour, the only one who defended you. Remember me as the person I forgot I was, a child of God, one who was created good for love's sake. Remember me as one of your disciples, who did not follow you long but was faithful at the end. Forget everything else about me but this, my final testimony.

Obviously at his core he was a good man, though a failure in many ways, not unlike you or me. Here on his cross he was a dying and desperate man. Death was imminent. Yet his basic decency compelled him to attest to the innocence of Jesus. And hence, Jesus promised that this very day he would be with him in paradise. Finally when it mattered the most, the good thief receives something that no one else, before or since, has ever received, the surety of eternal life in paradise.

The Burial and Anointing of Jesus

In light of the fact that this is a post-Easter accounting, it is obvious it was written with the fact of the empty tomb in mind. Notwithstanding, scholars agree that this does not seem to be a fabrication in which Joseph Arimathaea, a member of the Sanhedrin and a pious Jew ("one who looked for the true reign of God") gave Jesus a hasty burial without any assistance by any of his own disciples either out of sympathy or respect for the prescription of Deuteronomy 21:22–23, which enjoined the burial of a *criminal* immediately after his death. Whatever the reason, haste was of the utmost importance. Considering that Jesus died at or about 3:00 p.m., there was only three hours till the conclusion of the day of preparation before the Passover (the first day of unleavened bread) and the beginning of the Sabbath, which coincided in the year of Jesus' death. Joseph could not wait. Time was of the essence. One other item is of importance here. Mark (Mark 15:40) tells us that three women, Mary of Magdala, Mary the mother of James the younger and Joset, and Salome, witnessed the burial of Jesus. This is indicative of Mark's recognition that often women do what the male disciples fail to do. Mary Magdala, a resident of the Galilean town of Magdala, contrary to popular opinion is not the same woman as the prostitute described in Luke 7:37. She is probably the woman "out of whom Jesus drove seven devils" in Luke 8:2. The other Mary is more of a mystery. We simply don't know who either she or Salome was.

Joseph of Arimathaea, according to Matthew 27:57–61, is a rich man, a follower of Jesus, and "one who expected the reign of God." Matthew suggests that Joseph was not favorably inclined toward the spurious messianism of the Pharisees, the Sadducees, or the zealots. The tomb in which Jesus was buried was originally intended for Joseph. The actual burial was a simple affair (covering the body in a new linen shroud and placing it on a sort of shelf hewn out of the rock, rolling in front of the entrance to the tomb a circular stone that was sealed to prevent any unlawful entry to the tomb. This is similar to the first century CE graves that can still be seen in the Jerusalem vicinity.

Matthew adds an element to Jesus' burial not found in any of the accounts by the other evangelists, namely the placement of a guard at the tomb (Matthew 27:62–66). This apparently took place on the Sabbath, the day after Jesus' death. McKenzie[10] finds it of particular interest that the priests and Pharisees possessed considerable and accurate knowledge of Jesus' prediction that he would rise from the dead. He also finds it remarkable that Pilate had no problem granting a guard, even though he probably thought that to do so was absurd. McKenzie concludes from this revelation that this is what is behind the charge by the Jews that his disciples stole the body of Jesus upon finding out that the tomb was empty on the third day.

Luke's (Luke 23:50–56) description of Joseph of Arimathaea is that he was a good and just man, good toward his fellow men and women and just toward God. He possessed a deep faith that God would fulfill his promises about the kingdom. Unlike Matthew, Luke asserts that Joseph was a member of the council that had not consented to its plans to arrest and prosecute Jesus. Luke's account of the burial corroborates Mark's story in that he says that Jesus is simply wrapped in a shroud and laid in the tomb, but Luke adds that at the same time several women watch and then leave to prepare the spices so that they might anoint him after the Sabbath is over. The clear implication is that he was laid without being anointed. It was important to anoint the corpse so as to hinder the process of decomposition, which almost certainly began before they could get there on the third day. Although rabbinical law allowed the care of a dead body on Passover, had Joseph taken care of Jesus' corpse, he would have become unclean for taking part in sacred ceremonies.

John (19:38–42) asserts that Joseph of Arimathaea was a secret disciple of Jesus and a respected member of the Sanhedrin. With his colleague, Nicodemus, he asks Pilate for the body of Jesus. Apparently Nicodemus was also a secret disciple. Only at this point in time did both men come forward and declare themselves. The description of the burial process differs from

Mark. Instead of simply covering Jesus' body, it was wrapped (bound) "in linen cloths" with a mixture of spices, "myrrh and aloes, weighing about a hundred pounds." John tells us this was the customary procedure for royalty. He also adds that the site of Jesus' burial was an enclosed place outside the city walls in the proximity of where Jesus had been crucified. The garden in which the tomb was located apparently belonged to a private individual, probably Joseph himself.

To summarize, Joseph of Arimathaea, a good man by all accounts, despite some discrepancy among the evangelists as to his membership in the Sanhedrin or his status as simply a rich man, is the key figure in Jesus' burial. Only John mentions that Joseph bound Jesus in linen cloths and used a mixture of spices. However, we will soon see that the women followers of Jesus were also prepared to give his corpse a proper anointing.

Endnotes

[1] Calivas, Alkiviadis, (2003) Theophan the Recluse cited in Homily for Palm Sunday, Greek Orthodox Archdiocese of America; http://goarch.org/ourfaith/ourfaith8434

[2] Mally, Edward J., *The Jerome Biblical Commentary*, vol. 2, edited by Raymond Brown et al. (Englewood Cliff, NJ: Prentice Hall, 1968), 46.

[3] Greggs, Tom, Barth, Origin, and Universal Salvation: Restoring Particularity, (Oxford, England: Oxford University Press, 2009), 79.

[4] Marmion, D. Columba, *Christ the Life of the Soul* (St. Louis: B. Herder Book Co., 1925), 23.

[5] Eucharistic Doctrine, The Presence of Christ in *Statement of the First Anglican/ Roman Catholic International Commission,* http://www.vatican.va/roman_curia/pontifical_councils/chrstuni/angl-comm-docs/rc_pc_chrstuni_doc_1971_eucharistic-doctrine_en.html, Accessed August 18, 2014

[6] Since the earliest days of the Church, Holy Communion was received in the forms of consecrated bread and wine. This was in fulfillment of Jesus' command at the Last Supper: " ake and eat … take and drink." Receiving Holy Communion in this way is the norm until the late 11th century when the practice of distributing the Eucharist in the form of bread alone became popular. By the 15th century, the Church decreed that Holy Communion would be distributed to the faithful in the form of bread alone. In the early 1960s, the Second Vatican Council authorized reception of Holy Communion in both forms. Holy Communion has a more complete form as a sign when it is received in both bread and wine. (Loyola Press)

7   Neuner, J., and J. Dupuis, *The Christian Faith in the Doctrinal Documents of the Catholic Church*, seventh edition, edited by Jacques Dupuis, "The General Council of Trent's Thirteenth Session: The Decree on the Most Holy Eucharist, Canons 1526–1527" (New York: Alba House, 2001), 621.

8   Pope Benedict XVI, *Presiding in Doctrine and Presiding in Love* (Vatican: L'Osservatore Romano, 2005).

9   Camille, Alice, *Invitation to Catholicism* (Chicago: ACTA Publications, 2001).

10 McKenzie, John L., "Matthew 43," *The Jerome Biblical Commentary*, vol. 2, edited by Raymond Brown et al. 113–202.

CHAPTER 19

HE IS RISEN, ALLELUIA!
THE RESURRECTION

The resurrection together with the incarnation and the crucifixion is the fundamental reality or dogma of our Christian faith concerning Jesus of Nazareth, and it constitutes the core of salvation history. It is the decisive event in the eschatological order of salvation. This chapter provides the reader with an account of the various renderings of this event.

It must be noted that in none of the gospels is there given an accounting of the actual resurrection, probably because to do so would be impossible. One can only offer conjecture. The women in each of the gospels are the closest we have to actual witnesses. Also the linen cloths lying on the ground in John's account would seem to be evidence that the body was not stolen but Jesus had indeed risen miraculously.

Also, I have approached this seminal event by commenting on each evangelist's account rather than harmonizing them. This approach allows the reader to concentrate on and appreciate the particular perspective of each one.

The Empty Tomb: Mark 16:1–8

> There is no need to be amazed.
> You are looking for Jesus of Nazareth,
> who was crucified: he is risen, he is not here.
> —Mark 16:6

The Sabbath is over. The sun is rising in the early morning on the first day of the week, Sunday. Mary of Magdala, Mary (the mother of James), and Salome arrive at the tomb bearing spices with which to anoint Jesus. According to rabbinical law, they could have anointed him on the Sabbath, but for some reason it seems that they did not purchase the oils and salves on the Sabbath, choosing to wait. Perhaps it was because by the time Jesus was laid in the tomb provided by Joseph of Arimathaea, sundown and the Sabbath was upon them. Whatever the reason, they had to wait until sunrise on the first day of the week. Of real concern to them was who would roll back the heavy stone that closed the grave. This stone was heavy, circular, and flat. It was placed on its edge on a stone track, and it required considerable strength to move it.

As they approached the tomb, they were surprised to see the stone had been rolled back. They entered and found a young man dressed in a white robe who greeted them, "You are looking for Jesus of Nazareth, who was crucified; he has risen, he is not here. See, here is the place where they laid him … go and tell his disciples and Peter, 'He is going ahead of you to Galilee; that is where you will see him, just as he told you" (Mark 16:6–7).

The empty tomb speaks for itself. It is evident that Jesus is not present. However, the presence of an angel and his words, "As he told you," plainly shows that Jesus had predicted his resurrection. It would also lead one to believe that in spite of their cowardice in deserting him, Jesus was far more interested in comforting the penitent sinner than in punishing him for his sin. He was quite aware of the remorse and sorrow Peter and the other disciples were feeling at their disloyalty and wrongdoing. He knew of their self-torture. Yet they would continue to be his disciples as they were prior to his execution.

Of course the women did not understand this, for they were terrified, though amazed that they had been in the presence of an angel, which they more than likely presumed the young man to be. They had come to the tomb expecting to pay their last respects to a dead body by anointing it with spices and ointments. Along with the disciples they were still grieving over Friday's tragedy. Quite frankly the angel's presence frightened them out of their wits. They fled the tomb and failed to carry out his instructions.

Notwithstanding their dismay, Mark underscores the reality that Jesus' resurrection as the key to his whole life and the ground of our faith as his followers. St. Paul (Corinthians 15:14–17) says that without this victory over death, all of our preaching would be useless and our faith in vain. The resurrection of Jesus is the high point of our redemption and the central reality of our faith. After twenty centuries the fact of his resurrection is the supreme argument for Jesus' divinity. He who died on the cross has risen. He has triumphed over death and overcome the Prince of Darkness. He has risen indeed. *Alleluia.*

Matthew 28:1–10

> And suddenly there was a violent earthquake,
> for an angel of the Lord descending from heaven,
> came and rolled away the stone and sat on it.
> His face was like lightning, his robe as white as snow.
>
> —Matthew 28:2–3

Matthew builds on Mark's account of the empty tomb, although he says nothing about why the women were there. He also reduces their number from three to two, Mary Magdala, and the other Mary, both of whom had been present at Jesus' crucifixion. Just as with Mark, he says it was dawn on the day after the Sabbath. Matthew has the women witness a violent earthquake and an angel descending from heaven, removing the stone, and sitting on it. Whereas Mark makes no mention of the guards, Matthew speaks of them as having been overcome by the apparition of the angel. The angel, like the young man of Mark's gospel, was also dressed in white. "His face was like lightening, his robe white as snow." We are told that he spoke to the women, "There is no need for you to be afraid. I know you are looking for Jesus, who was crucified. He is not here, for he has risen, as he said he would. Come and see the place where he lay, then go quickly and tell his disciples, 'He has risen from the dead and now he is going ahead of you to Galilee; that is where you will see him.' Look! I have told you." (Mathew 28:5-7)

Unlike Mark, Matthew has the women overcome with awe and great joy as they run to tell the disciples what they have seen. On the way they come upon Jesus, who greets them. The women fall down before him and grasp his feet. Jesus tells them to not be afraid and repeats the instructions of the angel to go tell his brothers to meet him in Galilee.

The admonition to the women by both the angel and Jesus not to be afraid is an indication of how singular their experience was. After all, the guards had fainted with fear at the earthquake and the appearance of an angel. Yet the women were joyous as they departed in a hurry from the tomb. For them joy and love had conquered dread and fear. Yes, they were trembling and probably confused and not a little fearful. After all, even though Jesus had spoken several times of his rising from the dead, it never quite registered with them. No one seriously expected anything like this to really happen. But it did, and the sight of Jesus and his instructions gave their mission a sense of urgency. They were the first to see the empty tomb. They were the first to see the risen Christ. They were the first to receive the joy of the resurrection.

Yet the message of the resurrection goes well beyond joy. It is an indication of God making real his promise in the garden to put an enmity between the seed of the Serpent and that of the woman. Satan was the seed of the former, Jesus the seed of the latter. The living God is powerfully, and he is at work here. His mercy and forgiveness is overturning the rule of sin and death. The women were the first to see evidence of this cosmic defeat of the Devil.

And so Jesus tells the women to take his message to his brothers—his disciples—and tell them that they are to meet him in Galilee. He knows they have run away after his arrest and the first signs of danger. Despite their protests that they were ready to die to defend him, each one in the final analysis ran away, leaving him alone to face his accusers and eventual death. Even Peter had denied him three times. Yet Jesus still calls them his brothers. He will meet them in Galilee. This brings to mind his prediction that they would "all fall away from me tonight, for the scripture says: 'I shall strike the shepherd and the sheep of the flock will be scattered,' but after my resurrection I shall go ahead of you to Galilee" (Matthew 26:31–32).

He knew that they would desert him and that Satan would have his way with them. But just as he had prayed for Peter, he would pray that the others would not be overcome. In Galilee they would start anew. They would become in earnest "fishers of men." Once again he would issue his call, "Come follow me!" They would become witnesses of and give testimony to his resurrection. Upon them he would build his church, and the onslaughts of hell would not prevail against it. And so once again he sends forth his call to you and me that we follow the Lord anew and afresh from this point forward. Amen. So be it!

Luke 24:1–12

> Why look among dead for someone who is alive?
> He is not here; he has risen.
>
> —Luke 24:5

Luke's account of the resurrection is by far the lengthiest of the synoptic accounts. The reference to the empty tomb episode is a theological rendering modeled after the transfiguration event. He describes the initial scene much the same way as Mark does. However, in his account when the women entered the tomb and did not find the body of Jesus, they were puzzled. Suddenly two men "in brilliant clothes" appeared before them. The women were terrified. "But the two said to them. 'Why look among the dead for someone who is alive? He is not here; he has risen. Remember what he told you when he was still in Galilee: that the son of man was destined to be handed over into the power of sinful men and be crucified, and rise again on the third day.'" (Luke 24: 5-7) Note that the angels did not tell the women to go tell anyone what they had witnessed. They simply remembered their words.

Pope Francis[1] in his first Easter homily in 2013 reminds us that the women had gone to the tomb "to perform an act of compassion, a traditional act of affection and love for a dear departed person, just as we would." Jesus's words had stirred their hearts. Their love for him was simple and deep. Unlike their male counterparts, they had accompanied him to the end, to Calvary, and to the place where they thought was his final resting place. Were they in for a surprise! In the words of Francis, "Something completely new and unexpected happens, something which upsets their hearts and their plans, something which will upset their whole life; they see the stone removed from before the tomb … they do not find the Lord's body." They are stunned. They are confused. Remember, these women did not believe in resurrection despite Jesus' six references to his death and resurrection. They had not gone to the tomb to see if Jesus was still there. On Friday evening before the Sabbath they had purchased spices and ointments, expecting to anoint his decaying body. They had with them this very early Sunday morning these spices and ointments.

Their first hint that something was not normal was the heavy stone that had been rolled away from the grave. They were worried that they would not be able to roll it away themselves. But there it was, already revealing the entry to the grave. Suddenly before them are these two men in dazzling clothes who say to them, "Why do you look for the living among the dead? He is not here; but has risen" (Luke 24:5–6). Needless to say, just as in the other resurrection accounts, the women are frightened and perplexed. They bow to the earth in reverence. Then the angels ask them to recall the prediction and promise Jesus made to them in Galilee that he, the Son of Man, would be delivered into the hands of sinful men, be crucified, and rise on the third day. They should not be surprised. They had no need for these spices and ointments to preserve Jesus' body. And just as in the other gospel accounts, these men instruct the women to go to tell the disciples to meet him in Galilee.

So the women run off to tell the eleven what they had witnessed. Luke names Mary Magdala, Joanna, and Mary, the mother of James. Although the others discount what the women tell them, Peter goes to the tomb to see for himself and is amazed at what he sees, nothing but the linen cloths. It is just as the women have reported. It is empty. One can only imagine what must have raced through his mind. Could it be true? Did he really rise from the dead as he said he would? He must have. He is not in the tomb. He departs, wondering and marveling at what has transpired and perhaps contemplating what the future portends. What is really interesting is that Peter, who had denied his relationship with Jesus—and every one of the other disciples knew of this denial—had the moral courage to go out to the tomb to verify for himself what the women had told them. Peter was on the way to becoming the Rock.

Luke 24:13–35

> Did not our hearts burn within us as he talked to us on the road
> and explained the scriptures to us?
>
> —Luke 24:32

Luke (Luke 24:13–35) provides us with a second account of Jesus' resurrection, this time Jesus' encounter with two travelers leaving Jerusalem on the road to Emmaus. The actual site of Emmaus is disputed in that it was about twenty miles away from the city on the road to Jaffa. This is considerably more than the seven miles mentioned in the narration. The names of the men have come down to us as Cleopas, reputedly the brother of Joseph, Jesus' foster father and the father of Symeon, who succeeded James as bishop of Jerusalem. Although this is highly speculative, the point that commentators have tried to attribute to these names is that the "brethren of Jesus," his close relatives did not completely reject him.[2] Notwithstanding, this story by Luke is one of the most dramatic stories in the New Testament.

It is apparent that Luke had an independent source for his narration. In contrast to Mark's description of the women as frightened and failing to carry out the angel's instructions, they readily pass on to the Eleven what they had seen and heard. Perhaps the difference is the fact that they were not given a message to convey to the Eleven. Unfortunately, other than Peter, the others thought their story was sheer nonsense.

In this pericope we find two men, ostensibly followers of Jesus, on the road to a town named Emmaus. They are troubled and are arguing among themselves about the events of the past three days. Suddenly a third man joins them and asks what they were arguing about. The other two are incredulous. One of them responds, "You must be the only person in Jerusalem who does not know the things that have been happening there these last few days." To the third man's follow-up question, "What things?" they answer that they have been speaking of Jesus of Nazareth, who they had come to believe was a prophet "powerful in action and speech before God and the whole people" (Luke 24:19).

They spoke of how the chief priests and leaders of the people had handed Jesus over to the Roman procurator because they claimed that he had violated the Sabbath and claimed to be the Christ, the Son of God. They were disturbed and saddened that he had to suffer an ignominious death on a cross reserved for common criminals. They had hoped that Jesus was the promised Messiah foretold of old, the one to set Israel free. The two travelers continue to tell the stranger about the women at the tomb and what they had seen. They also tell him of a rumor that several women disciples had reputedly been to the tomb in which he had been buried and had found it empty. They had even reported that they had seen the risen Jesus.

At this the stranger responds with a scolding, "You foolish men! So slow to believe all that the prophets have said" (Luke 24:25). He reminds them that Scripture foretold that the Christ would suffer at the hands of the priests and the public authorities but that he would be vindicated. It was necessary that these events would come to pass so that the Christ might be glorified. He explained to them all the passages in Scripture that had been revealed about him by the prophets, starting with Moses.

When they reach a fork in the road, he makes it seem as if he needs to go one way while they proceeded another way. But they invite him to stay with them because the hour is late. He joins them, and at supper during at the breaking of the bread, they recognize him. And to their amazement, he vanishes from their sight.

They recall how their hearts were burning as Jesus spoke with them. They realize a new appreciation of the events in Jerusalem and on Golgotha. All of a sudden the conversation on the road to Emmaus makes sense, and a mystery is solved.

At that instant they become excited and set off back to Jerusalem to tell the Eleven and the others what they had experienced. When they arrive, they are greeted, "The Lord has indeed risen and has appeared to Simon." What the women had told them was true. One can only imagine the flood of emotions in that place as more stories of Jesus' appearance flowed in. Yet there is more. Even as they were all talking about this turn of events, Jesus is standing in their midst and saying to them, "Peace be with you!"

This story of the encounter with Jesus on the road to Emmaus was frequently recited at liturgical gatherings by the early followers of the Way, which was the appellation attributed to the followers of Jesus before they were called Christians at Antioch. Other scholars believe that this is not so much a story of a chance encounter with Jesus as it is an account of how the Eucharistic meal unites the faithful to the living presence of the risen Lord. The breaking of the bread and its sharing is at the very center of the new community. It recalls the Last Supper and the fact that it is in the breaking of the bread and the drinking of the wine that the community realizes that Jesus reveals his presence after the resurrection. It is an event that will continue through every age until the end of time. In this act Jesus is indeed the Christ, the anointed one, the Messiah.

It is also interesting that we are told that Jesus appeared to Peter as well as the women. One of his first appearances is to the man who three times denied he knew him. Once again here is evidence that he loves the sinner, giving the penitent sinner back his self-respect.

Luke 24:36–49

> Peace be with you …
> See by my hands and by my feet that it is I myself.
> Touch me and see for yourself.
>
> —Luke 24:36, 39

The third act in the Easter drama as recounted by Luke is Jesus' appearance before the Eleven when he shows them the wounds on his hands and feet and eats a piece of grilled fish to demonstrate his physicality and that he was real. Once they are convinced, he reminds them that everything that had been written or spoken about him by the law of Moses, the prophets, and in the psalms had been fulfilled. He continues with this last instruction to his apostles, "So it is written that the Christ would suffer and on the third day rise from the dead, and that, in his name, repentance for the forgiveness of sins would be preached to all nations, beginning from Jerusalem. You are witnesses to this. And now I am sending upon you what the Father has promised" (Luke 24:46–47).

It is interesting that this is one of the very few places in the New Testament in which Jesus refers to himself as Christ. This is a title, not a name. The title Christ is from the Greek Christos, which references the *anointed one*. It is a translation of the Hebrew word for Messiah, which refers to a king anointed at God's direction and with his approval. Jesus is identified as the Messiah as foretold by the Hebrew prophets. This title takes on great significance in the celebration of the Eucharistic celebration, which is a seminal point in this narration.

Jesus' final appearance before the Eleven and his last instructions to them occurred on the outskirts of Bethany, where he ascended into heaven after he blessed. The disciples then leave Bethany for Jerusalem to await the Paraclete as Jesus had instructed them.

In Luke, a consistent theme throughout his narrative is that the suffering, death, and resurrection of Jesus were accomplished in fulfillment of Hebrew scriptural promises and Jewish hopes. In his second volume, Acts, Luke will argue that Christianity is the fulfillment of the hopes of Pharisaic Judaism and its logical development. We now turn to John's account of the resurrection.

John 20:1–29

> They have taken the Lord out of the tomb ...
> and we don't know where they have put him.
>
> —John 20:2

John's account of the resurrection appearances is divided into seven sections.[3]

1. Mary and the two disciples visit the tomb.
2. Mary sees the Lord.
3. The disciples see the Lord.
4. Thomas sees the Lord.
5. John concludes his book for the first time – the meaning of these signs.
6. Jesus shows himself to the disciples by the Sea of Tiberias, and
7. John concludes his book for the second time – the disciples' commission.

1. Mary and the two disciples visit the tomb (John 20:1–10).

This is probably the best known of all accounts of the resurrection. Mary of Magdala is one of the most arresting characters in the New Testament. Not much is really known about her. The prevailing opinion is that prior to meeting Jesus she had been possessed by evil spirits. Jesus expelled them from her. From that moment forward she became a beloved disciple. She loved him with an extraordinary love. This early morning she goes to the tomb and notices that the stone had been moved. Frightened, she runs to tell Peter, and we presume John, crying, "They have taken the Lord out of the tomb." She obviously believes that either grave robbers or the authorities have stolen the body. The two disciples immediately run to the tomb, the youngest getting there first. He bends down and looks into the tomb to see the linen cloths lying on the ground. When Peter gets there, he goes into the tomb and also sees the linen cloths (the grave cloths) lying on the ground and another cloth rolled up by itself where the head of the corpse would normally be. The other disciple follows Peter, sees, and believes the Scripture that foretold that Jesus "must rise from the dead." They then leave.

2. Mary sees the Lord (John 20:11–18).

Meanwhile Mary remains outside the tomb at its entrance. She is weeping. She looks inside. Instead of seeing the linen cloths, she sees two angels in white sitting where the corpse of Jesus had been. They ask her why she is weeping. She responds, "They have taken my Lord away ... I don't know where they have put him." She feels the presence of someone behind her and thinks it is the gardener. He also asks why she is weeping and who she is looking for. She replies, "Sir, if you have taken him away, tell me where you have put him, and I will go and remove him." The man, who is actually Jesus, says, "Mary." She immediately recognizes his voice and turns around, saying, "Rabbuni!" which in Hebrew means *master* or *teacher*. Her first reaction is to hug him, but Jesus says to her, "Do not cling to me, because I have not yet ascended to the Father. But go to the brothers, and tell them; I am ascending to my Father and your Father, to my God and your God." With that Mary returns to Peter and the disciples to tell them what Jesus had commissioned her to say. To her belongs the glory of being the first person to whom he revealed himself after his resurrection. In truth she is also the first of the apostles.

3. The disciples see the Lord (John 20:19–23).

That same day in the evening the disciples were together behind closed doors, fearful of the Jews. Suddenly there is Jesus standing in their midst. He greets them, "Peace be with you." He shows them his wounds. The disciples were beside themselves with joy. Again Jesus says, "Peace be with you. As the Father sent me, so am I sending you." And breathing on them, he continues, "Receive the Holy Spirit. If you forgive anyone's sins, they are forgiven; if you retain anyone's sins, they are retained."

4. Thomas sees the Lord (John 20:24-29).

Thomas had not been present when Jesus first appeared to the disciples. They had told him about his appearance, but he refused to believe, saying that unless he saw Jesus' wounds and could touch them, he would not believe. Eight days later Jesus reappears and singles out Thomas by saying, "Put your finger here; look, here are my hands. Give me your hand; put it into my side. Do not be unbelieving any more but believe." To this Thomas exclaims, "My Lord and my God!" and Jesus replies to him, "You believe because you can see me. Blessed are those who have not seen and yet believe."

5. The first conclusion – the meaning of these signs that you might have faith (John 20:30)

The gospel writer tells us that Jesus worked many other signs that are not recorded in this book. What is here is here so that we might believe that Jesus Christ is the Son of God and we might have life through his name. There is considerable conjecture that John's gospel properly ends at this point. Vawter[4] suggests that the gospel writer had by this point exposed all the divine mysteries of Jesus' death and resurrection as well as provided the reader with enough historical background to establish the fact that the resurrection did indeed take place. Hence, Thomas's expression, "My Lord and my God!" is a fitting ending in that it is the most explicit expression of faith found in this gospel. The following episode in some circles is seen as an addition by an early redactor. At best it might well be an independent writing.

6. Jesus shows himself to the disciples by the Sea of Tiberias (John 20:1–23).

The disciples go fishing on the Sea of Tiberius (probably the Sea of Galilee). They are out all night and catch nothing. When morning comes, they see Jesus standing on the seashore, calling out to them, "Haven't you caught anything, friends?" They reply that they have not. Jesus then tells them to cast their net to the starboard side. This they do and pull in a quantity of fish so large they almost break their net. Realizing it is Jesus who is on the shore, Peter jumps out of the boat and makes his way to Jesus. Soon they are all ashore. Jesus starts a fire and cooks some fish. He invites them to have breakfast.

When they had eaten, Jesus and Peter take a walk along the shore. Three times he asks Peter if he loves him. Each time Peter responds in the affirmative with increasing discomfort and obvious feelings of personal hurt. The three questions and Peter's three confessions of his love lead to three replies by Jesus, "Feed my lambs; Look after my sheep; Feed my sheep." Satisfied with Peter's answers and, as some scholars contend, underscoring his forgiveness of Peter's three denials, he then indicates to Peter that he is to be the pastor or shepherd of Jesus' people and the kind of death he would face. "In all truth I tell you, when you were young you put on your own belt and walked where you liked; but when you grow old you will stretch out your hands, and somebody else will put a belt round you and take you where you would rather not go ... Follow me." Like Jesus, he will give his life, laying down his life for the faithful. He, too, will die on a cross.

7. The second conclusion – the disciples' commission and the final testimony, John 21:15-25

This conclusion is similar to the first. When one reads John's account of the resurrection,one cannot but be impressed with the role played in this drama by Mary of Magdala and Peter. In truth, one could conclude that Mary is indeed the first apostle if one believes that an apostle is one who is called or commissioned by a deity to be a herald and to convey a message—in this instance that Jesus is risen from the dead. The disciples must wait for their commission. It is unfortunate that given the customs of the time and over the centuries other women apostles, such as Mary, have been pushed aside by a decidedly male-oriented church. This is particularly galling when one realizes that it was women, such as Mary of Magdala, the other Mary, and Salome, who with great humility and incredible love supported Jesus and his disciples throughout his ministry with money and toil and who have down through the ages continued this support and love of his church with little recompense. As for Peter, what can I say? Here is this rough-hewn man, the salt of the earth, one without guile, sometimes brash and bullheaded, more often than not one who loved deeply, but a flawed human being like all of us. In Peter, Jesus saw the person to whom he would entrust his church. In Peter, we see our pastor.

Conclusion

For almost two thousand years Christians have been remembering and celebrating the resurrection from the dead of this itinerant preacher from Galilee. It has become the central reality of the Christian faith and has been preached as such throughout the ages. Today his followers—one third of mankind—are found on every continent in the world. His legacy has been profound in terms of the sheer numbers who have been touched by or benefited from his message of love and compassion through those institutions that address their physical, intellectual, and spiritual needs in his name and through the kindness and love of his disciples for one another over the centuries. His resurrection has been put forth as the supreme argument that he was God made man. By his death on the cross and his resurrection, we have been saved from the power of sin, the snares of the Devil, and eternal damnation. But the real truth is that sending to us his Son was an act of love by the Father, and by raising Jesus from the dead, the Father shows us that He is love. Morton Kelsey[5] writes,

> The true miracle is what this resurrection reveals—the inhumanly loving God. In spite of the evil, ugliness, and pain of the world, at the center of reality abides the divine Lover keeping watch above us all. In spite of our failures, our rejection of love, our destructiveness, our pettiness, our violence, God loves us and continues to reach out to us. Jesus came into our world, lived, died, and rose again before we human beings even considered responding to God, simply to demonstrate that love for us, to manifest the truth that God is love.

And so on Easter Sunday morning, let the eyes of high and low, young and old, people throughout the world, those in city and in hamlet, and those on mountaintop and in valley focus on the empty tomb and join in joyous song, "The Lord is risen from the dead. Alleluia!"

Endnotes

1   Pope Francis, *Easter Vigil Homily* (Vatican City: Libreria Editrice Vaticana, 2013).

2   Stuhlmueller, C.P., Carroll; "The Gospel According to Luke," in *The Jerome Biblical Commentary*. Ed, Raymond E. Brown, S.S., Joseph A. Fitzmyer, S.J., Roland E. Murphy, O.Carm. (Englewood Cliff, NJ: Prentice Hall, Inc., 1968) 79.

3   Vawter, Bruce, *The Gospel According to John: The Jerome Biblical Commentary*, edited by Raymond E. Brown et al. 464

4   Ibid

5   Morton, Kelsey, *The Drama of the Resurrection: Transforming Christianity* (Hyde Park, NY: New City Press, 1999), 133.

CHAPTER 20

THE COMING OF THE ADVOCATE AND THE FOUNDING OF JESUS' CHURCH

Come Holy Spirit come … Heal our wounds, our strength renew;
On our dryness pour your dew; wash the stains of guilt away
Bend the stubborn hearts and will; melt the frozen, warm the chill
Guide the steps that go astray … give them joys that never end. Amen.

—Sequence for Pentecost Sunday

The Birthday of the Church

For the Jews Pentecost occurred fifty days after Passover, when they celebrated the exodus of the Israelites from bondage in Egypt and when they also celebrated the gift of the Decalogue on Mount Sinai. For Christians Pentecost takes on a new meaning. Fifty days after the death and resurrection of Jesus, we celebrate a new covenant whereby the Holy Spirit descends upon his disciples and marks the birth of his church. The coming of the Paraclete or advocate, "the Lord and Giver of Life," had been promised to the disciples

In Acts 2:1–4, the disciples were gathered in the upper room of a building in Jerusalem. We don't know where this upper room was. Perhaps it was the room in which Jesus had washed their feet and broken bread with them. One thing seems to be certain. They were all frightened. They were low on money. In fact, their accounts had been in disarray since Judas's betrayal of Jesus. Some were doubtful if they could hold out much longer. There was no way they could afford to carry out his mission to the entire world. Others contended that it was too dangerous to go outside. They were marked men. Who would do the work they had been commissioned to do if they were killed or thrown into prison? Still others doubted their ability to evangelize. They were too old, too tired, or too poorly educated. The upper room must have felt rather safe if not comfortable. If they stayed put, maybe others would come from the outside and join them. And then—

Suddenly a sound came from heaven like a rushing wind that filled the entire house. Tongues of fire appeared and sat upon the head of each of the disciples, apostles, and others filled with the Holy Spirit, and each began to speak in other languages as directed by the Spirit. At this point they went out into the city and began to preach and bear witness to the risen Christ.

Now there were many people in Jerusalem for the Jewish feast of Pentecost. People from throughout the Roman Empire were gathered in the city. When they heard the sound, they were most curious. And then they started to hear their own languages being spoken by the apostles (Acts 2:5–6). People were amazed when they saw that several of those speaking their languages were Galileans. They thought that perhaps the apostles were drunk.

Peter, hearing their comments, stood up in their midst and began to speak. He assured the crowd that his colleagues were not drunk because it was only the third hour of the day. He spoke of those prophecies about the coming of the Holy Spirit, Jesus of Nazareth, his death by crucifixion, and his resurrection on the third day. The people were amazed and asked Peter what they should do. "Repent," said Peter. "Be baptized in the name of Jesus Christ for the forgiveness of your sins, and you will receive the gift of the Holy Spirit" (Acts 2:38–39).

That very day more than three thousand were baptized. The apostles continued to preach the good news. The disciples met each day for fellowship, the breaking of bread, and prayer. Many signs and miracles were performed by the apostles. And many more were baptized. Jesus' church had been launched.

The events that took place that day in Jerusalem were very different from the events that took place at the Tower of Babel in Genesis, when God used language to confuse men who tried to be like gods. On that Pentecost day God used language to bring men and women together. The miracle of Pentecost was not so much the apostles speaking in foreign tongues but the Holy Spirit speaking through these unlettered Galileans as they proclaimed the gospel so that every person present at the time could hear it in his or her own native language.

On this day Jesus' church began its public ministry with the fruition of Jesus' promise to send the Paraclete.

The Holy Spirit

The Hebrew word for spirit is *ruach*. It means "air in motion, wind, spirit, or breath." It also means *life*, often the principle of life and activity in human beings given by God and withdrawn by him. Prophets and charismatic leaders receive the Spirit of God in a special way for a special task. In the last days the Spirit is to be poured out on the whole people and on individuals in a new covenant.

In the New Testament the Spirit that comes upon Jesus' early community is seen to be guided by the Spirit. Similarly in Paul the Spirit (the Spirit of God or the Spirit of Christ) makes Christians children of God and empowers them to Christian activity, including prayer and love. It teaches especially that this Spirit, the Paraclete, brings the continuing personal presence of Christ. That this spirit of God or Christ is a distinct person is implied by the frequent triadic formulae in Paul. The term Paraclete means "a helper, counsellor, or advocate." Jesus, himself a Paraclete, will send another Paraclete to guide his disciples into all truth. This will be the Holy Spirit.

We also know that the Holy Spirit possesses all the attributes of God. We know from Scripture that he is omnipresent (Psalm 139:7), omniscient (Isaiah 40:13; 1 Corinthians 2:10, 11), and omnipotent (Zachariah 4:6; John 16:7–13; Romans 16:25), and he is called God (Acts 5:4).

Both the Hebrew Scripture and the New Testament refer to him by many titles, which include:

- Counselor (John 14:16),
- Spirit above the Waters (Genesis 1:2),
- Spirit from on High (Isaiah 32:15),
- Spirit of Christ (Romans 8:9),
- Spirit of Counsel and Power (Isaiah 11:2),
- Spirit of Glory (1 Peter 4:14),
- Spirit of God (Genesis 41:38),
- Spirit of Holiness (Romans 1:4),
- Spirit of Jesus (Acts 16:7),
- Spirit of Justice (Isaiah 28:6),
- Spirit of Knowledge and of the Fear of the LORD (Isaiah 11:2),
- Spirit of the LORD (Micah 2:7),
- Spirit of Truth (John 14:17),
- Spirit of Your Father (Matthew 10:20), and
- Spirit of Wisdom and Understanding (Isaiah 11:2).

Scripture also refers to the Holy Spirit by means of symbols. Here are a few of these symbols:

- Anointing (1 John 2:27)
- Breath of the Almighty (Job 32:8; 33:4; 34:14–15)
- Breath of Life (Genesis 2:7)
- Breath of the LORD (Isaiah 40:7)
- Cloud and Light (Mark 9:7)
- Dove (Matthew 3:16)
- Fire (Acts 2:3)
- Firstfruits (Romans 8:23)
- Power of the Lord (Luke 5:17)
- Power of the Most High (Luke 1:35)
- The Spirit (Matthew 12:31)
- Streams of Living Water (John 7:38)

Who is the Holy Spirit? Actually we have no real name for the Holy Spirit in the same way that we call the first person of the Trinity God and the second person Jesus Christ. We simply know him as Holy Spirit. Throughout Scripture he is known by various attributes or designations that describe his office or the role he plays in salvation and history, but they really don't tell us much about his personality. In addition to being known as the Holy Spirit, he is also called among other things the Holy Ghost, the Spirit of the Lord, or the Comforter. We know him also by certain characteristics that describe him as a person in Scripture. He testifies (John 15:26). He can be lied to (Acts 5:3, 4). He directs (Acts 16:6, 7). He appoints (Acts 20:28). He can be grieved (Ephesians 4:30), and he intercedes (Romans 8:26).

The Gifts of the Holy Spirit

Through the agency of the church the Holy Spirit confers his many gifts. One of those gifts is courage, and it enabled the apostles to give powerful witness to Jesus throughout Jerusalem and throughout the world over the centuries even to our present day.

Courage is only one of the gifts of the Holy Spirit conferred on the church that day. Isaiah 11:2–3 and St. Paul in 1 Corinthians 12:4–11 describe the others. They include wisdom, understanding, counsel/right judgment, knowledge, piety, and fear of the Lord. Freely given by the Spirit, each of these gifts helps us individually and collectively in the Spirit's call to universal holiness. These gifts are infused with sanctifying grace and enable the Christian to respond to the Spirit's promptings just as Jesus himself would.

Wisdom is the primary and greatest gift of the Holy Spirit. It is the end point of the contemplative disposition and the perfection of faith. *The Catholic Encyclopedia* notes, "By detaching us from the world [wisdom] makes us relish and love only the things of heaven."[1] Wisdom helps us judge or order our relationship to the created world. This does not mean renouncing the world. Rather it helps us to love the world properly as the creation of God rather than for its own sake.

Understanding is the second gift of the Holy Spirit. Whereas wisdom is the desire to contemplate the things of God, understanding allows us "to penetrate the very core of revealed truths." It allows us to grasp (up to a point) the essence of the truths of the Christian faith and to gain certitude about our beliefs. It also allows us to arrive at an understanding of our relation to God and his role in our lives and in the world. Finally we are also enabled to see the world and our lives within it in the larger context of the eternal law.

Counsel, the third gift of the Holy Spirit, builds on both wisdom and understanding. It speaks to the heart as it informs us about the right thing to do in times of trouble and trial. *The Catholic Encyclopedia*[2] notes that counsel "enables us to see and choose correctly what will help most to the glory of God and our own salvation." Counsel also perfects the cardinal virtue of prudence. Through the gift of counsel the Holy Spirit guides us to judge what we should do in particular situations.

The Holy Spirit emboldened Peter and the apostles to leave the upper room, go out into the city, and convert the many thousands. The fourth gift of the Holy Spirit, fortitude, gives us the strength to follow the actions suggested by the gift of counsel. It goes well beyond what we normally think of as courage, allowing us to do extraordinary things in times of trials and tribulations. It is different in some ways from courage in that it is an act that emanates from reason. The person exercising fortitude does not seek danger for danger's sake. Only if it is necessary will he put himself in danger. Fortitude allows us to overcome fear in the face of danger. Prudence and justice are the virtues through which we decide what needs to be done. Fortitude gives us the strength to do it.

Knowledge is the fifth gift of the Holy Spirit. It helps us to ascertain the parameters and circumstances of our lives and to determine God's will. It shows us how to live according to this will and purpose. It enables us to discern the impulses of temptation and the promptings or inspirations of God. It also perfects the theological virtue of faith.

Piety, the sixth gift of the Holy Spirit, perfects the virtue of religion (i.e., the willingness to worship and serve God out of love). Piety instills in us a desire to do that which is pleasing to God. It is an act of love, an instinctive affection for God.

Finally fear of the Lord, the seventh gift of the Holy Spirit, perfects the theological virtue of hope. It arises out of love, going well beyond the desire not to offend God or a sense of duty. It gives us the desire to not offend God and the certainty that he will supply us with the grace and wherewithal to keep from offending him. It has been stated that "the fear of the Lord is not servile but filial." We are generally not frightened by or fearful of our parents, but we certainly do not want to offend them. It is the same with respect to our relationship with God. We respect and love him. And we desire to in no way offend him.

St. Paul (1 Corinthians 12:28–31) adds a second array of gifts. They include the gift of speaking with wisdom, knowledge, and faith. He also describes the gift of healing, the ability to perform miracles, and the gifts of prophecy, discerning spirits, speaking in tongues, and interpreting tongues. In Galatians 5:22–23, St. Paul lists what are today referred to as fruits of the Holy Spirit. They include charity, joy, peace, patience, goodness, kindness, long-suffering, humility, faithfulness, modesty, continence, and chastity.

Endnotes

[1]   Joyce, G., "The Blessed Trinity," *The Catholic Encyclopedia* (New York: Robert Appleton Company, 1912), retrieved June 9, 2009, from New Advent at http://www.newadvent.org/cathen.

[2]   ibid.

Epilogue
The Sign of Jonah

This is an evil generation; it is asking for a sign.
The only sign it will be given is the sign of Jonah.
For just as Jonah became a sign to the people of Nineveh,
so will the son of man be a sign to this generation.
On Judgment Day the Queen of the South will stand up against
the people of this generation and be their condemnation,
because she came from the ends of the earth
to hear the wisdom of Solomon;
and look, there is something greater than Solomon here.
On Judgment Day the men of Nineveh will appear
against this generation and be its condemnation,
because when Jonah preached they repented;
and look, there is something greater than Jonah here.

—Luke 11:26–32

Many readers of the Bible take it quite literally, forgetting that to do so often misses the essence of holy writ. They miss the metaphor or allegory that enriches this fascinating set of writings. A perfect example is the story of Johan and the whale. Stated simply, Jonah seeks to run away rather than carry out God's command that he go to preach to the Ninevites, an Assyrian people once located in modern northwest Iraq. He takes passage on a commercial ship bound for a distant shore far away from Nineveh. A storm comes up, threatening to capsize or destroy the ship with its cargo and sailors. In the meantime Jonah is fast asleep in the ship's hold. The sailors draw lots to determine with whom the gods are angry. The lot falls to Jonah. They find and awaken him, querying him as to why the gods are angry with him. He forthwith confesses that he is a prophet on the run. He suggests that they throw him overboard to calm the seas. After some wrangling the sailors with much consternation do so. The seas calm down, and Jonah is swallowed by a large fish, a whale.

For three days and three nights he is in the belly of the whale until he is vomited upon the shores of Nineveh, from whence he had been running. But while he is in the whale, Jonah began to have a change of heart, and turning to God, he vowed to be obedient to him and carry out his initial mission.

Of course there is much more to this fanciful story. The whale is rich in symbolism among people the world over. In Middle Eastern mythology the whale is the ark that sails over the waters of the flood. It calls to mind Noah and the ark. It is a symbol of containment not unlike a sort of chalice. When the whale swallows Jonah, he descends into the darkness into his unconscious, says Carl Jung. In the belly of the whale he dies to his *self* as he contends with known and unknown antagonistic yet creative impulses and instincts. He undergoes a transformation of the heart. When the whale vomits him up on the shores of Nineveh, he is given a second birth, emerging from a state of death and entombment to resurrection into a cosmic environment.

The message here is that when we learn to go deep within ourselves, our creative impulses are awaken, and our lives are resurrected. When we come out of the creativity-generating waters into the real world and use our newfound creative impulses in this outer world, we discover and build new and dynamic ways of being.

But how does this comport with Matthew and Luke's reference to Jonah and the whale? Answering the Pharisees and scribes' call for a sign that would show them that he was who he said he was, Jesus identifies them as being of an evil and unfaithful generation by saying that "the only sign it will be given is the sign of the prophet Jonah. For as Jonah remained in the belly of the sea-monster for three days and three nights, so will the Son of man be in the heart of the earth for three days and three nights" (Matthew 12:39–40).

Luke 11:30 adds, "For just as Jonah became a sign to the people of Nineveh, so will the Son of Man be a sign to this generation." Although the Pharisees and scribes, according to most New Testament translations, were asking for a sign, they more than likely were not expecting Jesus to respond with a symbol. A sign simply denotes or stands in for a particular object, whereas a symbol identifies something familiar but possesses a connotation in addition to its conventional or obvious meaning. It implies something vague, unknown, or hidden. In other words, although Jesus was predicting that he would soon repeat Jonah's experience and in due time this and succeeding generations would understand the meaning of this sign, he was using this metaphor of Jonah and the whale as a symbol for something deeper. Jesus' opponents thought of a sign simply in terms of a miracle. However, he spoke of a sign as a way of salvation.

Jonah is quite clearly a type of Jesus. He prefigured what Jesus would do centuries later. He was a prophet of God. So too was Jesus. Moreover, he is the Son of God. Jonah gave himself up to save the ship and its crew. Jesus gave himself up to save you and me and everyone else. Jonah went down into a metaphorical grave, spending three days and three nights in a fishy tomb. Jesus went to a very real grave and spent three days and three nights in a real tomb. After three days in the fish Jonah was vomited out on to dry land. After three days Jesus rose from the tomb, conquering death, raising himself to new life.

But there were differences. Jonah fell into his misfortune because he rebelled against God. He had run away. Jesus did not rebel against his Father. Instead he embraced his cross in obedience to the Father's will. Jonah did not really die. Jesus really died and did rise from the dead.

There is still more particularly with reference to Jonah.

It should be pointed out that Jonah acknowledged his rebellion and subsequent danger and knew that God was in determined pursuit of him. He knew that he could not save himself and that his only hope was to call on God, whom he knew loved him and longed to save him. He knew that he was simply incapable of saving himself even if he had wealth, cleverness, skills, or significant contacts. And finally Jonah knew that he had to act and carry out the mission he had received as a prophet. In doing so, he knew that his life would be changed.

Finale

We have been on quite a journey from the desert to the resurrection. In many ways this legend of Jonah summarizes its high points. During this period we have looked at our sinful ways and exposed ourselves to the teachings of an itinerant preacher from Galilee. In these forty days we have tried with varying degrees of success to face our inadequacies and rid ourselves of whatever is displeasing to God. Like the prophet Jonah, we have come to realize that we can run but we cannot hide from the Almighty. God has his ways to expose our pride and our presumptions. Sometimes these ways seem irrational and unfair, and so we take matters into our own hands and run. But as the psalmist says in Psalm 139, "Where can I go from your spirit … if I go up to the heavens you are there." Or as Francis Thompson[1], the poet, writes in the "Hound of Heaven,"

> I fled Him, down the nights and down the days;
> I fled Him, down the arches of the years;

I fled Him, down the labyrinthine ways
Of my own mind; and in the midst of tears
I hid from Him—

God gave Jonah a mission just as he has assigned you and me missions. Jonah could not bring himself to embrace his mission. He wanted to do his thing just as we want to follow our own egotistical wills. He could not understand how or why God wanted him to preach to the hated Assyrians, who were notorious for their atrocities and abominations with respect to those they had conquered and their lifestyles of immorality and gross malevolence.

It took three long days in the belly of the whale before Jonah came to his senses. During those long days he experienced the groanings and pain of rebirth or metanoia. Once he was spat out on the shores of Nineveh, he began to realize his true destiny. During our forty days in the desert hopefully we have undergone a similar experience. We have met our enemies and seen that they are ourselves replete with the tarnishing of sin. Perhaps we have begun to realize the chasm between God and ourselves, a chasm of our own making. Perhaps we have realized that those trials and struggles we have experienced in life have really been his way of bringing us closer to him. An example might well be the sudden realization that our relentless pursuit of money, power, popularity, and success at all costs actually cuts us off from God, who is the source of our lives. Perhaps this is why oftentimes when we look back over our lives, we see how empty, unrewarding, and unfulfilling all this striving has been in the final analysis.

But God gives us a second chance to get it right and reorient our lives during our sojourn in the desert just as he did with Jonah as he languished in the belly of the whale. To those of us who see the Jonah in ourselves, the question to you (and me) is whether or not you have reached the point where you know you cannot go it alone. When will we realize that our only hope is to call on God, who loves us and longs to save us? God has work for each of us to do. All we need do is to let go of our petty desires and goals and let God into our day-to-day living. He is still in pursuit of us.

Endnotes

[1]   Thompson, Francis, *The Hound of Heaven and Other Poems* (Wellesley, MA: Branden Books, 2000).

BIBLIOGRAPHY

1. Apple, Raymond Rabbi, "Evil in Man: The Jewish Point of View," *The Australian Journal of Forensic Sciences*, Volume 15, Issue 3, (1983), 125–132.

2. Aquinas, Thomas *The Summa Theologica*, in Basic Writings of Saint Thomas Aquinas ed. Anton C. Pegis, New York Random House, 1945

3. Aquinas, Thomas, COMPENDIUM OF THEOLOGY, translator Cyril Vollert, S.J., (St. Louis & London: B. Herder Book Co., 1947) http://dhspriory.org/thomas/Compendium.htm#114 (Accessed August 20, 2014)

4. Athanasius, "On the Incarnation" Kindle Electronic Edition

5. St. Athanasius, *St. Antony of the Desert,* Rockford, IL: TAN Books and Publishers, 1995.

6. St. Augustine, *City of God*, translators: Gerald Walsh, S.J. Demetrius B. Zema, S.J. Grace Monahan, O.S.U, Daniel J. Honnan, Garden City, NY: Image Book, 1958.

7. St. Augustine, *Confessions*, Kindle Electronic Edition.

8. Augustine, *On the Holy Trinity*, Translated Rev. Arthur West Haddan, 1887, in The complete Works of Saint Augustine, 2013 Kindle Electronic Edition

9. Augustine, *On Christian Doctrine*, Edited by Philip Shaff, Translated by James F. Shaw, 1887, in The Complete Works of Saint Augustine, 2013 Kindle Electronic Edition,

10. Aumann, Jordan, Spiritual Theology, London: Continuum, 1980.

11. Barclay, William, *The Gospel of John*, vol. 2 (Philadelphia, PA: The Westminster Press, 1975.

12. Barnstone, Willis, ed., *The Book of the Secrets of Enoch (2 Enoch) Jewish Pseudepigrapha,* San Francisco: Harper & Row Publishers, 1984

13. St. Benedict, *The Rule of Benedict in English,* Collegeville, MN: The Liturgical Press, 1981.

14. Bly, Robert, *A Little Book on the Human Shadow,* New York: HarperCollins Publishers, 1988

15. Bonhoeffer, Dietrich, *The Cost of Discipleship*, New York: Macmillan Publishing Co., 1963

16. Brown, S.S., Raymond E., Joseph A. Fitzmyer, S.J., Roland E. Murphy, O.Carm. eds. *The Jerome Biblical Commentary*, Englewood Cliff, NJ: Prentice Hall, Inc., 1968.

17. Calivas, Alkiviadis, (2003) Theophan the Recluse cited in Homily for Palm Sunday, Greek Orthodox Archdiocese of America; http://goarch. org/ourfaith/ourfaith8434

18. Camille, Alice, *Invitation to Catholicism,* Chicago: ACTA Publications, 2001.

19. Campbell, Joseph, *The Power of Myth,* New York: Anchor Books, 1991.

20. Cary, Sylvia, *The Alcoholic Man,* Los Angeles: RGA Publishing Group, 1990.

21. Casey, Michael, *The Undivided Heart,* Petersham, MA: St. Bede's Publications, 1994.

22. Cassian, John, *On the Eight Vices on Control of the Stomach,* London: Faber and Faber Limited, 1979.

23. Curry, Jennifer R. and Stephanie Dailey, *Exploring Spirituality Across the Lifespan with Timelines: Developmental Milestones, Defining Moments, Changing Beliefs and Practices Argosy University* http://www.aservic.org/ wp-content/uploads/2011/12/Module-9 (Accessed July 10, 2012)

24. Deagan, G., "St. Thomas and the Problem of Evil," *Universitas* 13, (Select Papers) Centre for Thomistic Studies, Sydney, Australia.

25. de Chardin, Teilhard, *The Phenomenon of Man,* New York: Harper and Row Publishers, Inc., 1959.

26. DeFrancisco, James, Original Sin and Ancestral Sin: Comparative Doctrines published for Miltha Ministries at www. aramaicbibleperspectives.com/uploads/ABP - ORIGINAL SIN OR ANCESTRAL SIN.pdf (2007).

27. DeMello, Anthony, *Taking Flight: A Book of Story Meditations*, New York: Image Book, a division of Doubleday, 1988.

28. DeMello, Anthony, *Awareness: The Perils and Opportunities of Reality,* New York: Image Book, a division of Doubleday, 1990.

29. de Waal, Esther, *A Life-Giving Way: A Commentary on the Rule of St. Benedict,* Collegeville, MI: The Liturgical Press, 1995.

30. Diamond, Stephen A., The Psychology of Evil, Devils, Demons, and the Daimonic, in Anger, Madness, and the Daimonic: The Psychological Genesis of Violence, Evil, and Creativity, State University of New York Press, 1999, Kindle Electronic Edition

31. Douglas-Klotz, Neil, *The Hidden Gospel: Decoding the Spiritual Message of the Aramaic Jesus,* Wheaton, IL: Quest Books Theosophical Publishing House, 1999.

32. Dubay, Thomas, *Fire Within: St. Teresa of Avila, St. John of the Cross, and the Gospel on Prayer,* San Francisco: Ignatius Press, 1989.

33. Eliade, Mercea, *Myth and Reality,* New York: Harper Row, 1963

34. Eliade, Mercea, *A History of Religious Ideas, vol. 1,* translated by Willard R. Trask, Chicago: The University of Chicago Press, 1978.

35. English, S.J. John J., *Spiritual Freedom, From an Experience of the Ignatian Exercises to the Art of Spiritual Guidance,* 2nd Edition, Chicago, ILL: Loyola Press, 1995.

36. Eucharistic Doctrine, The Presence of Christ in *Statement of the First Anglican/Roman Catholic International Commission,* http://www.vatican.va/roman_curia/pontifical_councils/chrstuni/angl-comm-docs/rc_pc_chrstuni_doc_1971_eucharistic-doctrine_en.html, Accessed August 18, 2014.

37. Eusebius, *Ecclesiastical History,* Kindle Electronic Edition

38. Foucauld, Charles, Cry the Gospel With Your Life, Mesnil Saint-Loup, France: Edition Le Livre Ouvert, 1944.

39. Frankl, Victor, *Man's Search for Meaning,* New York: Washington Square Press, 1959.

40. Frey-Rohn L., *Evil from the Psychological Point of View: Essays by Carl Kerenyi and Others,* Evanston, IL: Northwestern University Press 1967.

41. Garrigou-Lagrange, Reginald, *Three Ways of the Spiritual Life,* Publisher unknown, 1938, Kindle Electronic Edition

42. Gilbert, Christopher, Grades of Freedom: Augustine and Descartes, in *Pacific Philosophical Quarterly* 86 (2005): 201-224

43. St. Gregory of Nyssa, "The Lord's Prayer/The Beatitudes," translator, Hilda C. Graej in *Ancient Christian Writers: The Works of the Fathers in Translation,* editors Johannes Quasten, S.T.D., and Joseph C Plumpe, No. 18, New York, NY: Paulist Press, 1954.

44. Greggs, Tom, *Barth, Origin, and Universal Salvation: Restoring Particularity,* Oxford, England: Oxford University Press, 2009.

45. Heschel, Abraham Joshua, *God in Search of Man: A Philosophy of Judaism,* New York: Farrar, Strauss and Giroux, 1955.

46. Heschel, Abraham Joshua, *Man Is Not Alone: A Philosophy of Religion,* New York: Farrar, Strauss and Giroux, 1951.

47. Hick, John, *Evil and the God of Love,* Houndmills, Basingstoke, Hampshire, England: Palgrave Macmillan, 2010.

48. Ignatius Loyola, *The Spiritual Exercises of St. Ignatius,* translated by Anthony Motola, New York: Doubleday Image, 1964.

49. Irenaeus, *Proof of the Apostolic Preaching,* Translated and Annotated by Joseph P. Smith, S.J., Ancient Christian Writers Volume 16, Mahweh, NJ: Paulist Press, 1956.

50. Ireneaus, *Against Heresies,* Kindle Electronic Edition

51. Johnson, Luke Timothy, *The Creed" What Christians Believe and Why It Matters,* New York: Image Book, Doubleday, 2003.

52. Jung, C. G. *A Review of the Complex Theory: The Structure and Dynamics of the Psyche,* Princeton, NJ: Princeton University Press, 1960.

53. Jung, C. G., Civilization in Transition**,** *Collected Works of C. G. Jung* Translators: Gerhard Adler and R. F.C. Hull, Princeton, NJ: Princeton University Press; 2nd edition 1970.

54. Jung, C. G., *Psychological Types* in Bollingen Series, Princeton, NJ: Princeton University Press, 1971.

55. Karmiris, John, *A Synopsis of the Dogmatic Theology of the Orthodox Catholic Church,* translated from the Greek by the Reverend George Dimopoulos, Scranton, PA: Christian Orthodox Edition, 1973

56. Kerestzy, Roch A., *Jesus Christ, Fundamentals of Christology,* Staten Island, NY: the Society of St. Paul, Abba House, 2002.

57. King, Jr., Martin Luther, "What is Man?" in *The Measure of a Man,* Philadelphia: Fortress Press, 1959.

58. Kinsella, Nivard, *Unprofitable Servants: Conferences on Humility,* Chicago: Franciscan Herald Press, 1960.

59. Lane, Dermot A., *The Reality of Jesus,* New York: Paulist Press, 1975.

60. Latourette, Kenneth Scott, *A History of Christianity,* New York: Harper & Brothers, Publishers; First Edition, 1953.

61. St. Leo the Great, "Sermon on the Beatitudes, Matthew 5:1–9" sermon 95. In *Nicene and Post-Nicene Fathers—Second Series*, vol. 12, edited by Philip Schaff and Henry Wace; translated by Charles Lett Feltoe, Buffalo, NY: Christian Literature Publishing Co., 1895, revised and edited for New Advent (2009) by Kevin Knight at http://www.newadvent.org/fathers/360395.htm

62. Lewis, C. S., *The Screwtape Letters* in The Complete C. S. Lewis Signature Classics, San Francisco: HarperSanFrancisco, 2002.

63. Lonsdale, Herman Lilienthal, *Lent Past and Present: A Study of the Primitive Origin of Lent, Its Purpose and Usages*, Princeton, NJ: Princeton University Internet Archives, 1895; reissued Memphis, TN: General Books, LLC, 2009.

64. Louf, Andre, *The Cistercian Way*, Kalamazoo, MI: Cistercian Publications, 1983.

65. Luther, Martin, *Commentary on Romans*, translated by Theodore Mueller, Grand Rapids, MI: Kriegel Publications, 1976.

66. Marius, Nel. Daniel 7, "Mythology and the Creation Combat Myths," OTE 1 (2006): 156-170.

67. Marmion, D. Columba, *Christ the Life of the Soul*, St. Louis: B. Herder Book Co., 1925.

68. McGraph, Alister E. McGrath, *An Introduction to Christianity*, Cambridge: Blackwell, 1997.

69. Merton, Thomas, *Seeds of Contemplation*, New York: Dell Publishing Company, 1960.

70. Merton, Thomas, *New Seeds of Contemplation*, New York: New Directions Publishing Corporation, 1961a.

71. Merton, Thomas, *The New Man*, New York: Bantam Books, Inc., 1961b.

72. Merton, Thomas, *Contemplative Prayer*, Garden City, NY: Image Books Doubleday, 1971.

73. Merton, Thomas, *The Inner Experience, Notes on Contemplation*, San Francisco: HarperSanFrancisco, Harper Collins Publishers, 2003.

74. Meyendorff, John, *Byzantine Theology: Historical Trends and Doctrinal Themes*, New York: Fordham University Press, 1974.

75. Minns, Dennis *Irenaeus, An Introduction*, London, England: T & T Clark International, 2010.

76. Morton, Kelsey, *The Drama of the Resurrection: Transforming Christianity*, Hyde Park, NY: New City Press, 1999.

77. Neuner, J, and J. Dupois, *The Christian Faith in the Doctrinal Documents of the Catholic Faith*, edited by Jacques Dupuis, Bangalore, India: Theological Publications in India, 2001.

78. Newman, John Henry, *Sermons Preached on Various Occasions*, eight sermons preached before the Catholic University of Ireland in 1856, 1857, the first year of the opening of its church, New York: Longmans, Green and Co., 1908.

79. Nouwen, Henri, *The Way of the Heart*, New York: Ballantine Books, Random House, 1981.

80. O'Connell, Timothy E., *Principles for a Catholic Morality*, New York: The Seabury Press, 1978.

81. Peck, M. Scott, *People of the Lie: The Hope for Healing Human Evil*, New York: Simon and Schuster, 1983.

82. Pontifical Council for Promoting Christian Unity, "The Greek and Latin Traditions Regarding the Procession of the Holy Spirit" L'Osservatore Romano, September 20. 1995, Weekly Edition in English http://www.ewtn.com/library/curia/pccufilq.htm (Accessed August 18, 2014)

83. Pristas, Lauren, *The Theological Anthropology of John Cassian*, unpublished PhD dissertation (Boston: Boston College, 1993).

84. Prevalett, Elaine, *Toward a Spirituality for Global Justice: A Call to Kinship,* Louisville, KY: Sowers Books & Videos, 2005.

85. Rahner, Karl, *Spiritual Exercises,* New York: Herder and Herder, 1956.

86. Rahner, Karl, *Foundations of Christian Faith: An Introduction to the Idea of Christianity*, New York: The Seabury Press, 1978.

87. Ratzinger, Joseph Cardinal with Vittorio Messori, *The Ratzinger Report,* San Francisco: Ignatius Press, 1985.

88. Ratzinger, Joseph, *In the Beginning— A Catholic Understanding of the Story of Creation and the Fall,* Grand Rapids, MI: Wm. B. Eerdmans Publishing Co., 1986.

89. Reid, Francis and Deborah Hoffmann, Filmmakers, Long Night's Journey into Day, South Africa's Search for Truth and Reconciliation (Berkeley. CA: Iris Films, 2000)

90. Røsok, Ingvild, "Unconditional Surrender and Love, How Spirituality Illuminates the Theology of Karl Rahner," The Way, vol. 50/4 (October 2011): 121–132.

91. Russo, Nicholas V. "The Early History of Lent," in *Christian Reflection* (Waco, TX: The Center for Christian Ethics at Baylor University, 2013) 18-26.

92. Samuels, Andrew, Bani Shorter and Fred Plaut's *A Critical Dictionary of Jungian Analysis,* New York: Routledge & Kegan Paul, 1986.

93. Schoonenberg, Piet, "Sin and Guilt," *Encyclopedia of Theology: The Concise Sacramentum Mundi*, ed. Karl Rahner, New York: Seabury, 1975.

94. Second Vatican Council's Constitution of the Sacred Liturgy, *Sacrosanctum Concilium*, Washington, DC: National Catholic Welfare Conference, 1963.

95. Seeskin, Kenneth, *Searching for a Distant God*, New York: Oxford University Press, 2000.

96. Tanquerey, Adolphe, The Spiritual Life: A Treatise on Ascetical and Mystical Theology, CreateSpace Independent Publishing Platform, 2013.

97. Thompson, Francis, *The Hound of Heaven and Other Poems,* Wellesley, MA: Branden Books, 2000.

98. Theodorus the Great Ascetic, circa 200 CE, *A Century of Spiritual Texts*, The Philokalia, Volume Two, Compiled by St. Nikodimos of the Holy Mountain and St. Makarios of Corinth; translated from the Greek and edited by G.E.H, Palmer, Philip Sherrod, and Kallistos Ware, London: Faber and Faber, 1990.

99. St. Theophan the Recluse, "On Prayer, letters 42 and 51." *Orthodox Life*, vol. 32, no. 4 (July-August, 1982): 21-30. Translated from the Russian by Fr. Stefan Pavlenko.

100. US Conference of Catholic Bishops, *Compendium of the Catechism of the Catholic Church,* Washington, DC: USCCB Publishing, 2006.

101. Ware, Timothy, *The Orthodox Church,* London: Penguin, 1997.

102. Welch, John, *Spiritual Pilgrims: Carl Jung and Teresa of Avila,* New York: Paulist Press, 1982.

103. Wilson, William Griffith, and Robert Holbrook Smith, *Alcoholic Anonymous*, revised as *The Story of How Many Thousands of Men and Women Have Recovered from Alcoholism*, 4th edition, New York: Alcoholic Anonymous World Services, Inc., 2014.

104. Zweig, Connie, and Steven Wolf, *Romancing the Shadow: A Guide to Soul Work for a Vital, Authentic Life*, New York: Random House Ballantine Publishing Group, 1997).

INDEX

CPSIA information can be obtained at www.ICGtesting.com
Printed in the USA
LVOW06s1008311214

420956LV00003B/5/P